Charles Dickens

Charles Dickens,
The Uses of Time

James E. Marlow,

Selinsgrove: Susquehanna University Press
London and Toronto: Associated University Presses

© 1994 by Associated University Presses, Inc.

All rights reserved. Authorization to photocopy items for internal or personal use, or the internal or personal use of specific clients, is granted by the copyright owner, provided that a base fee of $10.00, plus eight cents per page, per copy is paid directly to the Copyright Clearance Center, 27 Congress Street, Salem, Massachusetts 01970. [0-945636-48-2/94 $10.00+8¢ pp, pc.]

Associated University Presses
440 Forsgate Drive
Cranbury, NJ 08512

Associated University Presses
25 Sicilian Avenue
London WC1A 2QH, England

Associated University Presses
P.O. Box 338, Port Credit
Mississauga, Ontario
Canada L5G 4L8

The paper used in this publication meets the requirements of the American National Standard for Permanence of Paper for Printed Library Materials Z39.48-1984.

Library of Congress Cataloging-in-Publication Data

Marlow, James E., 1938–
    Charles Dickens : the uses of time / James E. Marlow.
      p. cm.
    Includes bibliographical references and index.
    ISBN 0-945636-48-2 (alk. paper)
    1. Dickens, Charles, 1812–1870—Criticism and interpretation.
2. Time in literature. I. Title.
PR4582.T5Z77   1994
823'.8—dc20   92-50683
                                                           CIP

PRINTED IN THE UNITED STATES OF AMERICA

For Corinne, *sine quack non*

When dealing with the problem of organic life we have, first and foremost to free ourselves from what Whitehead calls the principle of "simple location." The organism is never located in a single instant. In its life the three modes of time—the past, the present, and the future—form a whole which cannot be split up into individual elements.
—Ernst Cassirer, *An Essay on Man*

Contents

List of Abbreviations	9
Acknowledgments	11
Introduction	13

Part One: The Abuses of Time

1. The Dead Hand of the Past	35
2. The Presence of Hunger	69
3. Great Expectations: Fixtures of the Future	96

Part Two: The Uses of Time

4. The Battle of Life	125
5. Trust in the Present	154
6. Beyond Forgetting: The Uses of the Past	191

Part Three: Conclusion

7. Transcending Time: "Out of the Ruined Place"	223
Notes	241
Bibliography	255
Index	263

Abbreviations

AN	American Notes
BH	Bleak House
BL	The Battle of Life
BR	Barnaby Rudge
CB	Christmas Books
CC	A Christmas Carol
CH	The Cricket on the Hearth
CHE	A Child's History of England
CS	Christmas Stories
DC	David Copperfield
DS	Dombey and Son
ED	The Mystery of Edwin Drood
GE	Great Expectations
HM	The Haunted Man
HT	Hard Times
LD	Little Dorrit
MC	Martin Chuzzlewit
NN	Nicholas Nickleby
OCS	The Old Curiosity Shop
OMF	Our Mutual Friend
OT	Oliver Twist
PI	Pictures from Italy
PP	Pickwick Papers
RP	Reprinted Pieces
SB	Sketches by Boz
TC	The Chimes
TTC	A Tale of Two Cities
UT	The Uncommercial Traveller

Because so many editions of Dickens's novels are in use, references to them in parentheses in the text will be made to chapter number rather than page number. When, in the later novels, Dickens divided his novels into books as well, the book number will precede the chapter number. In those collected works without chapter numbers, I have used the page number (preceded by a *p.*) of the Oxford Illustrated Edition.

* * *

Besides these novels and collected pieces, Dickens wrote copiously in his two periodicals, *Household Words* and *All the Year Round.* He often added words, sentences, and paragraphs to the work of others, issued suggestions and criticisms, and used the cutting knife so that both periodicals spoke in the unambiguous voice of their editor-in-chief.

Acknowledgments

Those who have richly influenced how I and hundreds of others read are J. Hillis Miller and Ralph Cohen, with whom I was lucky enough to have studied on NEH Summer Seminars. I learned to admire Dickens's works studying under two fervent Dickensians at the University of California at Davis, Prof. Gwendolyn Needham and Prof. Elliot Gilbert, whose love for the writings of Dickens are reflected in seminal articles and hundreds of students. Ulrich Knoepflmacher was also kind enough to help with my early attempts to write critically on Dickens. And finally, I was among many who were influenced by Miss Grace Baker, who at Central High in Aberdeen, South Dakota, many years ago, managed to instill a respect for literature in many young women and rough-and-tumble young men who thought she had not. Thank you.

Libraries are of course essential for the study of an author active a century and a half ago. I wish to thank the New York Public Library, the Boston Public Library, the Widener and Houghton Library at Harvard and the research department at the University of Massachusetts at Dartmouth, as well as Professor Richard Upchurch of the Computer Science Department. I also wish to thank Prof. Richard Larschan of the University of Massachusetts, Dartmouth, for his early and essential help with this study.

Introduction

It has been said that the nineteenth century was the first modern century. With a weakening in the belief in eternity, action replaced God. In *Faust,* for example, the deity is defined as activity, and his commandment for man is a call to action. Since action requires a world, time became a primary focus of Victorian consciousness. The very lay of the land had been temporalized by Lyell's geology. Railroad timetables were read as diligently as ever prayer books were; watches and their chains formed a pale of incorruptible gold behind which every man took his refuge; the steeples of those cathedrals of activity—factories—were topped by clocks. The past, the present, and the future of the individual, the nation, and the human race were common topics of conversation. If action was the Holy Ghost, time was the Father, and the human being the Redeemer of the world.

The premise of this book is that Dickens himself was acutely conscious of time and that his work may be read as a dialogue with his readers about the topics that were at the forefront of the Victorian imagination: time and one's conscious address to it. Mildred Newcomb has pointed out, in discussing the images of marsh and river, that "Dickens makes this sensitivity to time—ultimately attentiveness to one's own mortality—the critical test of life in his characters."[1] Patrick Creevy has noted five hundred references to time in *Bleak House* alone.[2] For no one, it strikes me, is Steiner's axiom truer than it is for Dickens: "The past-present-future axis is a feature of grammar which runs through our experience of self and of being like a palpable backbone."[3] The most cursory readings of Dickens's biographies, letters, or novels, I believe, leads one to the sense that concerns about the past and the future were constantly—ineluctably—part of his consciousness. In this book, I argue that these concerns were so much a part of Dickens's thinking that he was always in the throes of imagining a stance toward one of these three periods of time that could satisfy all of his psychological needs. But with each stance that he took, his dialectical mind saw the other side. "It is a leading characteristic of Dickens's mind," wrote John Carey, "that he is able to see almost everything from two opposed points of view."[4] This is certainly true of the way Dickens looked at his own experimental stances toward memory, current circumstances, and expectation. Once he tried out a stance toward, say, the past, he soon came to see that it failed to give him satisfaction; and in a succeeding novel he would try to correct the stance by adopting an alternative one. Arnold Kettle once wrote, "The history of the novel is, in this sense, the history of the novelists search for an adequate philosophy of life."[5] A "philosophy of life" is another way of saying an attitude toward time—or of saying an appropriate use, for example, for memories. The history of Dickens's work is truly the history of this search.

Therefore, I shall be following his search from novel to novel, attempting not to explicate or honor the form of each separate work but to treat each novel as a kind of existential experiment. This practice has the prior endorsement of perhaps the greatest of Dickens's critics, G. K. Chesterton: "Dickens's work is not to be reckoned by novels at all. . . . There is no such novel as *Our Mutual Friend*. They are simply lengths cut from the flowing and mixed substance called Dickens—a substance of which any given length will be certain to contain a given proportion of brilliant and bad stuff."[6] Obviously, much excellent criticism has succeeded in showing that the novels are integral and offer great aesthetic satisfaction in themselves. But because I am interested in pursuing the ongoing stances toward time—and take as my assumption the notion that Dickens, the works, and the readers are caught in the flood of time and respond constantly to each other as a consequence—I will not seek to judge the individual novels as works of art.

In the past decade or so, many of the studies on Dickens—especially the monographs and the recent monumental biographies by Fred Kaplan and Peter Ackroyd[7]—consider his work as a whole. In most of these studies, two approaches may be distinguished: the diachronic and the synchronic. The diachronic approach to Dickens and his work can be found in the biographies by Kaplan and Ackroyd. Developments in the psychology of Dickens and in the construction of his novels constitute the primary focus of their approach. These biographers have seen Dickens as someone who took ever greater risks in his efforts to articulate the dilemmas of human beings in modern society, and they have assumed that Dickens was constantly reaching ever further to integrate his own personality. The premise of their approach, like that of mine, is that Dickens matured as an artist and human being as he tried to articulate an authentic human existence over the course of his career. Lawrence Frank has spoken, for example, of the "Autobiographical Imperative" in Dickens's work: his premise is that there is an ontological need to be in transition and that everything in the world changes except for the need to change. (Hence, we see that paradox has gained respectability in criticism at the end of the twentieth century.) *David Copperfield* reflects "a vision of man as a narrative being."[8] However, in John Jasper's failure to escape the "inertia of the society he has rejected" and Crisparkle's "embodiment of conventional consciousness"[10] and Edwin Drood's revelation that "he has acquiesced more than he knows to the conventional world,"[11] it seems clear to Frank that Dickens had not succeeded in creating a character (and, by unexamined implication, a self) who had his "own center, ontological and ethical"[12] by the time he had written his last novel. However debatable this notion, the Romantic self that Frank has postulated for Dickens is probably acceptable to other critics of this diachronic school.

Badri Raina, describing his view as a third-world perspective (by which he has meant, I think, a socially responsible perspective), has seen in the novels a "dialectic" in which Dickens returns "with ever-increasing rigor to the one central contradiction of his career, that which involves his simultaneous roles as aspiring, successful and disgusted Victorian"[13]—that is, Raina has cited Dickens's inner conflict between his need for the security provided by so-called bourgeois respectability and his need for the authentic selfhood provided by Romantic notions of human meaning. Dickens's self-contradiction is reflected in *Oliver Twist,* in which Dickens successfully "demythologized middle-class polemics about crimes and criminals"[14] but his vision is finally "rendered infructuous by the quality of Oliver's separate and exceptional destiny."[15] In *Dombey and Son,* Dickens was "able to initiate a more honest and self-assured adjustment of his ideological problematic."[16] However, Raina has written that in *David Copperfield* Dickens's "undifferentiated ambivalence toward David remains morally and artistically disquieting."[17] In that novel Dickens's treatment of and (implied in David's) opinions about Heep and Micawber, as opposed to Steerforth, show him to have been an as yet unreconstructed Victorian. But Dickens's dialectic reaches its goal in *Great Expectations:* "The story of Pip is the achieving of an authentic self."[18]

What is problematic about this diachronic approach is its tendency to lead to a kind of intentional fallacy—that is, one first argues conditionally that Dickens's novels provide sufficient evidence to postulate a pattern of significance, and then one holds Dickens up to judgment for not having developed fully down the lines established by the pattern. Thus a schema that is erected for heuristic purposes is sometimes transformed into a frame within which to judge Dickens's art. This tendency arraigns the specific work by some criterion ostensibly extracted from several works and their apparent intentions, but it does not justify the application of the criterion in any particular case. Hence, by knowing what Dickens ought to have done, the diachronic approach can ironically cease to tolerate evolution and creation (i.e., diachronicity).

Another recent version of the diachronic approach is that of Dirk den Hartog. He has found in Dickens's works a "legacy of Romanticism within the alien framework of mainstream Victorian values, a persistence which functioned as an adversary sub-culture within the parent body."[19] From Wordsworth, Dickens accepted the notion that "to keep vitally in touch with the childhood self was both a psychological desideratum and a moral value."[20] Dombey, for example, lacks this continuity. "Dickens's striking recognition . . . [is] that the only cure to Dombey's psychological disease is his complete sloughing off of the strong egotistic identity that has functioned as a false solution to his childhood deprivation."[21] William Dorrit, in contrast, "could be argued to represent Dickens's negative version of the Wordsworthian continuity idea, in its sense of the liability of the past to implode destructively upon the present."[22] By the time of *Great Expectations,* Dickens had come around 180 degrees from Wordsworth: "The un-Wordsworthian paradox at the heart of Dickens's argument *is,* I think, that the wish for uncommonness also expresses a profound need of Pip's being."[23] Hence, Dickens's "creative thinking" took place "within the ideological contradictions of the age in a continual effort of self-disentanglement and self-clarification."[24] Clearly, den Hartog has expressed the belief that Dickens changed his mind, developed artistically, and revealed contradictions. This growth in negative capability—this critical capacity to accept the inconsistencies in life—is the great virtue of Ackroyd's biography as well: Ackroyd, despite his desire for coherence in his own tale, has insisted on letting the many contradictions in Dickens's life and ideas stand.

Whatever the differences in premises, these diachronic critics have in common the belief that Dickens's novels show over time a continuous moral struggle, with greater integration coming at the later stages in his career. Whatever their differences in focus, they tend to agree that the later novels attain greater artistic coherence and value than the earlier ones.

A contrary approach—with a synchronic predilection—results in different evaluations. At its worst, this school could be represented by crude Marxists or crude Freudians who discover in every novel a similar criticism of capitalism and its agents or repression and its agents. At its best, it could be represented by Mildred Newcomb, Edwin Eigner, and S. J. Newman. Perhaps the most influential member of this camp is John Carey. He appears to construct his *Here Comes Dickens* dialectically—that is, his argument moves from violence to order, and from humour to corpses and effigies. However, his approach is in fact essentialist and static, for Carey's analysis rests on the point "that Dickens is essentially a comic writer."[25] Knowing this essence—knowing, therefore, Dickens's authentic as opposed to inauthentic worldviews—Carey had all he needed to judge each novel as a work of art. For example, Carey has written that "Headstone proves a failure because he is fabricated out of the author's social prejudices, instead of being impelled, as Quilp is, by his author's savage humour, self-criticism, and emancipation from the cant and sentimentality that were threatening to kill Dickens's art."[26]

The bias is evident. One can as reasonably argue that Headstone carries much more of Dickens's affect in comparison to Wrayburn (OMF) than Quilp does in comparison to Little Nell (OCS). Carey's core bias is this: "What is noticeable is that Dickens has stopped feeling, and has started to write well."[27] It seems, therefore, that Dickens failed to write well when he ceased to be a kind of Augustan Radical. For Carey, Dickens is a comic writer; and when his humour "fails his imagination seldom survives it for more than a few sentences."[28] Even if one cannot accept all the exclusions dictated by Carey's premises, nevertheless his trenchant assessments of particular scenes and characters are of great value. Moreover, Carey rights the previous imbalance in Dickens criticism in two important ways: (1) he has argued that the early novels—in which the "anarchic" side of Dickens reigns—deserve more attention than they have recently had; and (2) he has argued that Dickens's "violent, anarchic side" is in a constant state of war with Dickens's pieties and conventionalities. In *The Old Curiosity Shop*, for example, Quilp is the revenge this "anarchic" side takes on the conventionalities that Dickens admits into the novel. Paradoxically, then, Carey's position has discovered a kind of dialectic: in every book an incessant civil war is waged between the artistic and inartistic side of Dickens's being, with the quality of the book depending on more battles being won by the "anarchic" side. What is particularly appealing here is the opening Carey's view allows for the consideration of Dickens's novels within the framework of Bakhtin's thinking on the dialogical novel.

If Carey had no use whatsoever for the melodramatic element in Dickens's work, Edwin Eigner has considered it to be as legitimate as the anarchic element. In the best scholarly fashion, Eigner has noted the many allusions to English traditional pantomime in Dickens's early essays—and has then traced the influence of the pantomimic characters upon the characterization in Dickens's novels, focusing finally on *David Copperfield*. Two particularly suggestive points have been provided by Eigner. One is that Dickens made an "association between pantomime and our everyday lives [that] is essential in terms of the carnivalesque in his work."[29] Besides this allusion to a part of M. M. Bakhtin's work, Eigner has also made the very fruitful suggestion that "pantomime sets up one genre in order to move on to another."[30] Eigner's suggestion speaks to the issue of the rapid shifting of voices and modes of presentation in Dickens, which has been shown by Susan Horton to be a primary problem in reading Dickens.[31] It is a feature of Dickens's art that has received too little attention and explanation.

S. J. Newman has made reference, apparently, to this same feature by noting that "the beauty of *Sketches* lies in its employment of a wide range of fictive linguistic devices in order to approximate to what Iris Murdoch calls 'the weird stuff, human consciousness.'"[32] The "growing awareness of incongruity" becomes "one of the organising principles of Dickens's later art";[33] in this art Dickens's sentences become "vertiginously fantastic"[34] and, for example, create in *The Old Curiosity Shop* "the first decisive emergence of post-rationalist art."[35] Like John Carey (whose work Newman has considered the best on Dickens since that of Edmund Wilson), Newman has expressed his belief that comedy is the sine qua non of Dickens's art and that "it is the nature of comic art to come possessed by language."[36] In novels like *Martin Chuzzlewit*, therefore, Newman has said that we must "unlearn interpretative systems in which language is finally at the service of the idea."[37] Dickens's was a mythic imagination that created its own reality out of verbal play and not out of a prior intellection.

These synchronic approaches have several features in common. Even though Carey and Newcomb, for example, range over the entire spectrum of Dickens's work, they have not considered the novels either as single works of art or even as markers in a personal or artistic evolution. The atemporal focus on the comic, on the one hand, and imagery, on the other, provides for no development, no feedback, no dialogue with earlier works or an earlier artistic personae. What is more, these critics have made no pretense of considering each novel in what Medvedev and Bakhtin call the "concrete unity of the historical phenomenon-utterance."[38] These critics have ignored the fact that the work has an organic connection that "exists only for the given utterance and only under the given conditions of its utterance."[39] Hence, the ahistorical or decontextualized evaluations do justice neither to the unity of the separate novels nor to the historical drama of the writer's growing consciousness of his own dilemmas and his own articulations of those dilemmas. What Susan Horton has said of thematic criticism is true of some synchronic approaches: "The model is essentially mystical, in that it does not pretend to say what makes us choose one detail or part over another."[40]

On the other hand, these synchronic approaches—especially those of Newman and Carey—have discussed Dickens's writing without indulging in what Roy Harris called the "telementation," or "fixed code fallacy," which "fails to come to terms with linguistic creativity."[41] They focus on what Peter Ackroyd has described as Dickens's "need to rewrite the world."[42] By concentrating on Dickens's verbal play, these critics have safely passed by the shibboleths of deconstructionism. As Jacques Derrida has said, "Nietzsche has written that writing—and first of all his own—is not originally subordinate to the logos and the truth."[43] Their attention to the anarchic and subversive in Dickens's language deprecates a faith in achieving the presence of truth. Dickens's writing is no longer seen as a mere conveyance of previously devised meanings—as a mere telementation; it is, rather, a poesis—a making. His writing is not a mere transmission—it is a mission itself. This attention to Dickens's *writing* is a vital contribution to the literary criticism of Dickens's works.

Thus, the synchronic approach has created a different hierarchy of interpretive operations. By highlighting the carnivalesque, the synchronic approach has revived earlier evaluations of Dickens's novels—preferring the novels with mythic characters like Mrs. Gamp, Quilp, and Pecksniff to the so-called dark novels, the later novels with clearer thematic and imagistic patterns. To redress the injustice done to the earlier novels is a valuable service; and one cannot but feel compelled by criticism that can both account for a nearly universal attraction to those earlier characters and yet accord with the recently exploited work of M. M. Bakhtin, which accommodates the anarchic and carnivalesque as integral parts of the literary experience.

The insights of both kinds of approaches leave us with an enhanced sense of the complexity of Dickens's art and of the difficulty of writing about it within the non-contradictory principles of Western thinking. The synchronic critics have discovered eternal motion in the anarchic essence of Dickens's art; the diachronic critics have discovered a teleological essence in the dialectic movement of his life and art. These forms of dialogic interpretation, then—with or without the use of Bakhtin—have tried to do justice to the polyphonic structure of Dickens's art; and this concurrence seems to dominate the criticism at the end of the twentieth century. Both of these approaches—entailing a tolerance of paradox—have greatly increased our understanding of Dickens's novels; but their very existence has complicated our own reading.

Susan Horton has elucidated the difficulties by alerting us to the "hermeneutic circle" that one encounters with every act of reading: "The interpreter isolates a part of the text that he takes to be central for the understanding of the whole. In turn, the whole that he projects on the basis of his comprehension of the part comes to explain and give significance to all the remaining parts of the text."[44] Horton has made obvious that every meaning a critic derives from a Dickens text is the direct result of a previous valorization of a detail or part by the critic. Hence, a critic must be willing to make conscious and public what Peter J. Rabinowitz has called the "rules of notice."[45] If all of the features of a novel receive equally close attention, the text, according to Rabinowitz, "becomes an infinite and impenetrable web of relationships."[46] Although rules of notice serve to prevent chaos, Rabinowitz has argued that each set of rules is determined by the "politics of interpretation"—and, therefore, must be debated.

This debate must be waged on multitudes of intersecting planes, and each plane may be divided into binary opposites. For example, those who, like E. D. Hirsch, have conceived a text to offer an objective validity, an intrinsic genre, which the reader uncovers, may be opposed to those who, like Bleich and Fish, have conceived the meaning of the text to be wholly subjective. Those who favor content may be compared to those who favor structure. Many readers assume a "negative capability" in the artist; others assume the artist to be determined by conscious, subconscious, or socio-economic powers. Those who hold that Dickens can best be read as one "flowing and mixed substance" stand opposite to those who set each novel apart, as if each novel were unrelated to the previous and following novels. Those who weight influence balance those who weight innovation. Dialogism contrasts with monologism, essentialists with existentialists, and so forth. John Forster has quoted a workman as saying of Dickens, "The more you want of the master, the more you'll find in him."[47] Forster could have had no conception of the truth of that notion in modern criticism. Obviously, our rules of notice are dictated by our political choices—whether national, partisan, aesthetic, or anagogic. The justification for our political choices, however, lies in what they achieve as interpretation—in the help they give a reader in reading. All a critic can do, then, is to declare his interpretive allegiances and to get on with it in the hope that the end will justify the means.

As for the declaration of my critical faith, let me sketch here the principles that guide my rules of notice. First, I intend to use, so far as possible, Dickens's own language as indexes of organizing themes. While acknowledging that words do not contain a meaning, I propose to argue that fewer errors of interpretation are likely to occur if one stays within Dickens's circle of signifiers than if one were to translate his themes into our circles. I hope that using Dickens's own phrasing—such as "the battle of life"—will enable us to trace the permutations of meaning without multiplying terms with which Dickens would not have been familiar. It is an effort, in other words, to speak a related language, at the very least. Conceding that one is not part of the original audience—by importing as few words as possible into the discussion—one can at least make a good faith effort to resuscitate something of the relationship between author and reader that originally obtained.

Second, whatever other functions a novel may serve, it is above all an act of communication in language. As such, it is rule-guided, goal-oriented behavior. As Roman Jakobson has written, "In point of fact, any verbal behavior is goal-oriented, but the aims are different."[48] Language, according to Jakobson, has six functions which correspond with its constitutive factors: "An ADDRESSER sends a MESSAGE to the ADDRESSEE. To be operative the message requires a CONTEXT referred to."[49] In the case of a novel, the context is almost infinitely complex. The context includes: (1) ideas and things; (2) myths, science, religion, and all of what Cassirer has called the "symbolic forms"; (3) national history and interpretations of that history; (4) the economic infrastructure and notions of personal identity; and (5) the generic rules of the novel, developed down the years, which may be affirmed or subverted—and thus modified—by the novel in hand. Other factors constituting language include "a CODE, fully, or at least partially, common to the addresser and addressee" and, finally, "a

CONTACT, a physical channel and psychological connection" between addresser and addressee.[50]

Although each factor determines a different function—and, generally, one function is marked by the set towards one factor—"we could . . . hardly find verbal messages that would fulfill only one function."[51] For example, "It is hot today" could fulfill a set towards addresser, addressee, or context, at the very least.

One difficulty with Dickens's art is that it is constantly rehearsing all of the six functions that Jakobson names: the emotive, the conative, the referential, the poetic, the metalingual (per code), and the phatic (per contact). As sharply concrete as many of Dickens's references are—and as evocative as are others—Dickens's prose is often felt to be intoxicated, almost self-indulgent. For example, a hypocritical peroration by Sarah Gamp or Pecksniff may go beyond any realistic conative, emotive, or referential function. Such a peroration may obviously go far beyond the needs of the plot or structure, as Henry James implied in using the phrase "great, baggy monsters" to describe Dickens's novels. Such speeches simply become a play—or display—of language itself. The language draws attention only to itself: its function is simply to be there; it is intransitive, opaque. "The set towards the MESSAGE, as such, focus on the message for its own sake, is the POETIC function of language."[52] This feature of Dickens's prose does not cooperate with certain kinds of interpretations; but it is so common that it cannot be ignored. The critic must account for such presentations.

The prose may also refer to several classes of objects. To refer to "the woman in white" is to assert a real woman whom Dickens may have either seen as a boy or heard discussed as a man—a woman whose existence he cannot doubt—or it is to postulate a fictive creature that in the world of words takes on for the reader an equivalent reality; but in either case, the poetic function may be quite as important as the referential one. There are times when the referential set may be marked by the tone rather than the index, as when Dickens repeated his father's expressions, such as "the sun has set up on him forever," or gave to Micawber and Squeers expressions like "As ye sow, so shall ye reap"—an expression of John Dickens that takes on different colorings depending on whether it is in the narrative voice or in that of Wilkins Micawber. Mimicry may reveal as much about the addresser as it does about the context—and, thus, may be more emotive than referential.

In any case, the referential function in a novel is not the same as it is in a natural speech-act situation. As Barbara Smith has said, "News, or information is what the listener values in natural discourse. It is obviously not what he seeks or expects in a twice-told tale."[53] The context in a novel is best seen not as an effort to exhaust the natural world—not as mimesis—but as a set of rules by which to evaluate the characters and their actions. It is not that one should ignore the specificity of many of the locales and allusions in Dickens; much of the early activity of *The Dickensian* was to chart in the real world the progress of fictive characters. One should, however, recognize that some other function may lie behind the apparent referential function—that is, a reference can often be best read in terms of an emotive, conative, poetic, phatic, or metalingual function.

In fiction—especially in the fiction of Charles Dickens—there is a continuous operation of the phatic function, the set toward contact. Here, as Jakobson wrote, the message serves to check the physical channel and to "attract the attention of the interlocutor or to confirm his continued attention."[54] Almost uncannily, one can hear Dickens reiterating the phatic: "Come in. Come in. *Do* you read me? Do you *read* me? Over." To take one example, Dickens referred in *Our Mutual Friend* to "the Southwark Bridge which is of iron and London Bridge which is of stone."[55] Afterward he can refer to their presence without naming them: the "stone" and "iron" toll the theme of necessity, which is made evident to the reader in other ways. While the bridges have poetic value then—cross-referencing to the world of words—they are also visible in the quotidian world; the reader is able to locate them—and even to touch them. By so doing, the reader can feel included in Dickens's world of words. Hence, the referential function is also a phatic function, for contact between the fictive world and the reader's world seems to be the primary purpose.

The so-called tag lines used by and signifying particular characters are another form of the phatic function. When, for example, a previously introduced character is described but not named for some pages at the beginning of a chapter or installment, Dickens's purpose appears to have been to challenge the reader to invest in his world, to cooperate with the communication. Contact, not meaning, appears to have been the purpose—and certainly is the result. References to fairy-tale or pantomime figures or topical allusions to personages from the popular theater—or to people or issues in the current news—are not, primarily, emotive but phatic. "You see?" Dickens seems to have been pointing out, "we share the same context. We are in this together." Even those scenes and speeches that twentieth-century critics derogate most as "melodramatic" or "sentimental" or "homiletic" would perhaps be better viewed as efforts at emphasis—renewing contact, constituting a community. The frequent changes in the "mode of presentation" to which Horton has referred—the virtuoso variations of voice—can also be viewed in this phatic light.

What the mutability of functions in Dickens's prose points to, I believe, is an intention on his part to create a complete world of words, "novels where," as Peter Ackroyd says, "he conquers his isolation and fears by creating a community of love, where he can create his own world as a blessed alternative to the one which so threatened him."[56] It is an intention which George Steiner finds universal: *"Language is the main instrument of man's refusal to accept the world as it is....* Ours is the ability, the need, to gainsay or unsay the world, to image and speak it otherwise."[57] Replacing the world with a community of love can also be seen as a motive in the large amount of time and energy that Dickens devoted to private theatricals, speeches, and readings.

This is not a solipsistic use of language. Such a community can be established only in a concrete speech-act situation (and for Dickens the writing of novels was such a situation), in which an interlocutor cooperates with the speaker "according," as John Searle said, "to a system of constitutive rules."[58] The illocutionary effect, which is achieved "by getting our audience to recognize what we are trying to do,"[59] is in Dickens's case to get the readers to recognize that they are in a speech-act situation—that is, to recognize that they participate not in a world of "brute facts" but in one of "institutional facts."[60] The content of the work, bleak or comic, is indifferent; the reading public, no less than the public that had once viewed tragedies, should recognize that the content or meaning of the works is already circumscribed within—and is secondary to—the fact of community. The community is "the triangle of author, work, and reading public"—in which, as Jauss wrote, "the latter is no passive part, no chain of mere reactions, but even history-making energy."[61]

The evidence is copious that Dickens sought to establish upon the author-novel-reader axis a surrogate family, a community of love and understanding. Peter Ackroyd has argued that the "idea of entertainment, of an audience sharing in a certain pleasure"[62] was for Dickens a constant during his life; and he has argued further "that the boundary between fiction and reality" tends to disappear.[63] According to Forster, Dickens not only wanted his "imaginary worlds" to afford "an occasional refuge to men busily engaged in the world,"[64] but he also wanted "all things [to be] happily brought within human sympathy."[65] He wanted to create an ideal world of *harmony*—to use a word he so often employs.

This ideal world is created as well as expressed by the theatricality of Dickens's prose and person. Flamboyant in dress, Dickens was equally flamboyant in writing style. This style creates the passionate tone which the contemporary French critic Taine noted. But Dickens's readers understood the rules of the game; it is a theatricality that insists on dressing up ordinary life, of dwelling "upon the romantic side of familiar things" (BH Preface), of portraying life in what Ruskin in *Unto This Last* called "a circle of stage fire." But Ruskin might have called it a circle of numinosity.

With God dead and the faiths dying, Dickens took the last step in the march of Puritanism to affirm the final importance of earthly particulars—not because they are still signs of a divine grace that will translate the soul into another world, but because they are signs of the humane grace that will enable the soul to accept this world. In his prose, Dickens cast the light of eschatology over earthly matters. This light could well be perceived as delusive; but it might be better perceived as edifying. S. J. Newman speaks of Dickens's work as *sub specie theatri*.[66] The play on words is appropriate: the theatre has replaced eternity; the speech community has replaced the congregation. Fred Kaplan's suggestion in his biography that Dickens had a "performance personality" strikes home. While the performance lasts, faith lasts; and while faith lasts so does the community. Hence, a style that seemed to Taine to resemble monomania, and seems to many modern critics to be a falsification of experience (of the referential mode of language) in fact constitutes experience; for the primary experience of the novel was, for Dickens, the creation of a world of words that both the author and the reader could inhabit. Thus, Dickens's theatricality—his continual changing of tones and modes of presentation—can keep us alert to our necessary inclusion. As Robert Buchanan said more than a century ago, Dickens is the "good genie of fiction";[66] Dickens is the prophet of the *parlor:* the word was with God and the word was God.

To stress the phatic function in Dickens's work is not the end, however. To assume that the network of author, work, and reader survives as an atemporal, isomorphic triangle would be to make Dickens's fiction into a dead, a stillborn, language. Susan Horton has posited "the temporal nature of the reading experience" with "a *moving* reader, moving in all senses of that word: moving through a text, and being moved—to have expectations, surprises, reactions."[68] Dickens's fiction is living discourse—and as such creatively renegotiates and continuously rules the community; it is a growing, developing enterprise in time. As George Steiner has said, "So far as we experience and realise them in linear progression, time and language are intimately related: they move and the arrow is never in the same place."[69]

Even before Plato, mankind attempted to sever the objects of discourse from time. Derrida has dwelt upon the point that the attempt to reach the truth, the origin—before and outside time—is the essential flaw in Western thinking.[70] Language exists only in time. As the aboriginal "I am," language produces time—for time requires the human subject. It is no accident that Sartre defined human existence in much the same words that Hegel had used to define time: that which is not what it is and is what it is not.[71] According to Henri Bergson, "In real time, in the life of consciousness, there is a perfect continuity, and our self is at every moment, as it were, in a state of being born, absorbing its past and creating its future."[72] As the addresser changes, his message changes; as the message works, the addressee changes. The reaction in the addressee gives rise to motives for making other changes in the message, thus signaling changes in the addresser. Meanwhile, changes in the context affect all three constituent factors—which, in turn, become elements of the context, which they alter. Thus, language is like a wheel that cannot cease turning.

In the temporal nature of language, what is signified is not transmitted all at once, not holistically—but moment by moment, word by word. To gather in the meaning of phrases, sentences, paragraphs, and texts, the reader proceeds in time, processing the message in a series of looping operations. An archaic positivistic view of language would assume that words ring up meaning as they are processed by the reader—much as grocery prices are automatically tolled by the laser scanner. But this is not how natural language is processed. We hold significances for individual words in suspension as we work our way to the end of the sentence, waiting for time and the form and content of the sentence to supply information adequate enough to enable us to make an informed guess about the significances of earlier words.

As a rather simple example, take the following sentence with its missing word: "The man came out of the bank and _____ at me." What one knows about the "man" is practically nil until that slot between "and" and "at" is filled. What the reader will loop back to assign to "man" will be far different if the missing word were "smiled" rather than "shouted"; and it will be far more different if the missing word were "shot." Messages work in series of such loops until one is satisfied that there is information enough to make a final loop enclosing the entire message. That different readers create different loops goes without saying. Writers, too, can scarcely say the same thing twice. The "As ye sow, so shall ye reap" phrase that Dickens heard from his father went through a half-dozen mutations in tone and significance over the course of his career. My point is that the changes are continuous and that the triangle is not frozen in the act of communication—or as a result of it. All communication is dialogue, and there is always another word to be said; thus the dialogue is not only lively but living. Dickens wanted above all to attain a vital communion with his readers. To achieve this relatedness, Dickens dealt with topics that were at the forefront of the Victorian imagination: time and consciousness. If his dialectic of time created, and grounded, the community he desired, his sense of personal mortality could be blunted.

George Orwell opined that "All art is propaganda.... Every novelist has a message."[73] If every novelist wrote but one novel—and that a monological one—one might be prepared to concede the point. But few of us may be prepared to deny that dialogism may inform a work or that a voice from within the work may contradict the apparent voice of the author; and few of us may be ready to dismiss the possibility of change in the human consciousness that conceived the work. Even Orwell notes that "in every attack Dickens makes upon society he is always pointing to a change of spirit ... a change of heart."[74] But hearts do not change if everyone is already armed with a final message; in that case there would be no reason to hope that the propaganda of the artist will result in "a change of heart" in the reader. By the same token, if the artist always broadcasts the same message—but does not change himself—it would be the height of vanity to believe that he or she could effect a change in the reader. But the continuous changes in Dickens's messages and medium, I hope to show, will shatter the notion of art as propaganda or telementation—in other words, as political or religious ideas in a finalized state. No, at its best Dickens's art is a questioning, not a dictation. For Dickens was constantly in transition: testing, learning—altering stances, stereotypes, and philosophies. Needless to say, in the course of his immense output, some techniques—some conventions of content or form—remained in place: the "tricks and manners" that had previously succeeded in the phatic function are not recklessly discarded. Dickens seems to have felt that innovation had to be measured against the stability that provides communion. But there is an amazing amount of experimentation in his fifteen long novels—even in his shorter works, such as "Mrs. Lirriper's Lodgings"; and in nothing was he so relentless in trying out as the stances toward time.

It is not always possible to reach agreement on where Dickens stands on every issue. Was Dickens's stance toward the present that of a preconscious communist, or of a hypocritical capitalist? What is the relation of the individual to his epoch? Is the individual always guilty? Did Dickens sentimentalize the past, or did he fear and hate it? Did he believe that investing the human spirit in the future was an act of immoral abandonment of the present condition of England?—or that it was the only moral guide for the present? The literature reveals critics on both sides of each question—and at every tab between. My point is, simply, that Dickens was never finished. The dialectic goes on. And dialectic is exploration, not propaganda.

Like Wordsworth, Dickens seems to have viewed his own life as representative of the age in which he lived. He felt that what concerned him concerned all. He internalized what the age expressed; the age internalized what he expressed. The history of England, for example, is not a sacred scripture. He took a personal position, unabashedly judging historical characters as if they were present. He felt no less personal about the present. We know of his disdain for politicians whose "falseness of talk, of bombastic eloquence"[75] about the condition of nineteenth-century England would preclude dialogue. Whether Malthusian or Millenarian, those politicians and preachers who would suppress the joy of the present aroused his anger. They were brokers of the future—and mortgaged the present in the process. Dickens saw that their speech was a circumlocution—a speech that went around the audience and made no contact, especially not with the poor, who most needed to hear of times other than the present, including "Once upon a time."

The very phrase "Once upon a *time*" respects the differences in time: what once was is not now, and what is now will not always be. It thus announces a profound consciousness of time. Time, without the solace of eternity, suffused the Victorian addresser, the addressee, and the context. All was in movement. This realization of the mutability of all the elements in the speech-act made necessary the continual recourse to the metalingual and the phatic. Dickens felt this mutability to such an extent that he defined the human being as "a parting and farewell-taking animal"—in other words, as the animal who knows time. So it should be no surprise that in his fiction Dickens engaged in a dialectic upon time. If every human being is now always suffused, as William James said, with "a consciousness of whence and whither,"[76] Dickens can be seen as trying to discover within this modern consciousness an adequate stance toward each of the divisions of time, a stance that would distinguish the divisions and fuse them—and in so doing, heal the divided soul of man. If successful, Dickens would create in his art a community that could be continually renewed—and, thus, extended perpetually through time.

Charles Dickens

Part One
The Abuses of Time

1
The Dead Hand of the Past

> . . . and all my realm
> Reels back into the beast.
> —Tennyson, *Morte d'Arthur*

One of the most difficult things for one who is trying to read in good faith is to boot up, so to speak, the worldview of another era. This is certainly true of reading Victorian literature. Because the twentieth century is an age during which, for the most part, it is the future which seems to lower—atomic cataclysms, AIDS, environmental disasters—it is difficult for us to appreciate the extent to which, for the nineteenth century, it was the past that was most threatening. Then, civilization was imaged as a progress up a slippery slope from barbarism. One slip, personal or cultural, and the individual or nation would slide into barbarity again—and the present would be swallowed up by the past—which seemed always to be lying in wait, so to speak, for national or personal failure to take its own back again. I cannot overemphasize this dread of the past, clutching like a reptile at the heels of those climbing out of the swamp of barbarism.

Charles Dickens dreaded this lowering past, for himself and for England. As a consequence, he appeared to many of his contemporaries to be enthralled with the Victorian present. Even John Ruskin believed that Dickens was "a pure modernist," a member of the "steam-whistle party *par excellence*."[1] Certainly the public stance of Charles Dickens was as a staunch defender of his contemporary world, with all its mechanical and technological advances:

> Happening to think that the infallibility of the grumblers and the pre-Raphaelites just a trifle doubtful, and that the doctrine of Progress seems to me a hair's breadth nearer the truth, I will count on my fingers the blessings which the past days had and those which they

had not; and then we can strike the balance, and say which is best off, the San Graalites or ourselves.[2]

On the counts of education, personal freedom and dignity for the majority, public morality, sanitation, and so forth, the present easily wins.

> Yet though we have risen, slowly, painfully, and with many a hard struggle, out of this social degradation and ignorance ... there are yet men so ungrateful for their blessings, or so ignorant of the truth, who look back to all this blind and brutal past with an admiration they will not grant to the present, and regret even its brutality for sake of the fuller flavour of animal life about it.[3]

But Dickens was no idolator of the present. The vehemence of his argument here only attests to the power he felt in the past. Although he was speaking of the rise of the human race, he might have been speaking of his own experience—for the past had a tenacious hold on Charles Dickens. He himself had had to rise "slowly, painfully"—both as a man and as an artist—out of its grip. His work, in fact, can be seen as an extensive dialectic, in which each novel employs a different strategy for dealing with the past.

The "panic fear; the fear of ruin, of being thrust down again into poverty,"[4] was acutely personal for Dickens—but it was also general. As is well known, the primary source of Dickens's own obsession with the past was probably the period when he was employed at the age of twelve in Warren's blacking warehouse and his father was imprisoned for debt.[5] Being "cast away at such an age"[6] there, enduring the blight of all his boyish hopes, was bad enough; but scarring him much more deeply was his mother's demand, after he had been momentarily retrieved, that he be returned to full-time employment. The tightly reined prose in which he, many years after, confessed the pain in an autobiographical fragment evinced the repression of great passion: "I never afterwards forgot, I never shall forget, I never can forget, that my mother was warm for my being sent back."[7] Two commonplaces of the criticism of Dickens are that the paucity of adequate mothers in his fiction is related to this traumatic experience and that David Copperfield's sense of a "loss or want of something" expresses his creator's ambivalence toward his mother. The importance Dickens attached to his personal "loss or want" is made clear when he wrote of Alfred the Great: "But he had—as most men do who grow up to be great and good are generally found to have had—an excellent mother" (CHE, 3). Those who are not so fortunate seem doomed to suffer in all the constituents of time: in memory, in initiative, and in hope.

To Charles Dickens in the beginning of his career, suffering was the ineluctable baggage of the past—both his own and, by extension, the national past. Cast away as an innocent and ambitious boy of twelve, Dickens felt that his past epitomized the waste of the lives of millions of people in England. The inevitable question for him therefore was, What does one make of the suffering of the innocent? To this universal question, every writer has proffered an answer. Dickens continually offered answers; in each novel, these answers are implicit in the strategy he employed to deal with the past. But as each answer fell short—or revealed a negative side—he created a new strategy for the subsequent novel. Hence, his entire literary career might well be considered a continuous response to this question about the suffering of the innocent—which was for him the first of questions.

In the first novels, in fact, Dickens simply attempted to ignore the claims of the past, in order to suppress his own pain. Samuel Pickwick has no past; and Oliver surmounts his deplorable childhood with great ease. Although Nicholas Nickleby has no important past, Smike (in that third novel) may well represent an igneous outcropping of Dickens's feelings from his own past. With *Barnaby Rudge,* Dickens's strategy changed: here past suffering finally asserts its power for evil, a power which *The Old Curiosity Shop* had previously admitted. With the Christmas Books, Dickens's strategy altered again: in them he sought to affirm the personal past, purveying the idea that, the pain notwithstanding, the positive influence of any memory outweighs the negative. But with *Dombey and Son* and *David Copperfield,* the burden of the past lies not so much in its pain as in it vacuity—that "vague unhappy loss or want of something," which can warp the present more than grief or resentment can.

Soon the strategy changed again: in *Bleak House, Little Dorrit,* and *A Tale of Two Cities*, the evil of the past is derived not so much from the suffering of the innocent or the absence of love as from the efforts to defeat the past. Just to have escaped the clutches of the past now seems to bring a new kind of suffering: guilt—the consciousness of which now haunts the present. How can this different kind of suffering be expiated? Furthermore, in these later novels, the personal pasts are more thoroughly intertwined with the national enterprise and ideology—and, thus, the guilt resonates. *Great Expectations, Our Mutual Friend,* and *Edwin Drood* continue the exploration of ways in which man can keep the past from petrifying the present and from destroying the vitality of the spirit. But everywhere the horrible power of the past is acknowledged.

In this dialectic of the past, Dickens could not find a single strategy that was guaranteed to eliminate all the modes of evil emanating from the past. Still, there can be no full understanding of his creative imagination without an analysis of these strategies for making the past safe for men—strategies that were meant to free himself, his characters, and his audience from what we will call the "dead hand of the past." Dickens never uses the exact phrase; but, as we shall see, his imagery justifies our use of "dead hand" as the term for the past that is allowed to infiltrate and undermine present happiness. In common with the origin of the English law of the *mortmain*, Dickens's concern was that the goods of this world should be turned to immediate personal and social uses of the living.

The law was not only the source of the trope *mortmain* but was also the paradigmatic instance of the power of the past to affect the present. The law served as the particular example of the general concept in *Pickwick, Oliver, Barnaby Rudge, Bleak House, Hard Times,* and *Little Dorrit*—if not, also, in *A Tale of Two Cities*. For Stephen Blackpool in *Hard Times*, there are laws aplenty to punish but "a God's name . . . show me the law to help me!" (HT, 1, 11). The result of all Gradgrind's "sifting" in his parliamentary "cinder-heap" is, as Stephen says, "a muddle" (2, 5). In the next novel, it is no less a muddle for Mr. Dorrit, who is put into Marshalsea Prison without ever quite understanding the details of his circumstances or the laws that put him there. Perhaps nowhere is Carlyle's influence on Dickens stronger than upon his thinking about the worth of the laws enacted by Parliament. The laws, such as the Poor Law of 1834, merely imposed chains upon the living.

The dead hand of the past extended far beyond formal law. For Dickens the past was given authority as the source of the institutions, conventions, and habits that supplanted active moral life. As *All the Year Round* put it: "Of course no law compels you to worship this fetish [of custom]; but then, remember, if you rebel in those things you fall under the shadow of another fetish—a terribly potent old Man of the Sea, whose name is Respectability, and whose kingdom is unlimited and whose power is without check."[8] J. Hillis Miller, laying full emphasis on what he has called the "tangible, material presence of the dead forms of the past," has eloquently described the *umwelt* of Dickens's later novels:

> Characters do not fall naked into a naked world, but find themselves in a world which everywhere already has a sense. This meaning has been given to it by the past generations of the dead. The world is everywhere heavy with the debris of history. It is as though one had been set down in the midst of the ruins of an ancient city and were forced to live the dead life appropriate to it because everything around was still fabricated and valued.[9]

The individual feels helpless in a world so freighted with custom and significance. The past may also dominate the present through its deposit of material influences—that is, the individual is shaped by the tangible, visible world in which he finds himself. A dirty, ugly unhygienic environment directly distorts the character. Personal experience of the physical and social world, therefore, seems to recommend the priority of the past.

The past was also assigned a priority in the affairs of men by pseudo-deductive logic. Commonly in the nineteenth century, the paradigm of material causality was imported by mechanistic philosophy and science into human affairs. Since the present is in succession to antecedents, it must also be a consequent of antecedents. Hence, the present should be seen to be a "victim of circumstances" determined in the past. This frequently used motif of the "victim of circumstances"—which would contradict a belief in free will—runs throughout Dickens's novels. Therefore, it was usually treated ironically.

Even John Stuart Mill had great difficulty in preserving the notion of free will in the face of such antecedents. Committed to a materialist conception of the universe, he could not see how the individual could be free when everything that forms him extends beyond his reach into the past. Dickens obviously faced the same philosophical problem, but as only an occasional materialist he did not find it impossible of solution. Carlyle felt that mere material causes could be transcended, and so did Dickens. Both could have agreed with perhaps the greatest contemporary critic of the ideologies of their period, Friedrich Nietzsche, who urged

> against the doctrine of the influence of the milieu and external causes: the force within is infinitely superior; much that looks like external influence is merely its adaptation from within. The very same milieus can be interpreted and exploited in opposite ways: there are no facts.—A genius is not explained in terms of such conditions of his origin.[10]

John Forster's description of the intention behind *Oliver Twist* says much the same thing in the Victorian literary idiom: "It is indeed the primary purpose of the tale to show its little hero, jostled as he is in the miserable crowd, preserved everywhere from the vice of its pollution, by the exquisite delicacy of natural sentiment which clings to him in every disadvantage." After all, in the Romantic tradition—since Coleridge's "primary imagination" is universal—every man is, in Blake's terms, a "Poetical genius" and thus is free of mere circumstances.[11]

Nevertheless, in the course of his career, Dickens often conceded the potential power of material surroundings. These surroundings were also considered a derivation of the past. The living conditions that made it so difficult for Will Fern to be "decent" (TC), the depressing dampness of Chesney Wold (BH), the restrictive Marshalsea (LD), the polysemic "meshes" in which Pip grows up (GE), the Stone Lodge in which the Gradgrinds are raised (HT), the world between the two bridges in which the Hexams live (OMF)—all these physical surroundings affect the characters of the people in them. Granted, Dickens used these environments as symbols of the ideologies that in some sense constituted them. But it is clear that Dickens was alert throughout his career to doctrines that claimed the primacy of the material environment in the formation of the human spirit and that would in effect deprive the present of its scope for free action and the future of its promise.

Dickens was, if anything, more aware of the other, immaterial circumstances that were held to determine the present. The great frequency of the word *influence* in his later novels, especially in *Bleak House*, indicates that Dickens was becoming attuned to notions of historical determinism and psychological suggestion—as well as to those of material determinism. The word had both a metaphorical and a literal sense in Dickens's use of it, and it was employed in the narratives to indicate both material and immaterial determinations. Fred Kaplan has ably examined the sense of the word that Dickens probably garnered from mesmerism.[12] Ostensibly material but operationally spiritual—perhaps even derived from Descartes's "animal spirits"—the "magnetic fluid" of Mesmer entered human subjects at the agency of the operator and achieved therapeutic benefits. This invisible fluid was part of a general tendency of the period to smuggle in for the service of mankind former spiritual powers of healing—exiled by the materialistic scientists—by calling them subtle but material phenomena. Therefore, the word *influence* had not yet lost its material suggestion, however strong its connotation of ideological or spiritual effect was becoming. But influence could either support or negate free will. Dickens was aware of the many voices that argued for prior determination of human character and actions. He knew that human freedom—and, thus, the loving community—would be held hostage by these many different kinds of circumstances. Therefore, as different sorts of determinative circumstances or influences appeared in his fiction, his strategies for the defense of human freedom altered. His dialectic of the past, therefore, traces his developing awareness of different kinds of influence.

After a rather blithe attempt to remain in an elastic, unending present in *Pickwick*,[13] in *Oliver*, and in *Nickleby*, Dickens abruptly confronted the power of the past and the influence of the dead in *The Old Curiosity Shop*. The doomed girl, Little Nell, is too much the creature of sentimental melodrama, perhaps, to please twentieth-century tastes. But Nell can be seen as the beleaguered soul in the life of the present—and, in fact, all the dimensions of time afflict her. First, Nell is, like Master Humphrey, perhaps too sensitive to the present, with its intolerable "footsteps . . . in the midst of pain and weariness" (OCS, 1). As Philip Rogers points out, Nell's mistaken fear of change is the reason for her flight from London.[14] Separation from her grandfather, the center of her loving community, is her greatest fear. The second affliction is her grandfather's desire to make Nell "a fine lady" and thus save her from the contingencies of life. This attempt to fix the future—this early version of "great expectations"—would split the present and future. But to me, the past is Nell's heaviest affliction. Dickens made the most of the contrast between those signs of the past, "the dust, the rust, and the worm that lives in the wood" and the primary sign of the present, "the beautiful child in her gentle slumber" (OCS, 1). The old curiosity shop that the characters leave behind is itself a symbol of the past; it is little more than "one of those receptacles for old and curious things." Filled with curious but apparently useless items, the shop nevertheless has a supernatural influence, as the narrative shows—a binding influence on the present. When Nell cries out to her grandfather, "Let us be gone from this place, and never turn back or think of it again" (OCS, 3), we can easily imagine Dickens speaking either of his experience at Warren's blacking warehouse, where he suffered so much—or, indeed, of prior centuries, when the common people suffered so much. Nell also indicts both the material and immaterial influences of the place when she warns against turning back to it or even thinking of it again.

To capture something of the power that this book had for its original readers, therefore, we must acknowledge the dread of the encroaching past that pervaded the nineteenth century. Nell fails to escape the past; and in her death an entire generation could mourn its own potential failure. One reason she fails is that the old man carries the contaminating past with them; for another, Nell, too, seems to have been contaminated—to have been touched by the dead hand of the past. Having learned about the warriors and monks buried in the graveyard, Nell has "some dreams of those old times" (OCS, 54) from which she awakens, wishing for their return. She is, like Paul Dombey later, old-fashioned after all. She feels a "curious kind of pleasure in lingering among these houses of the dead" (OCS, 17) and is clearly attracted to any "old silent place" or "very aged, ghostly place" that promises the peace of death. For Nell is weary of life; and despite her words, she wishes to escape "this place"—not into the trials of the present but into death. The hold of the past proves too strong for even so precious a child—a melancholy upshot, indeed, in a novel of the 1840s, when the past called to England so powerfully. By delineating in *The Old Curiosity Shop* how innocent youth falls victim to the powers of time—and especially to the past— Dickens was sounding one of the primary themes of his fiction.

In Chapter the Last of the novel, intuiting the shop's symbolic responsibility for the catastrophe, Dickens remembered to mark an end to that initial setting with its morbid influence: "The old house has long been pulled down and a fine broad road was in its place." It is all too appropriate an end for the cancerous old place to be sacrificed to that symbol of contemporary progress— a fine broad road. But this final assertion of progress is, for me, simply unpersuasive. Even the marriage of Dick Swiveller, which redeems the Marchioness from the nullity of her own past, cannot cancel out the impression of loss. For Nell is dead; help came too late, and death has indubitably consumed the best of the present.

Barnaby Rudge, Dickens's fifth novel, thoroughly treats the past as a pernicious influence on the present. In the plots of both *Oliver* and *The Old Curiosity Shop,* the past is partly redeemed because friends and relatives issue from it attempting to save young victims. And though *Pickwick* and *Nicholas Nickleby* are placed in the recent past, each is essentially ahistorical. But *Barnaby* is decidedly an historical novel, going beyond the memories of its readers for its milieu to the Gordon Riots of 1780. In *Barnaby,* frequent attacks are made on the "good old times," when there were a "vast number ... who could not read or write" (1) and "people were hung in batches every six weeks" (11). This heavily ironic treatment of the theme of the "good old times" may be due to Dickens's topical political concerns,[15] but the tone leaves little doubt about the virtues of the past.

Although one would assume that the Gordon Riots were revolutionary in nature—and, therefore, presumably future-oriented—we are amazed to find that the rioters were not revolutionaries at all. Rather, they desired to get rid of "the innovating spirit of the times . . . resist all change . . . [and] restore those good Old English customs [mentioned elsewhere by Dickens]" (8). Gordon, Chester, and Dennis the Hangman agree with Simon Tappertit and his apprentices that innovation and progress have gone too far in England. Dennis, for example, holds that the law was created to punish and that capital punishment, like all things truly "constitootional," must be preserved against innovation. To this motif of temporal counterrevolution, the plot adds, as groundtones, a phantom figure out of the past and a long-unsolved murder. Even Grip, Barnaby's pet raven, seems to be a symbol of the past's influence on the present. The effect of this influence is powerfully felt by Barnaby's mother, who "shuddered, as though the hand of Death were upon her" (5), despite the chained, bolted, and double-locked door between it and her. This *hand of death* is not what we called the dead hand of the past but death-in-life. In this case, it shows up in the form of her missing husband, the murderer. Hers is only a more intimate example of the general influence of the past on the living.

In *Barnaby Rudge,* Dickens was perhaps at last facing up to—and beginning a tactic intended to disarm—his own past. There had been several child characters through whom he probably vented some of the self-pity he had stored up from the blacking days. Oliver and his dying friend in the work-house (who has the significant name of Dick) are quite likely expressions of this pity; Smike and the other boys at the Dotheboys Hall, as well as Nell, continue the burden. In *Barnaby,* however, we see pity for the victim being transformed into scorn for the oppressor. One such oppressor is old Joe Willett, a "father of the good old English type" (30). The pity is also transformed into rage, expressed in the violence of Hugh: "What else should teach me—me, born as I was born, and reared as I have been—to hope for any mercy in his hardened cruel place. . . . On that black tree, of which I am the ripened fruit, I do invoke the curse of all its victims, past, present, and to come" (77). While Hugh means that he is personally the fruit of the gallows on which his mother died, the curse is national and inevitable—for fruit like Hugh always ripens into terror. To the extent that the gallows represents English society in the eighteenth century—as it does for Dennis—Hugh thus curses England, past and present.

There are neglected children perhaps in every novel, but with Hugh we see the outrage done to them burst into rage: this is an early emphasis of a motif that is to erupt in full force in the other historical novel, *A Tale of Two Cities*—namely, "As ye sow, so shall ye reap" (that favorite expression of Dickens's father). Whereas in several earlier novels a blighted youth comes forward to elicit pity from the reader—and then either dies or is saved—now the blighted youth blights the present, as Jo does in *Bleak House*. In his dialectic of the past, Dickens was now able to envision the past not as a dead hand reaching up to pull the living present down but as rage destroying the present from within. Hence, the past could no longer be simply buried or forgotten; it had to be confronted.

In the first pages of *Martin Chuzzlewit*, there is a satire on the supposed antiquity of the Chuzzlewit family. Undue pride in lineage is certainly one of the ways in which the past incapacitates the present. However, except for old Martin's distrust of the motives of others, there are few other signs in this novel of a concern over the dead hand of the past. Perhaps Dickens's loss of faith (in 1842) in the young American republic altered to some degree his perception of the English heritage. This novel is a transition in Dickens's development of the theme. It stands midway between a vision of the past as a curse and his new vision of the past as a kind of unexpected grace.

Ebenezer Scrooge annuls the past in two ways. As a utilitarian, he supposes that one can confront all institutions and practices with a magic question of utility: to what degree does each practice foster pleasure and limit pain? He supposes further that, learning the degree to be inadequate, one can simply abolish the institution with a wave of the hand, no matter how cherished or flourishing the institution was. Utilitarianism, then, assumed its own ahistoricalness—not unlike Marxism. It could cut off the past without a tremor or repercussion. This assumption suits Scrooge, for it is also his personal inclination to proscribe the past. There is too much pain in it for him, not only in what he has suffered but, pointedly, in what he has chosen not to suffer, through his own indulgence in great expectations. Thus, the essence of his character—his pathetic flaw, so to speak—is to deny the value of the past. Peter Ackroyd believes Scrooge is an "exaggerated aspect" of Dickens as he was when he wrote *A Christmas Carol*.

Those temporal revisionists, the Ghost of Marley and the Ghost of Christmas Past, are primary agents of altering Scrooge's ruthlessly utilitarian disposition—a disposition meant not to be subject to the past at all. The rendition of the sow and reap theme by Marley's Ghost is: "I wear the chain I forged in life . . . and of my own free will I wore it" (CC, 1). According, therefore, to Marley's Ghost, not even eternity is free of the actions of the historical past. Hence, Scrooge is in error if he stifles the past. As we glimpse the details of Scrooge's past, we realize that it is not so much the memory of pain as the fear of pain in the future that has changed him. His character in the present is a precipitate of the fear of life he succumbed to when he gave up Belle. Her words are precise: "You fear the world too much" (2). Her own "memory of what is past" is important enough to give her the hope that Scrooge can remain faithful to their past and future. But Scrooge's fear changes him. Still, it was of his own free will.

At Fezziwig's joyous Christmas party, Scrooge is part of a community of love. When he abandoned Belle, he had abandoned all hope for such a community. A community of love cannot withstand analysis by utility, and it has no market value in laissez-faire economics. Thus, the dead hand is, in Scrooge's case, made powerful through rational economic decisions; the same limited rationality rejects the effects of the losses. Scrooge's decision to concentrate on gaining financial security is clearly a Benthamite decision, which severs the past and present and shows no concern for spiritual losses. Utilitarian sloganeering provides Scrooge with enough sense of rational justification to blind him to the fact that it is fear that drives him.

Long before Breuer and Freud's "talking cure," Dickens suggested that only by recalling the past—both happy and unhappy—can one disarm it and gain freedom. The past must be subject to present discourse; but the present is also subject to the past—with mutual, continuous looping effects. To permit this reciprocal flow between the past and the present is what Scrooge vows: "I will honour Christmas in my heart, and try to keep it all the year. I will live in the Past, the Present, and the Future" (4). The decisive step for Dickens here was to admit that the past can be a force for life—that to confront memories is a movement towards freedom, an emancipation into the full present.[16]

The same vision appears to have animated Dickens, a year later, in *The Chimes*. Finding that the events of his own past still lay like burrs underneath the success of the present, Dickens's strategy was to uncover the past fully, to use his fiction to probe once more the effects of suppressing the past. He seemed determined to demonstrate what a mistake it is to ignore or to suppress the past—the precise strategies he had adopted in his earlier novels. Through Trotty Veck and Meg, Dickens has shown that it is the memories of the past that help us preserve our humanity in the present. Therefore, the past must be preserved against such members of the "steam whistle" school as Sir Joseph Bowley. Bowley epitomizes the forces of contemporary society that would completely negate the past and the human values that are necessarily temporal. "I allow nothing," he says, "to be carried into the New Year. Every description of account is settled in this house at the close of the old one" (TC, 2). This practice of closing the books on the past—this zero-based ethical bookkeeping—depresses Trotty Veck, who, as a result, hears the bells that used to comfort him now begin to say: "Put 'em down, Put 'em down! Good old Times, Good old Times! Facts and figures, Facts and Figures! Put 'em down, Put 'em down!" (1).

The phrase "Good old Times" evokes two values. Insofar as it refers to prior centuries, echoing Filer's famous words, "what times they were!" it is mockery. It is Trotty's doubt that causes his misreading of the bells, "the poor man's only music," as Coleridge said. But, insofar as the good old times are personal, as in Meg's case, the phrase loses its ironic cast. This slippage between *signifie* and *signifiant* makes reading Dickens difficult, but it is by no means peculiar to him. "J. S. Mill saw the phrase wisdom of ancestors as one of those which had begun as an expression of respect and homage and had in time become a sarcastic gibe of hatred and insult."[18] It would be difficult to find the original disposition towards "wisdom of our ancestors" in Dickens, but "good old times" is definitely backtracking semantically as Dickens's dialectic of time continues. The "good old times" here should be read in the light of Bowley's anti-affective diatribes.

In *The Chimes*, the Goblin of the Bell makes it clear that the past centuries have brought human progress: "Ages of darkness, wickedness, and violence, have come and gone—millions uncountable, have suffered, lived, and died—to point the way before" the living (3). The point here is that the living must not permit the sufferings of the dead to have been in vain. Thus: "Time is for [the human being's] advancement and improvement; for his greater worth, his greater happiness, his better life" (3). The present must build on the painful past.

The national past is intended to haunt the melodramatic events of the next *Christmas Book,* titled *The Battle of Life.* Life's moral battles take place, symbolically, over the very bones of those who fought and died in the past. That conceptual setting notwithstanding, the past has little influence upon the actual narrative events, except in two etiolated ways. First, Marion's self-sacrifice is apparently predicated on her prior knowledge of Grace's goodness and present love. Second, knowledge of the horrible and pointless sufferings of humanity in the past ages has prevented Dr. Jeddler from taking life in the present seriously. From the excruciating national past, he has derived the notion that all life is best seen as a great farce. Dr. Jeddler's lack of earnestness even causes him to laugh at Marion for being moved by fiction—a characteristic we cannot but judge against the biographical evidence of Dickens's desire to elevate his calling. Dickens's satirical treatment of Jeddler makes the dual point that neither novels nor the past are to be considered trivial. Otherwise, this *Christmas Book* has little to recommend it. But in prostrating Michael Warden by her unselfish act, Marion brings him to beg the pardon of those he had intended to wrong. The concluding sentiment is "forget and forgive." Jingle, Monks, Sikes, Fagin, Ralph Nickleby, Chester, John Willet, Quilp, Squeers, Pecksniff, and Jonas Chuzzlewit—all these sinning characters are punished, either by events or through retribution. But in the *Christmas Books* we find for the first time the case for charity rather than for vengeance upon past misdeeds. Judged by the new theme of "forget and forgive," by no means are most of Dickens's novels *Christmas Books.* But this difference shows that Dickens changed his mind often about the past; the dialectic continued. "Forget and forgive" could almost be an injunction from Dickens's conscious to his unconscious mind: an injunction about what he should do with the pain of his own past.

For Dickens, however, to forgive the past was not at all the same thing as to obliterate it. Utter obliteration of the past—with all its painful memories—was no doubt a constant temptation for Dickens; and it is the considered choice of Mr. Redlaw, the Haunted Man of the *Christmas Book* of that name published in 1848. But in *The Haunted Man,* Dickens affirmed the discovery just barely noticeable in *The Battle of Life:* the pain of the past is not in itself the source of a dead hand. Dickens's dialectic grows even more subtle: it is precisely the effort to obliterate the pain of the past that promotes the growth of evil from it. The proper stance toward the past is expressed by the motto on the picture, with its double meaning, "Lord, Keep my memory green" (HM,

3). But Redlaw, in keeping with his name, angrily expresses the opposite desire: "Let me blot it from my memory!" (HM, 3).

Perhaps affected by the narrow confines of *The Haunted Man,* Dickens has merely expounded on—but has not altogether convinced us of—the strength of Redlaw's motivation. Yet, the sound of Dickens's own voice is heard, I believe, in the explanation Redlaw gives; and it reveals Dickens's intense desire to obliterate his own painful past:

> "No mother's self-dying love," pursued the Phantom, "no father's counsel, aided *me.* A stranger came into my father's place when I was but a child, and I was easily an alien from my mother's heart. My parents, at the best, were of that sort whose care soon ends, and whose duty is soon done; who cast their offspring loose, early, as birds do theirs; and, if they do well, claim the merit; and, if ill, the pity." (1)

The slight displacement of biographical facts does not mislead us; indeed, in *David Copperfield*—the novel Dickens was contemplating even as he finished *The Haunted Man*—Redlaw's deeply resented deprivations are merely divided between Steerforth and David Copperfield. Even with a rejecting mother and an inadequate father in his own past, Dickens arrived at the position that one ought to retain rather than obliterate the past. Certainly his own efforts to forget came to nought; thus, the final *Christmas Book* reiterates the theme of them all: one must somehow embrace the past.

In *Dombey and Son,* the dead hand returns in force with the tradition that Mr. Dombey follows in desiring a son to keep the family name and firm going. By concerning himself with a name—an abstraction—Mr. Dombey neglects concrete reality, sacrificing Florence as well as his relationship with Edith to his faith in impersonal abstractions. In caring only for Paul, he *wills* the scope of his love—thus negating its essence. Dombey is obsessed with a fear of change, which was perhaps the primary source of the strength of the dead hand in Dickens's England, whether individual or societal. The son, Paul, is described as "old-fashioned" or "peculiar" (and rightly has a taste for things old): what else should the son of the ancient firm of Dombey and Son be? In his desire to avoid change himself, Paul eventually slips into the ultimate changelessness—death.

Mr. Dombey's inability to change remains part of his character almost to the very end. Bereft of Paul and his firm and—through his heartlessness—of Florence and Edith, Dombey broods alone in his desolate house. He passes hours listening to the voices of the past: "Let him remember it in that room, years to come" (DS, 59). He had driven Florence from him that day in that room; and by taking the past to be irrevocable, he indulges in more of his characteristic refusal to admit change:

> But that which he might have made so different in all the Past—which might have made the Past itself so different, though this he hardly thought of now—that which was his own work, that which he could so easily have wrought into a blessing, and had set himself so steadily for years to form into a curse: that was the sharp grief of his soul. (59)

Dickens created a masterly portrait when he showed that Dombey, for all of his remorse over Florence and his ruin, would not, even then, change his character, "so proud he was in his ruin, or so reminiscent of her, only as something that might have been his, but was lost beyond redemption—that if he could have heard her voice in an adjoining room, he would not have gone to her" (59). Dombey's ruling passion is always a desire for stasis, to stamp all time with the changeless initials of his firm. His whole being is pervaded with the spirit of the dead hand of the past. Now, he wills that his very sorrow and ruin go on unchanged. He fails to see that love is the only changeless element in this world and that all else changes whether one wills it or not.

As Dombey considers suicide—an act which would render his past permanent—Florence comes back, once more asking for forgiveness! Twentieth-century readers may have to overlook her melodramatic loyalty in the bright light of Dickens's theme. The narration summarizes Dombey's sudden realization of the nature of Florence: "Unchanged still. Of all the world, unchanged" (59). And when Florence asks her father to accept her son, Paul Dombey Gay, "for the sake of the name . . . you had a son of that name once" (59), the changelessness that ultimately transforms him is fully experienced by the reader. Ironically, the only thing in Dombey's past that is not included in his desire for stasis is the only thing that survives unchanged: Florence's love.

K. J. Fielding has written of *David Copperfield* that the "novel suggests that Dickens was still satisfied (or wanted to be satisfied), as he wrote in his autobiography, to 'know how all these things have worked together to make of me what I am.'"[19] Harold Bloom's suggestion that it "is the first therapeutic novel"[20] is closer to the urgencies I feel in the novel—although a study of Dickens's dialectic of the past certainly must assume that all the novels take their place as therapeutic efforts. In his biography of Dickens, Fred Kaplan has found many characters who are versions of living characters: "In Dombey Senior, he created a version of John Dickens transformed into a self-contained monster of personal pride and love of self, that very aspect that had resulted in Charles's being sent to the blacking factory."[21] Certainly, in this novel, Dickens seems to have been working out much of the bitterness of his own past, against his own father and mother. It is almost as if Dickens, like his character Traddles, were drawing skeletons during his misery, with the hope that he could draw the residue of the bitter sense of injustice and humiliation and its concomitant fears right out of himself, even as Traddles apparently succeeded in doing.

Traddles's peace with the past is illustrated when David, meeting Traddles years after their school days together, speaks bitterly of their sadistic taskmaster Creakle:

> "He was a brute to you, Traddles," said I, indignantly, for his own humor made me feel as if I had seen him beaten but yesterday.
> "Do you think so?" returned Traddles. "Really? Perhaps he was, rather. But it's all over, a long while. Old Creakle!" (27)

Dickens can all but be seen admonishing himself over his experience at the blacking factory: it's all over, Charles, a long while. Earlier in the novel, Aunt Betsey had given the implication of this attitude: "It's in vain, Trot, to recall the past, unless it works some influence on the present" (27). This was Dickens's strategy for achieving a declaration of peace with his past. The past can be made to render benefits to the present—specifically, the benefit of moving, softening the heart. Otherwise, it is vanity to recall the past; all other uses of past pain belong to the dead hand.

Ironically, although Aunt Betsey does not recall the past, it recalls her periodically in the form of her ex-husband. This little mystery is not a gothic excrescence upon the plot but possesses considerable thematic relevance. Betsey's attempts to deal with her own unhappy past are integral to the fabric of the novel. Betsey's problem reminds us that the power of the past is real and is not simply subject to the will. It cannot be wished or reasoned away. It will out. This insidious power of the past to interrupt the present is portrayed comically in the way King Charles I continually pops his errant head into Mr. Dick's memorial about current injustice. Mrs. Gummidge is another example of one who allows the past to dictate circumstances in the present. And Uriah Heep is a manifestation of Dickens's growing awareness of danger in the present emanating from the public past—namely, from the prior treatment of the poor. Heep's ambition and malignity are comprehensible to—if not compassionated by—Dickens. Heep is a Bill Sikes or Hugh of the Maypole, with equal power of devastation—but with greater caution. Heep's ultimate defeat does not mitigate this insidious power of the past. However, if the settings of *David Copperfield* are seen as a series of loving communities destroyed in turn by some form of the dead hand, the defeat of Heep saves the final community.

Perhaps the dead hand is given its ultimate representation by Mr. Spenlow, who considers it "the principle of a gentleman to take things as he found them" (33). It might be better said that he leaves things as he finds them, as his dying intestate shows. With Dora, the genteel principle has disastrous results. Her inability to adapt is a direct result of her undisciplined upbringing, which is consistent with the "principle of a gentleman." Hence, the novel moves from personal predilections to social and ideological implications.

This surprisingly open confrontation with his personal past in *David Copperfield* completed, Dickens in later novels would return to the themes of *A Christmas Carol* and *Dombey and Son*, probing the ways in which the dominant ideologies spread the curse of the dead hand into individual lives. The principle of the dead hand is the principle of no change: as it was in the past so it shall always be. This conservative principle has allies everywhere. Many of the ideals of Victorian society would save the individual from change. From *David Copperfield* on, for example, Dickens would make the point repeatedly that this "principle of a gentleman" was, as public policy, the root of the national evil. The poor, the principle implied, ye shall always have with ye and in their assigned stations, so meddle not with God's disposition. As unjust as this principle was for the poor (who would be spared by it the effort of social mobility), the rich were also harmed by this deference to the past, which would spare them the effort of emotional movement. The surest symptom of infection by the dead hand is manifest in the way in which so many wealthy characters in Dickens's novels are rendered careless, both in the sense of reckless and in the sense of passionless. A prime embodiment of both symptoms is Steerforth, who explicitly recognizes his kinship with "the bad boy" of the nursery tale "who didn't care." Dickens feared that England was raising an entire generation of middle-class men who lacked the ability to care. The English were being schooled,

Dickens felt, to be uncaring not only for the here and now of their own lives but for the there and now of others. In *David Copperfield,* the Steerforths and Rosa Dartle notoriously agree, ex cathedra, that the lower classes cannot feel deeply. The paradox is that in order to believe in this *apathia* in others, one must have been trained to be unfeeling.

An important transformation is evident here—one that links the internal sphere of feelings with the external world of action. The metaphor "to move" draws upon the Romantic idea of the moral effect of art—especially that of Wordsworth, who emphasized the meaning of the metaphor in "Tintern Abbey." Enhanced through the experiences of art, the capacity to be moved is, in the numerous adaptations of Shaftesbury's doctrine of "benevolism," a primary source of morality. By means of sympathetic imagination—what Shelley called "Love," or "a going out of our own nature"[22]—one is moved to acts of generosity and altruism. All this is well known. Equally well known is Dickens's personal addiction to physical movement—and even speed. In his novels, Dickens drew together the moral metaphor and the literal sense of "to move." For Dickens, anything that curtailed physical, social, and psychological forms of movement was wrong and must be fought; anything, in a word, that prompted an individual to stop where he was—to remain contained within himself—was the dead hand. Class divisions, reliance on precedent, dependence upon immutable abstractions—all of these human tendencies to stand pat endangered the capacity of the human being to continue to be moral. The human being was free only insofar as he or she was "fluid"—to use another frequent metaphor of Dickens's—or soft enough to be moved. Dickens's later novels constitute a compendium of the kinds of ways the dead hand can harden and immobilize the normal individual and the nation.

In *Bleak House,* the dead hand (which each human being harbors) is abetted by fetishes of the world of fashion and Chancery Court. Representative of governmental institutions at large, Chancery Court is characterized by that joke of a case, Jarndyce and Jarndyce, which is early on given the image of a malignant hand: "How many people out of the suit Jarndyce and Jarndyce has stretched forth its unwholesome hand to spoil and corrupt would be a very wide question" (1). John Jarndyce has seen the evil influence of Chancery Court; in his action and his advice, he warns the young people, "Don't found a hope or expectation on the family curse" (24).

But Richard cannot be saved; he admits that the case "has gone on unsettling me ever since" earliest childhood (23). And the evidence of its effect on him is provided much earlier and in terms we have come to expect: "Richard had a carelessness in his character" (9). Despite the fact that his "was as frank and generous a nature as there possibly can be" (9), the dead hand of the past in the guise of the Jarndyce case spoils him. He wages a losing battle against the immense "influences of mace and seal" loosed by the case. As John Jarndyce admits, "The character of much older and steadier people may be even changed by the circumstances surrounding them" (13). But even John's well-meaning advice to take the past for granted, Esther's good efforts, and Ada's love cannot dissuade Richard from settling down into the enveloping case. Because Jarndyce and Jarndyce *is,* it deserves to be brought to a conclusion—or so we can suppose Richard's rationalization to come down to. In other words, because the past was and still is unfinished, the present cannot move. As he did so often by playing with words, Dickens has shown us that the Jarndyce case has *jaundiced* Richard's perception of reality. Richard does not realize that the past is never finished.

In fashionable society, or the so-called World, the dead hand also rules: "Both the world of fashion and the Court of Chancery are things of precedent and usage" (2). Even though Lady Dedlock seems to set most of the precedents that this world slavishly follows, we find both her freedom and her capacity to care as much curtailed as those of the rankest parvenu. To gain her position, Lady Dedlock had to forsake her natural feelings; and the result is that she lives in a "desolation of boredom and the clutch of Giant Despair." Her persistent boredom is eloquent testimony to her abandonment of her human prerogative to care. But the discovery that her daughter is alive brings the heart of Lady Dedlock to life again, if only to support a few noble actions: to announce herself to Esther; to save her young servant Rosa from scandal by sending her away; and, finally, to seek her ex-lover's grave. But otherwise, Lady Dedlock (as her name suggests), like a beau ideal of Victorian society, was

> so long accustomed to suppress emotion and keep down reality, so long schooled for her own purposes in that destructive school which shuts up natural feelings of the heart like flies in amber and spreads one uniform and dreary gloss over the good and the bad, the feeling and the unfeeling, the sensible and the senseless, she had subdued her wonder until now. (55)

Wonder, as we are to discover from Gradgrind (HT) and Mrs.

General (LD), is a most unrespectable emotion and must be considered the first target of the dead hand. In *Bleak House,* "respectability" becomes a code name for—and a major force of—the dead hand.

"Respectability" has many forms in *Bleak House,* and all of them are fatal to natural feelings and affections. There is at the one extreme old Turveydrop, who has in the name of Deportment transformed himself into a tailor's dummy: "He had established such a long prescriptive right to this Deportment" (50) that the younger generation does not even question it. To Turveydrop, the "past" really does consist of the "good old times." The present has unfortunately "degenerated," he says, for a "levelling age is not favourable to deportment. It spreads vulgarity" (14). As Chester in *Barnaby Rudge* would agree, manners are to come before feelings. At the other extreme of "respectability"—but equally resistant to natural emotions—is the lawyer Vholes. Everything he does in his profession is supposedly warranted by his concern for his aged father and three daughters. But the reader should have no difficulty in discerning that Vholes's commitments are more abstract than that: "Dressed in black, black-gloved, and buttoned to the chin, there was nothing so remarkable in him as a tireless manner" (37). For this apt representative of the dead hand, it is appropriate that his "place was last painted or whitewashed beyond the memory of man" (39). Tulkinghorn naturally speaks approvingly of Vholes: "Mr. Vholes is considered, in the profession, a *most* respectable man."

What neither Vholes nor Tulkinghorn can tolerate "is a family name compromised" (48). All considerations of morality and of feeling must yield to that Moloch, the family name. They would have served Dombey well. Vholes and his ilk demand respect and remuneration as the reward for their devotion to the dead hand of the past—"for continually doing duty, like a piece of timber, to shore up some decayed foundation that has become a pitfall and a nuisance" (39). For Dickens, what went by the name of respectability had by this time forfeited all claim to respect: reactionary, callous, superficial, and self-serving, respectable men and women were inevitably in the hire of past precedent—and precedent, in turn, was in the hire of injustice. While it had been possible for Dickens to use the word *respectable* in a positive sense heretofore, with the writing of *Bleak House* it acquired a pejorative sense which, with but few exceptions, it retained in all his following novels.

The injustice of the social system is stressed in *Bleak House,* wherein life with justice and hope—like a Laocoön—is strangled by the several kinds of precedent that dominated Victorian ideology. Under the guise of precedent, the dead hand makes many kinds of assaults upon living beings. All the assaults have one element in common: success is assured when the victim's will to care is withered. This carelessness is manifested in several ways, but they are summed up in the generic term, *dandyism*. According to the narrator of *Bleak House,* there are dandies in all stations of life who,

> in mere lackadaisical want of an emotion, have agreed upon a little dandy talk about the Vulgar wanting faith in things in general; meaning in the things that have been tried and found wanting, as though a low fellow should unaccountably lose faith in a bad shilling, after finding it out! Who would make the Vulgar very picturesque and faithful, by putting back the hands upon the Clock of Time, and cancelling a few hundred years of history. (12)

These dandies "have found out the perpetual stoppage" (12). While Young England may have been the manifest target here—just as the Pre-Raphaelites were for much the same reason[23]—the dandyism that Dickens upbraided was no mere fad: it was an ideology that had dominated human thought for ages. Its Victorian version was detectable by the "smooth glaze" it put over its subjects, who, above all, were "to rejoice at nothing and be sorry for nothing"—who were to be, in a word, careless. This smooth glaze is Mrs. General's ideal in *Little Dorrit*. Her very name suggests that the dandyish form of the dead hand is alien to specific, personal relationships and thrives only in the abstract and dehumanized ideals of the culture.

When dandyism is defined as "a practice that renders people careless," we see that Thomas Gradgrind in *Hard Times* qualifies as a dandy. Despite all his newfangled ideas on child rearing, education, and the nature of social relationships, Gradgrind condones any attempt to legislate the feelings out of human experience. A feeling, after all, is not a hard, quantifiable fact that he, like all of Dickens's utilitarians, believes solely to embody the truth. On this basis, we can distinguish the difference between Gradgrind and someone like Sir Leicester Dedlock, with whom Gradgrind would seem to have a great deal in common. But a comparison reveals—and this is of great moment to Dickens's own dialectic of the past—that Sir Leicester does, after all, care much for his Lady. Although his family is as old as the hills, Sir Leicester has not let his sense of his own priority petrify his heart. Moreover, we find too that Mrs. Rouncewell truly cares for Sir Leicester. It is a testimony to the honesty of Dickens's dialectic that almost the last excellent servant in the novels gives her allegiance to a baronet of such antiquity.[24] The example of Sir Leicester shows that carelessness is not necessarily part of the inheritance of an individual with ancient lineage.

Although ostensibly a Philosophical Radical, Gradgrind is hardly to be distinguished from those defenders of precedent who have been called to Chancery Court. When his daughter Louisa speaks to him about life, he points out mechanically that her life is "governed by the laws which govern lives in the aggregate" (1, 15). Gradgrind, habituated to speaking in generalities, cannot see that his own daughter is appealing, as he says later, not for "the wisdom of the Head" but for "a wisdom of the Heart" (3, 1). Although Gradgrind has been, as Louisa goes on to say, so "careful of me," he is even more careful of his ideology. Like all dandies—such as those dandy appreciators of art that Dickens has described in *Pictures from Italy*—Gradgrind is not at home in the concrete, human fact of life. He has let a glaze of ideas intervene between his natural feelings and his actions.

Far from being truly radical, Gradgrind is, in fact, rather toothlessly bourgeois. Not only is he taken in by Bounderby's bogus claims, but he takes up Mr. James Harthouse—a dandy by any definition. In both cases, the old ailment of the bourgeoisie—the need for respectability—has infected and befuddled Gradgrind. When Louisa admits to an antisocial thought (being tired of everything), Gradgrind is scandalized in the best unreflective, unphilosophical fashion: "What would your best friends say, Louisa? Do you attach no value to their good opinion? What would Mr. Bounderby say?" The narrator adds that Gradgrind spoke "as if Mr. Bounderby had been Mrs. Grundy" (4). Respectability, not analysis, is the first principle of such Radicalism, and marks it with the dead hand.

By recruiting Harthouse for his political party, Gradgrind shows a nose for precedent and respectability. For, says the narrator, those in charge of the Gradgrind School "liked fine gentlemen; they pretended they did not, but they did" (2, 2). Dickens was not the only person to see the form of the dead hand under the capitalist glove; but in *Hard Times,* he showed precisely how the old aristocracy and the new plutocracy united on the plane of carelessness. For the laissez-faire capitalists, carelessness was enjoined by economic principle. Charity was counterproductive.

The system could function beneficially for all only if well-meaning but misguided efforts to curb capitalistic excesses were renounced. "Verb neuter," as Tom Gradgrind says (2, 3), "not to care" seems to be the psychological corollary of the aboriginal economic law of supply and demand.

For the aristocracy, on the other hand, a pretense of ease and carelessness had become habitual—an unquestioned centuries-old precedent created by the ideal of *sprezzatura*. Whereas the explicit philosophy of the bourgeoisie induced uncaring public behavior, the implicit philosophy of the aristocrats boiled down to uncaring private behavior. In both cases, caring had been ruled out of modern life. James Harthouse sums it up:

> I assure you I attach not the least importance to any opinions. The result of the varieties of boredom I have undergone is a conviction (unless conviction is too industrious a word for the lazy sentiment I entertain on the subject), that any set of ideas will do just as much good as any other set, and just as much harm as any other set. There's an English family with a charming Italian motto. What will be, will be. It's the only truth going. (2, 2)

Such a motto expresses a cynicism that is one of the worst imprints of the dead hand, for it denies to the present the power to alter itself and the future through responsible action. Of course, for the privileged, such fatalism has the benefit of deprecating personal responsibility for the social ills surrounding them.

Harthouse does manifest a slight interest in seduction and believes that he sees in the unhappily married Louisa Bounderby a likely object for his interests. Noticing the importance to Louisa of her brother Tom, Harthouse muses that the "whelp is the only creature she cares for. So, so." Tom unconsciously encourages Harthouse by saying, "My sister Loo? . . . *She* never cared for old Bounderby" (2, 3). Dickens was touching a deep level of commitment in the Victorian era—marital loyalty. Dickens could find no stronger anxiety with which to arm his dialectic. He would have the reader know that loyalty depends not upon principles, economic or otherwise, but upon affection. A doctrine that attempts to do without caring is therefore a doctrine that must do without moral pretensions. Loyalty requires morality; and without loyalty, there is no loving community. The virtue of individuals—and of society—is a function of their ability to care. But Gradgrind's utilitarianism is preeminently a doctrine that omits human caring. Tom sums it up again: "Verb neuter, not to care. Indicative mood, present tense. First person singular, I do not care; second person singular, thou dost not care; third person singular, she does not care" (2, 3). To care is the wisdom of the heart that Gradgrind must learn through his own humiliation and suffering.

With the Steerforths and Spenlows, we observed some of the ways family pride and family tradition can become part of the dead hand of the past. But the case of Gradgrind brings out Dickens's new dialectical position, for Dickens recognized that a child's present can be corrupted not only by a family's carelessness (as in his own experience) but also by too much carefulness. Much of this carefulness is wholly selfish, as in the case of the family of Traddles's Sophy. "You see," says Traddles, in the naive mode of narration that is endemic to David's own narration and that works by upsetting the readers so much that they arrive at the unspoken truth, "Sophy being of so much use in the family, none of them could endure the thought of her ever being married" (DC, 61). Caddie is in the same bind with Mrs. Jellyby—as is Prince with Mr. Turveydrop. If Dickens's own childhood was maimed by the carelessness of his family, he eventually grew to see that even ostensibly selfless care for the family honor—represented by Chester, Dombey, Steerforth, Mrs. Sparsit, Mrs. Merdle, Mrs. Gowan, Mrs. Pocket, Mrs. Wilfer, Podsnap, and many others—can be as destructive of the individual's spirit as the carelessness of Miss Murdstone, Mrs. Clennam, or Mrs. Joe. This realization was not a small step in Dickens's development.

In *Hard Times,* Dickens did not miss the opportunity to show that the working class—immune to the spiritual afflictions of the aristocracy and plutocracy—can still care. Stephen Blackpool, with "the rugged earnestness of his place and character," speaks of his fellow workers:

> "They're true to one another, faithfo to one another, fectionate to one another, e'en to death. Be poor amoong 'em, be sick amoong 'em, grieve amoong 'em for onny o th moony causes that carries grief to the poor man's door, an they'll be tender wi you, gentle wi yo, comfortable wi yo, Chrisen wi yo. Be sure o that, ma'am. They'd be riven to bits, ere ever they'd be different." (2, 5)

Sissy Jupe is a particular example of the natural feelings of the poor that have not yet been expunged by political doctrine, education, social custom, or economic theory. But the novel warns that even in the children of the poor the natural capacity to be concrete and caring—and, therefore, moral—is being rooted out by the

M'Choakumchilds on the one hand and the Bounderbys on the other. Such a training in carelessness is another operation of the dead hand. With Stephen Blackpool's inability to obtain a divorce from his alcoholic wife, Dickens broached in *Hard Times* one of the ways that the dead hand afflicted him personally.

Little Dorrit, K. J. Fielding has observed, is "very much a novel of the past, of memory, and deeply concerned with how to treat a determined dwelling on past wrongs and seeking for past happiness."[25] Fielding is right: *Little Dorrit* is Dickens's most searching examination of his sense of sclerosis and of the social entropy that derives from the manifold forms of the dead hand.

Although Lionel Trilling has felt compelled to argue for the continued relevance of *Little Dorrit* in a world so improved that the "dead hand of outworn tradition no longer supports special privilege in England,"[26] we do not see that the relevance of the novel is a problem—taking "dead hand" in the metaphoric way we have been using it. The dead hand has as many manifestations now as it had then. All of these manifestations have in common the freezing of feeling and of action by precedent, fashion, or political stance. This is so profusely illustrated in *Little Dorrit* that K. J. Fielding's reading of the intention behind the novel almost understates the case: "For as well as being about the characters who refuse to accept the past, the novel—as far as it concerns both Arthur Clennam and Little Dorrit—is also largely about the return to the scene of an unhappy and even wronged childhood to find freedom and fulfillment."[27] With the exception of Doyce and perhaps of Meagles—and certainly of Maggie who has a past that goes back only to the hospital room from which she emerged, eternally ten years old—nearly all the other characters in the novel are coerced by the past to conform in characteristic ways.

Although William Dorrit, while in Marshalsea prison, wished that his children might see him as he was in the past—upon being freed, he wants to erase the nearly twenty-four years of prison life; and he directs his children never to refer to it. In prison, he not only accepted the past, he invoked it. He founded his position as Father of the Marshalsea on it. Afterward, in Italy, he would deprecate it; but it is not to be effaced—and consumes him at last. Whether the scene is set in the Marshalsea or in Italy, prison imagery dominates the narrative, implying that constraints on freedom are elected by individuals throughout society. In accepting the social system upon which he builds his present—both in the Marshalsea and in Italy—Dorrit is, in essence, taking the dead hand of the past into his own. He may deplore certain antecedents; but he nevertheless gives himself over—except for rare moments—to the dead hand of the past. He may wish to "sweep it off the face of the earth and begin afresh" (2, 5); but such words are vain when one begins afresh each time with a mind that is set in the most ancient patterns available.

Amy's brother and sister reflect the power of the dead hand in their own ways. Tip—who, like Tom Gradgrind, is so easily "tired of everything" (1, 7)—is to have about him forever the shadow of the prison wall. To obviate the pernicious power of the past, one must act. But what Tip's past has done is precisely to eviscerate his energy to act. Fanny's case is slightly more complex. After Fanny changes from a dancer to an heiress, there is a marvelous depiction of how she and Mrs. Merdle tacitly conspire to ignore the past—in which Mrs. Merdle had prevented a relationship from developing between Fanny and her son, Sparkler. It would seem, then, that they have conspired to eviscerate the past of its power. But, in fact, Fanny is far from free of it. Her reason for marrying Sparkler is clear: "Especially as I should have many opportunities, afterwards, of treating that woman, his mother, in her own style. Which I most decidedly should not be slow to avail myself of, Amy" (2, 7). To live for revenge is obviously to defer to the past. Dickens seems to have been commenting to himself that even to wreak the revenge desired is to give one's self up to life under the dead hand.

Similarly, Fanny's reproach of Amy for walking in the company of the pauper, Old Nandy, reveals the extent to which mere respectability dominates her vision of life. Even her exclamation, "I have told you already, so don't fly in the face of Providence by attempting to deny it!" (1, 31) admits her bias towards the dead hand—and, incidentally, shows a facet of the dead hand that can be called, after its arch-proponent, "Podsnappery." Even when Amy tries to talk Fanny out of the marriage with Sparkler, Fanny confesses the extent to which the past possesses her: "Other girls, differently reared and differently circumstanced altogether, might wonder at what I say or do. Let them. They are driven by their lives and characters; I am driven by mine" (2, 14). But Amy, who under similar circumstances is not similarly driven, is next to her; and the reader sees that Fanny is not being passively driven but is herself the driver. Fanny merely uses the idea of antecedents as an excuse; by accepting the dead hand, she becomes engaged not to Sparkler but to the past.

With almost every character in *Little Dorrit*, Dickens has illuminated another facet of the dead hand. Rigaud displays the malady in two ways. As a "gentleman"—whom he defines as one who never works—he insists on a social distinction now moribund. Moreover, his self-definitions could be used by Sartre as studies in bad faith. "Frankness is part of my characters" (1), he says; being enraged under certain given circumstances is also an inalienable given of his character. Having accepted this heteronomous definition of himself, Rigaud ceases to define himself; thus, he gives up autonomy. He has transformed himself into an *en-soi*. But in the superstitious scheme of traditional society, both of these given characteristics mark him as a "gentleman"—which provide him with definite benefits in such a society.

On the other hand, Mrs. Clennam—going even farther back than the aristocratic precedent for a pattern for her practice—models her stance toward the world upon the prophets of the Old Testament. Her whole present is predicated on her sufferings. By continuing to suffer—or, as she paradoxically calls it, "to submit"—she justifies a perpetuation of her revenge. "I have done," says Mrs. Clennam, "what was given to me to do. I have set myself against evil! not against good. I have been an instrument of severity against sin" (2, 31). The word "severity" totally judges her in Dickens's perspective. Her motto, D. N. F. (Do Not Forget), in effect also means Do Not Forgive; thus, she keeps the past disparate, mute, and unnegotiable. Dickens himself agreed with Haredale in *Barnaby Rudge*, who says: "All good ends can be worked out by good means. Those that cannot, are bad" (79). Thus Mrs. Clennam and a certain religious style in England stand judged. Furthermore, her suggestion that she was called—that she had to do as she did—bespeaks a fatalism that would deny meaningful human choice, putting all eventualities into the reins of the dead hand. Whenever one conforms to mere precedent—legal, social, ideological, or psychological—one ceases to take active care. To cease to take active care is not only "How Not To Do It"—as that important theme in the novel puts it—it is also to operate as if consequences can be divorced from personal responsibility.

Two other characters in *Little Dorrit* show how daring Dickens had become in his exploration of the phenomena of the dead hand. He looked at the undersides, first, of what appears to be a call to individual freedom, and, second, of a Carlylean call to work. The first is Miss Wade's call to Tattycoram to assert her personal dignity and freedom. To put this affecting cry for personal freedom in the mouth of a fatalist is a potent irony. Miss

Wade's radical—like Mrs. Clennam's orthodox—fatalism alienates event and human intention. In neither case is one to bear responsibility for what must, by ancient impulse, happen. The Carlylean call is represented by Pancks's submission to the Victorian work ethic; and it accomplishes the same thing as Wade's fatalism. Pancks accepts no responsibility for the future, for the consequences of his actions. He believes doing his work is "The Whole Duty of Man" (1, 13), all that can be asked of him. Both kinds of call disguise ruthlessness and petrify the heart. They sever past from present, individual from individual. Because such beliefs deny viable choices in life, they serve the dead hand, not the virtue they name.

Many critics have called *Little Dorrit* the darkest of Dickens's novels. Certainly, a sort of entropy seems to prevail because (1) many characters who try to act see their actions suffer a moral short circuit; (2) there is a Circumlocution Office; (3) the protagonist Arthur Clennam believes he has no will; and (4) even the good-hearted people like Flora live in the past—she being, significantly, "wholly destitute of the power of separating herself and him from their bygone characters" (1, 13). But if we inspect the power of the past—which is amply represented by Flora's housemates, the Patriarch and Mr. F's aunt—we see how comically hollow that power is. Hence, in this novel the "darkness" may be more shadow than substance. We soon learn that the Last of the Patriarchs is all appearance; he is so "grey, so slow, so quiet, so unpassionate, so very bumpy in the head" (1, 13) that he has no substantial power. But perhaps the epitome of the dead hand in its feckless aspect is Mr. F's aunt. "When we lived at Henley, Barnes's gander was stole by tinkers" (1, 13). So random a comment—so irrelevant a memory—is absurd; but Arthur, because of his obsession with the past, is in awe of Mr. F's aunt. To the reader, the old lady is comic and powerless; to Arthur, her ridiculous remarks—such as "I hate a fool!"—seem quite personal, pertinent, and "Solomonic." His trepidation before her is more than a little demeaning. Clearly, Arthur, who has not yet learned to comport himself like a man towards his own past, represents his creator's realization that the very concern over the past is a large part of its power. Mr. F's aunt is, literally, vestigial; she is but a comic channel by which the pointless past is imported into the present and rendered innocuous. As such, she serves to defuse the reader's sense of the power of the dead hand.

Of all the novels by Dickens, *Little Dorrit* may illustrate the hardest and most thorough struggle over the rights and dangers of the past. Nevertheless, the struggle continues in *A Tale of Two Cities*. Albert Hutter says that "the overt and seemingly relentless subtext of this novel is to give meaning to death or to the past, to disinter the historical moment and make it come alive."[28] The French Revolution is depicted as a natural effect of the injustices of the past; and the excesses of the revolution are a result of the carelessness and indifference broadcast by the aristocracy in the past. The warning to England was obvious: "It was much too much the way of native British orthodoxy, to talk of this terrible Revolution as if it were the one only harvest ever known under the skies that had not been sown" (2, 24). But the savagery had been sown—even as it was being sown in England, Dickens feared, in 1859.

Dickens set up the dead hand theme by treating respectable institutions with withering irony. Even venerable Tellson's Bank and its partners come in for scorn through their refusal to consider altering their old building: "In this respect the House was much on a par with the Country, which did very often disinherit its sons for suggesting improvements in laws and customs that had long been highly objectionable, but were only the more respectable" (2, 1). And the narrator grows even more incensed, reminding us of Tellson's complicity with the "putting to death [that] was a recipe so much in vogue" in the previous century. As a representative, then, of the "good old times" (garnering much of its current respectability from its antiquity), Tellson's Bank—a synecdoche for the principles of the dead hand, upon which its operation is run—is shown to be worthy of nothing but ridicule.

To the extent that the aristocrats in France depended upon the past for their privilege, to that extent did the crimes of the past have the power to destroy them. The Marquis de Evrémonde, who epitomizes the French aristocracy, sounds a reactionary note that echoes in England: "France in all such things is changed for the worse. Our not remote ancestors held the right of life and death over the surrounding vulgar" (2, 9). But the Defarges are in agreement, desiring only to maintain this ultimate right for their own use. The Defarges are the natural outgrowth of exercising such rights—the harvest of such a sowing. If Monseigneur's principles create the revolutionaries, the revolutionaries are, in their very acts of revenge, the self-appointed heirs of the very past that they are trying to extirpate. By replicating the ruthlessness of their oppressors, the victims yield to the dead hand. Their suffering has caused the sclerosis of reaction, not true change. Therefore, the dead hand does both the sowing and the reaping; and the harvest can only be death.

Resurrection is the counter-theme of *A Tale of Two Cities*. Ironically, what hope for the resurrection of humanity there is seems to be assigned to the ambivalent Jerry Cruncher and the Resurrection Men. But this is a parody of the theme, a game with the reader that Dickens could not resist playing. However, without ambivalence, Lucy is shown to be a fountain of life. Obvious and melodramatic though her function in the plot may be, the character is essential to the novel—as she and her creator are aware. "Can I not recall you" (2, 13), she says to Carton—sounding Lorry's earlier, cryptic phrase, which initiated the important motif which serves as title to Book the First, "Recalled to Life." All of France, and all of England, needed to be recalled to true life. But Carton is the prime object for resurrection because, as he says, "I am like one who died young. All my life might have been" (2, 13). Carton breaks the Dickensian mold: here is a character whose past is—nothing. It is not even suffering and humiliation. Insofar as it is "wasted forces," it is merely dead. It is as if his dialectic of the past brought Dickens again to see that suffering is not the worst legacy of the past. What is worse is a past that conveys into the present nothing to care for. In the character of Carton—often said to be in the Byronic mold of Steerforth—Dickens at last concluded that the Steerforths of the world were more unfortunate than the Copperfields. Although Edgar Johnson decried the "overindulged sentiment" in certain scenes in *A Tale of Two Cities*,[29] the novel is an important stage in Dickens's dialectic; and it surely conveys power both in its articulation through the themes of the dead hand of the potential for renewed life, and even in the biblical resonance of Carton's last words: "I am the Resurrection and the Life, saith the Lord" (3, 15).

Revenge for past injustice is as significant a motif in *Great Expectations* as it is in *Little Dorrit* and *A Tale of Two Cities*. "In the little world in which children have their existence, whosoever brings them up, there is nothing so finely perceived and so finely felt as injustice" (GE, 8). Again, Dickens has worked through the telling phrase: being brought up "by hand" means, in effect, that Pip has a dead hand, equipped with Tickler the whip, hovering over him from his earliest memory. At home, Mrs. Joe and her dinner guests insist on Pip's show of gratitude for this stifling and uncaring oppression. Pip knows full well "all the times she had wished me in my grave" (4). The opening scene of the novel—at the family's grave-site—supports this feeling. With the hand of death and the dead hand so intermingled for Pip, it is little wonder that he would do nearly anything to escape their range. It is little wonder, too, that the desire for revenge, explicit and implicit, should dominate so much of the action.

Even Joe is to some extent dominated by a dead hand—for the memory of his own father's cruelty to his mother prevents him from rising against Mrs. Joe for Pip's sake. But the primary embodiment of the dead hand in this novel—and perhaps in all of the novels—is Miss Havisham. Like Madame Defarge, Miss Havisham lives to revenge herself upon a whole class of fellow creatures—males. Magwitch, too, is motivated by revenge: by making Pip a "gentleman" and claiming to be "the owner of such," Magwitch is symbolically asserting his power over Compeyson for all the injustice he was done by him and by the system that he represents and that has empowered him with the status of a "gentleman." For Pip, to possess great expectations turns out to be merely another vain strategy in dealing with the past. His great expectations, ironically, are derived from the past—as are all dreams of revenge. In so far as Pip attempts to escape from his past, so far is he a victim of the dead hand.

Our Mutual Friend differs from *Little Dorrit* and the intervening novels largely in its emphasis on the benefits accrued by accepting the dead hand. By minimizing the apparent costs of accepting it, Dickens—having gained some sense of victory through his long dialectic—seems to have been determined to dress the dead hand with every possible advantage for this final showdown. Old Harmon's will is a transparent move out of the past to control the present. Old Harmon intends through it to force his recalcitrant son to marry Bella, whose name implies both beauty and war in her character. For her part, Bella finds the wealth very attractive from a distance. Thus has Dickens filled the dead hand with gold, enticing both John and Bella to accept their destinies. And if *Our Mutual Friend* seems a brighter novel than the previous five or so, it is because Dickens meant to make the temptations of the dead hand stronger and more subtle than it was for the characters and readers in those earlier novels—and, thus, to make the defeat of the dead hand more inspiring.

Our Mutual Friend is another manual of the numerous ways in which the dead hand can act upon the living. One way is Jenny Wren's father's excuse that his drunkenness is merely "circumstances over which no control" (2, 2). Once again, the character's language says more than the character intended: for in omitting a human subject and a verb, the signifier bears an indexical relationship to the signified. Boffin's (pretended) two-valued ethic is another way in which the dead hand acts upon the living: "There's nothing betwixt stiffening yourself up, and throwing yourself away" (2, 5). Similarly, Mr. Podsnap's notion that the arts should reflect his life of unthinking habit—as well as his ludicrous assumption that the status quo is the manifest design of Providence—are further ways of invoking the dead hand. Having apparently learned the same theories as Gradgrind, Podsnap cannot think of his daughter Georgiana as a particular young woman—but only as a generalization. The Young Person is an impersonal institution that perpetuates past and pat respectability in its—to use the unfortunate Georgiana's term—most "awful" form. But Headstone and Wrayburn are the most dramatic examples in the novel of the deathliness of Respectability.

Wrayburn, for all his irony towards the phenomenon of respectability at the Veneerings, cannot by himself even conceive of the unrespectable idea of marriage to a working-class girl like Lizzie.[30] So as not to know what his pursuit of her is likely to bring about—Lizzie's moral destruction—he finds several subterfuges. In response to Lightwood's moral warning, he pretends to have forgotten past experience so that he can claim ignorance of the likely course of events. One does not defeat the dead hand by suppressing history; and, as we have seen in his dialectic, Dickens of all men did not believe suppression was possible. Wrayburn, who had taken refuge in frank confession, "was sorry, but his sympathy did not move his carelessness to do anything but feel sorry" (3, 10). Careless to the Dickensian depth of the word—too careless to be moved enough to change or to act—Wrayburn can only follow the long established pattern à la Steerforth of seduction and, presumably, eventual abandonment. Wrayburn, for all his wit and intelligence, is a victim of the dead hand. He even accounts for his obeisance to it by the most hackneyed necessitarian argument: "She must go through with her nature, as I must go through with mine" (4, 6). He sounds like a decadent Miss Wade. He speaks as if human beings were objects in motion on a collision course. But Bradley Headstone, by the same thinking, must also go through with his nature, which directs him to intervene between Lizzie and Wrayburn—to separate Wrayburn's unreflective intention from its likely consequence; and he must literally bring the dead hand of the past down upon his rival—and to leave Wrayburn for dead.

As Lawrence Frank has said, Headstone is a "monument" to his "dead or dying" self, whose name proclaims his "paralysis."[31] In trying to repress his miserable past—in utterly repudiating it—Headstone commits Redlaw's (HM) error. All that poor Headstone wants is a respectable position in society wholly separated from the past. He attempts to become the self-made man, sui generis, with no relation of either joy or pain to the past. But he also desires Lizzie, who unmakes him again. In his pursuit of her, he has to endure the gibes of Wrayburn—which evokes his inescapable past—and has to endure the knowledge that Lizzie has a power over him sufficient to make him throw away his hard-won respectability. Lizzie is the polar opposite of respectability not only for the class-conscious Wrayburn but also for Headstone, in her power to make him care. In contrast to Headstone, Lizzie shows, in her defense of her father's good name, that the past is important to her.

After the attack on Wrayburn, Headstone is abandoned by Charlie with the words, "Every effort I make towards perfect respectability is impeded" (4, 7), thus implying that he now finds Headstone an encumbrance rather than an assistance in his own drive toward respectability. Charlie gives ample proof as to the character of those who feel no allegiance to the past. He readily jettisons father, sister, and then mentor in favor of respectability. Like the capping of a joke upon Headstone, Rogue Riderhood harps on respectability as he tries to blackmail the teacher: "Yours is a 'spectable calling. To save your 'spectability, it's worth your while to pawn every article of clothes you've got" (4, 15). Riderhood's demand—that Headstone, in effect, cover his nakedness with respectability alone—must have sounded to poor Headstone like a Wrayburnian parody, especially with the vulgar contraction, "spectability," which suggests utter visibility.

Having given himself so completely over to respectability, Headstone has suppressed his vitality and paralyzed his will. His violence derives from this suppressed vitality, revenging itself upon his respectability—revenging itself on his own cowardly spirit that had not gone to sea where it could have come into its own. But the sea must be matched with a spiritual fluidity; and Headstone locates his personal safety not in harmony with the moving present but (as his name indicates) in stasis.

Dickens's work is a chronicle of his bitter struggle to come to terms with his own past. Certainly the novels are much more than that, even in respect to time; but in his efforts to reconcile himself with his own past pain, he tried one strategy after another—and these were incorporated into the repertoires of his novels. The pain was at first assuaged by his preachment of social change.

Oliver Twist and *Nicholas Nickleby* would serve to help alter—or to eliminate—those archaic institutions or principles that harmed many young Olivers. But with the *Christmas Books,* the value of the past—both as pain and as fond memory—is discovered. With this positive value granted to the past, David Copperfield discovers not so much a pain as a void in his own history. This lack of affect—this absence of a past—is seen as the more horrible curse. In *Bleak House* and the following novels, the past takes on the more ominous forms of ritual, habit, precedent, moribund institutions—and, in *Hard Times,* of rigorous ideology. Through these forms the individual is dominated by the strictures of the past—both personal and national. This theme is carried on in *Edwin Drood,* when the wills of deceased parents would coerce two young people, Edwin and Rosa, into a loveless marriage. Edwin and Rosa—like the Boffins, Harmon, Bella, Lizzie, and finally Wrayburn in *Our Mutual Friend*—are able to stand against domination by the past. They free themselves. But for Dickens, the struggle with the past was a long dialectic, the ever-increasing complexity of which is an attestation of Dickens's continuing development as an artist and a human being.

2
The Presence of Hunger

> Black mutinous discontent devours them; simply the miserablest feeling that can inhabit the heart of man.
> —Thomas Carlyle, *Chartism*

When one glances at it, the Victorian era may well appear to be evenly divided between people who looked backward and people who looked forward.[1] A moiety of the public was turned toward the past, either from personal nostalgia, aesthetic medievalism, political conservatism, secular and religious primitivism, or simple fear of change. To those who looked backward, the present was a sad decline from "the good old times." But, as I have argued, Dickens showed in ample detail that orienting toward the past to find meaning or satisfaction in life was to invite great spiritual danger. On the other hand, a moiety of the public looked to the future; from either personal and national ambition, imaginative license, political utopianism, scientific and social evolutionism, or simple desire for diversion, as they compared to the present what they saw in the future—and called it progress. In the next chapter—under the heading of "Great Expectations"—I will examine the dangers of that effort.

It would seem to follow that the individual ought to fix upon the present. Yet everywhere in Dickens we find the present shown to be hard, repulsive, and downright threatening. The trajectories of desire for the past or the future, which we find crisscrossing his work, result in great measure from a profound dissatisfaction with the present. For in the 1830s and 1840s, Dickens and his contemporaries found themselves staring into the teeth of hunger. Stark, physical hunger stalked the land. The great majority of Britons seemed only a step ahead of starvation, and millions suffered from periodic famines. Everywhere in England, the meagre and wan faces of the poor were visible. Douglas Jerrold writes of "the bony outline of a human thing, with toil and want, cut, as with an iron tool, upon him. . . . This man toils and starves, starves and toils, even as the markets vary."[2]

Hunger was a common fact, known personally by many of the people. But it was more. Hunger dominated the ideology of the age. In the nineteenth century, scarcity—long deemed part of the curse of the Fall—was no longer a mere theological contingency; it was credited as a historical necessity. I do not believe it is possible to exaggerate the extent to which the spectres of starvation and its offspring dominated the conceptual landscape of the early Victorian era. Hunger utterly pervaded the people's system of beliefs. The idea of hunger crept into and inhabited the philosophical foundations of Western thought—rotting hope at its core by denying that time had any use but for feeding.

The philosophy of hunger came largely from the mathematical demonstration by the Reverend Thomas Malthus that human population must inevitably outstrip the production of food.[3] Originally engaged in merely showing the logical gaps in the utopian visions of human perfectibility propounded by Condorcet and Godwin, Malthus succeeded in darkening the horizon of every individual Briton for a century. Although men of every stamp—clerical and secular, arguing from diverse final causes—rose up in refutation, Malthus's ideas had the great rhetorical advantage of clarity. His vision of the necessity of hunger thoroughly dominated the thought of the age. Much is made of Darwin's debt to Malthus; but the fact is that nearly every writer of note in the century wrote with the figure of Malthus lowering in the back of the mind.

Everything Carlyle wrote, for example, was written under the shadow of the Malthusian spectres. Carlyle's works *The French Revolution* and *Sartor Resartus* are filled with the imagery of the voracity Malthus diagnosed.[4] But Carlyle's universe was one in which genuine work would never fail to sustain the body and spirit of the worker. Unlike Malthus, then, Carlyle saw that it was not the constitution of the world but false human institutions that caused people to go hungry. Carlyle perceived the world to be full of work to do—"where boundless Plains and Prairies [are] unbroken with the plough"—and, therefore, full of sustenance. The only question was, as he put it in *Chartism,* Can the labouring man "who is willing to work, find work, and subsistence by his work?"[6] The answer was no, not because the world could not sustain its present population—for "Canadian forests stand unfelled"—but because present human institutions were grossly ineffectual in getting people into work and food into people.

Carlyle held the conviction that the human being was on earth to work. In keeping with his Calvinist heritage, Carlyle converted the fact of human hunger into a boon. Human work was the sole means of converting time into spirit; but without the momentum of hunger, who would work? Since output was multiplied by organization and direction, each human being had the primary obligation of obedience to his natural leader, or foreman. For this reason, Carlyle felt a good deal of sympathy for "captains of industry" and for capitalism, insofar as it was informed by the Protestant work ethic. Certainly, he recognized the evil of the cyclical booms and busts that seemed indigenous to capitalism. Workers, he wrote in *Chartism,* live "like gamblers, now in luxurious superfluity, now in starvation."[7] Neither the one condition nor the other is favorable for spiritual work. As Carlyle wrote, the consequence is that "black mutinous discontent devours them [workers]."[8] Carlyle's diction here has etched out the two themes upon which Dickens constructed his depiction of the present: the themes of human dissatisfaction—or alienation—and the dread of being consumed. But, by and large, Carlyle felt that the impulse of capitalism was positive. Therefore, he could not comprehend why Manchester capitalists included Malthus's vision of hunger in their theory of political economy: "Laissez-faire and Malthus, Malthus and laissez-faire: ought not *those* two at length to part company?"[9] If one can judge from the fiction, Dickens understood better than his mentor Carlyle the benefit capitalism derived from the theology of hunger.

It is too complicated to discuss at length here the interrelationship of (1) utilitarianism, (2) scientific materialism, (3) neo-Smithean theories of political economy, (4) those moral and religious convictions that emphasize the results of the fall from Eden generalized as *lapsarian,* and (5) the Malthusian principle of population. Let me only suggest that capitalism gained an inestimable advantage from having hunger as the premise of all arguments about political economy. That premise—combined with a general acceptance of the rights of private property—created a logical fortification protecting the status quo that seemed unassailable. Indeed, Malthus's recommendations for dealing with the poor are wholly consistent with conservatism. By withdrawing parish subsidies from the poor—so that some suffered immediately—Malthus's policies promised to prevent many of the poor from suffering future large-scale hardships that might lead to revolutionary change endangering the status quo.

The conviction that self-interest was the single human motivation underlay both laissez-faire economics and Bentham's philosophical radicalism; both the so-called economic man and the hedonist[10] found sanction in Malthus's description of the struggle for existence among the poor. The struggle was said to be the natural consequence of hunger, of preordained scarcity—and it was only natural that man, like any other organism, should attempt to acquire a sufficiency for his sole self. Competition, therefore, appeared to be the natural response to a niggardly world. Competition implied a world in which people accepted as necessity the policy of letting the devil take the hindmost. Max Weber has thoroughly illuminated the confluence of Puritan piety and capitalistic principles.[11]

If political economists in theory and practice contributed to and benefited from a general theory of Hunger, another group—composed of members of the religious community—also helped to establish the theory. This religious group believed that the cycle of hunger and plenty was the work of the seasons, caused not only by the Malthusian "fact" of scarcity but also by the "fact" that men are fallen creatures in a world of time. Summer and winter thus provided these defenders of capitalism with an analogy to excuse the natural cycle of dearth and glut in capitalism. But since belief in Malthus implied a loss of faith in a providential world order, the religious-minded found themselves divided. On the one hand, many Christians continued to believe that Providence sustained the world—no doubt the English part of it, especially; on the other hand, many Christians felt the need for a renewed emphasis on the consequences of the Fall. These lapsarians stressed the biblical injunction that the children of Adam must earn their bread by the sweat of their brow (it is a total scoundrel in Dickens, Rogue Riderhood in *Our Mutual Friend,* who hypocritically employs this injunction). Whereas Carlyle laid stress on the felicity of labor that this myth of the fall contained, many religious-minded people saw work not as spiritual opportunity but as proof of the curse of man. In general, the world these people saw was inhospitable; and, therefore, it came as no surprise to them that men should hunger. Because the Bible testifies that "the poor always ye have with you" (John 12:8), the religious-minded saw no reason to better apportion the goods of this world. I wish only to stress that the underside of the Protestant work ethic was the implication that many—the unsaved, it was hoped—would go hungry in this world.

These four allied doctrines—Malthusian, capitalistic, utilitarian (which included philosophical and scientific materialism), and lapsarian—conspired to construct a world with hunger at its heart. Dickens saw that life for the mass of the English people was all but unbearable; and as his career unfolded, he realized ever more clearly that the many faces of dissatisfaction and hunger that he saw in England stemmed from the Hunger that these dominant ideologies inscribed in the nation's charter of belief. He made his fiction a continual effort to expose this vision of Hunger for what it was, and he never ceased to attempt to deconstruct its constituting premises.

The present life that these ideologies authorized for the majority of English people filled Dickens with contempt and anger. The possibilities of the present were constantly being distorted by these ideologies: the Malthusians would piously repair God's mistake of supplying the poor with reproductive organs; the Sabbatarians would eviscerate the taste for beer and decent pleasures of all kinds—at least in the working classes and on Sundays;[12] and the utilitarians, following Bentham, would lobotomize the faculty of the imagination—and, thus, the capacity to care for another person. These ideologies sought only to strip people down—to cheat their hungers in some way—rather than satisfy the hungers and enrich them. The present world was one in which not only the laws but the very ideals of society seemed to encourage a rapacious accumulation of wealth and power—at the expense of the pocket, the stomach, and the spirit of the lower classes. Although his fiction fully acknowledges the presence of hunger in nineteenth-century England, Dickens from the first categorically denied the *necessity* of that hunger—denied the truth of Hunger.

Like Carlyle, Dickens had personally suffered from hunger as a boy. In *Sketches by Boz,* Dickens wrote of "small office lads in large hats" for whom it required a "considerable mental struggle to avoid investing part of a day's dinner-money in the purchase of the stale tarts so temptingly exposed in dusty bins" (p. 51). As a child, he occasionally lost the mental struggle—and had no money left to quiet his hunger at night. At the height of his career, he deplored the "enormous black cloud of poverty in every town which is spreading and deepening every hour, and no one man in two thousand knowing anything about, or even believing in, its existence; with a non-working aristocracy, and a silent parliament, and everybody for himself and nobody for the rest."[13] Everywhere in his work there is evidence of the insufficiency gripping England; everywhere Dickens confronted the spectre evoked by Malthus and confirmed by the Manchester school of political economy and a thousand Protestant chapels. Even as late as the

1860s, he witnessed in his visits to the underworld of London privation and degradation as terrible as he had seen in the 1830s. Progress had bypassed the poorest. Although his own success relieved him personally from the danger of starvation, Dickens never lost sight of the hunger in the land—and never ceased to show the relationship of hunger to Hunger. From Dingley Dell to Fleet prison—from *Pickwick* to *A Tale of Two Cities*—all of his fiction was part of the lifelong debate Dickens pursued with Malthus and his allies.

As with the dialectic of the past, the strategies for exposing Hunger constantly underwent change. Throughout his fiction, however, Dickens used images of deprivation, of food, and of voracious individuals. Readers have always felt how important food is in the aesthetic economy of Dickens's work. Barbara Hardy has effectively generalized the "moral values [which] are attached to meals—to the giving, receiving, eating and serving of food. These values might be summed up as good appetite without greed, hospitality without show and ceremony without pride or condescension."[14] Such meals certainly exist in *Pickwick*—where there is an emphasis on abundant food and boon companionship,[15]—and throughout the fiction and journalism.[16] But perhaps disproportionate attention can be given to the positive intentions of meals, such as those at Dingley Dell. For even in this first and most genial novel, Dickens inaugurated the theme of voracity.

In *Pickwick Papers,* voracity serves to invoke ridicule.[17] The Methodist preacher—the red-nosed deputy "shepherd," the Reverend Mr. Stiggins—reveals his true character by the manner in which he eats. "The rednosed man," says Tony Weller, "warn't by no means the sort of person you'd like to grub by contract, but he was nothing to the shepherd" (22). Visiting home unexpectedly, Sam is initially in some doubt whether the red-nosed man he sees in the company of his stepmother is the deputy shepherd—that is, until the deputy shepherd "commenced on the toast with fierce voracity": from the moment that Sam sees the red-nosed man eating, "all doubt on the subject was removed" (27). Stiggins is lanky, but intent upon swallowing as much of this world as possible: his *piety* has been narrowed down by Dickens to *pie*.

Early in the novel, Jingle's attention circles continuously around food. In Jingle's first appearance—after ordering a beefsteak for Snodgrass's blackened eye—he orders "glasses round—brandy and water, hot and strong, and sweet, and plenty" for himself and the rest of the Pickwickians. His first comic story is of the tall lady who lost her head while eating, "sandwich in her hand—no mouth to put it in" (2). The knowledge of the difficulty of joining mouth and sandwich in this world—of joining cup and lip, to use the phrase featured in *Our Mutual Friend*[18]—is the constant motive behind Jingle's behavior. His language, like his story, reflects his experience of the most basic form of alienation—that between body and soul. Arriving in Rochester with the Pickwickians and asked to dine, this displaced picaro glibly responds: "Great pleasure—not presume to dictate, but broiled fowl and mushrooms—capital thing!" (2). Evidently, Jingle knows the culinary resources of every inn on the road. It is a matter of survival.

Jingle is not the first character in English fiction to talk in broken sentences—in a staccato, elliptical, looping fashion, or what might well be called the revisionist style. But when we study his idiolect and recall the "thinness of his body, and the length of his legs" (2)—as well as the fact that his "face was thin and haggard"—we realize that Dickens has done what he so often has—namely, physiognomized his prose; that is, he has informed with significance the speech habit of a character, rendering the sign iconic by molding the surface structure of the sentence around the contours of meaning. "Glasses round," Jingle says first, "brandy and water"; and then he begins to specify modifications to the original substance—"hot and strong, sweet, and plenty" (2). This revisionism, it strikes me, is the speech of a man who is used to eating on the run, who takes what he can get first—and only then looks for embellishments to the original substance. His speech habit, in other words, is that of a man whose existence is literally hand-to-mouth. It is no wonder, given this primary motivation, that he later agrees so readily to an immediate compensation for giving up Rachael Wardle. He takes what he can get now. The chance for a larger accumulation of capital by marriage is not for the likes of Jingle. Eating is one form of gratification that cannot be deferred in this Dickensian world of hunger.

Pickwick perceives little about Jingle's nature—or, better, the exigencies of Jingle's world—until the latter has run off with Rachael. But then, Pickwick had a good deal to learn about the world. He had to learn, for one thing, that for most of the English the world is far more like Mrs. Leo Hunter's "public breakfast" than it is like a meal at Dingley Dell—that is, the world is a place where, "the refreshment-room being thrown open," the worldly wise, "all the people who had ever been there before," scramble in "with all possible dispatch: Mrs. Leo Hunter's usual course of proceeding, being, to issue cards for a hundred, and breakfast for fifty, or in other words to feed only the very particular lions, and let the smaller animals take care of themselves" (15). Even in civilized circles, it seems, the struggle for survival is rampant. This scene could serve as a comic emblem of the political economy that Dickens saw established in England.

Only after he is imprisoned in the Fleet does Pickwick come to realize the full extent of deprivation in England. In seeing the Chancery prisoner die of neglect and in meeting the emaciated Jingle—who is literally "down in the mouth"—Pickwick is suddenly forced to look at the other side of his world, the face of hunger. Even his comical response to Jingle's explanation of his recent mode of survival reveals his ignorance: "Lived for three weeks upon a pair of boots, and a silk umbrella with an ivory handle!" (42) exclaimed Mr. Pickwick, who had only heard of such things in shipwrecks or read of them in *Constable's Miscellany*. His innocence of the procedures by which goods are converted into food is comic. But Pickwick gains depth as a character when he recognizes the necessity of such conversions—and understands that Jingle is what he is because he must eat. It is Jingle's pathetic condition which explodes Pickwick's naive world: close to starvation, Jingle has been transformed into the very spectre of hunger—a hunger which can no longer be ignored.

Thus, in *Pickwick Papers*, Dickens took three preliminary steps towards a criticism of England by means of the theme of voracity. First, Pickwick is able at last to recognize the true nature of human existence: it is not all "'taturs, tarts, and tidiness," as in the Saracen's Head in Towcester (51). Second, Pickwick shows enough spirit to refuse complicity with the sharkish nature of the social world—as is proved by his insistence upon telling Dodson and Fogg of his contempt for them, notwithstanding his own lawyer's pleas not to. Finally, we see in Job Trotter's loyalty to the down-and-out Jingle, as well as in Sam's loyalty to Pickwick, that poverty and even hunger are not alone sufficient to ruin the spirit of human beings—who live for something more than merely to eat. Thus, hunger may be a fact—but Hunger, and its sanctioned brutishness, is not.

In *Pickwick Papers*, Dickens highlighted the fact of hunger; starting with *Oliver Twist*, he began to scrutinize what might be called the fiction of Hunger. He set himself the task of undermining the Malthusian faith in the ever-present necessity of hungering. Both motives—to acknowledge real hunger and to deride theoretical hunger—are present hereafter in all of his work, fully articulating his vision of the present.

Oliver Twist seems, in a number of ways, designed to complement *Pickwick Papers*: it emphasizes the theme of voracity, which had so emphatically surfaced in the first novel—and yet, paradoxically, it asserts the individual's capacity to resist the circumstances that tend to dehumanize the poor. Critics of the book attacked the verisimilitude of Nancy; but even more difficult for Victorian readers to accept was the revelation of the facts of hunger in England—hunger of both body and soul. To both kinds of incredulity could Dickens say: "I am glad to have had it doubted, for in that circumstance I should find a sufficient assurance (if I wanted any) that it needed to be told" (OT, Preface). Seditious as it was, it needed to be told.

In terms of the theme of voracity, the advance Dickens made in *Oliver* is the description of how society has institutionalized—and thus perpetuated—the tendency of one man to feed at the expense of another. By showing us Bumble, Dickens immediately made explicit the inequities of distribution in England. We are told that Mr. Bumble is a fat man; and one of the first things we see him do is to stir a gin-and-water and swallow half of it at a gulp. The master of the workhouse, too, is "a fat, healthy man" (2); and the governing board is represented by a gentleman whose stuffed "white waistcoat" leaves little doubt about his ruling passion. Meanwhile, the victims of the new Poor Law and its dietary regimen of "three meals of thin gruel a day—with an onion twice a week, and half a roll on Sundays"—waste away and die.

> Oliver Twist and his companions suffered the tortures of slow starvation for three months; at last they got so voracious and wild with hunger, that one boy, who was tall for his age, and hadn't been used to that sort of thing (for his father had kept a small cookshop), hinted darkly to his companions that unless he had another basin of gruel *per diem*, he was afraid he might some night happen to eat the boy who slept next to him, who happened to be a weakly youth of tender age. He had a wild, hungry eye; and they implicitly believed him. (2)

The very rhythm of the prose is impetuous and voracious. Although the cannibalistic hint is made with a degree of humor (it would be less laughable as Dickens developed the theme in his later novels), the voracity is more insistent here than it was in *Pickwick Papers*. The insistence is enough for the reader to believe that Oliver, "desperate with hunger, and reckless with misery" (2), could confront the awful masters of his destiny with a request for "more."

The consequences for English society of tolerating such institutions are evident. If even Oliver could be made "reckless with misery," what must be the result of misery on others who are less well endowed spiritually than Oliver? Although in the foreground Oliver retains the conventional goodness of a popular hero, the majority of boys in the background are problematic. The implications should have caused concern in the Victorian middle class. If cannibalism was spoken of by boys, would it not be spoken of and implemented—in a figurative way at least—by men? Dickens had not yet formulated his warning as explicitly as he was able to do twenty years later in *A Tale of Two Cities;* but the point can scarcely be missed here: English society seemed to be doing everything it could to raise a generation of anthropophagists. If the society had not yet wholly succeeded—as it had not with Nancy or Oliver—that fact merely showed (as Dickens meant the novel to show) the depth of good in human nature. But in Bill Sikes, the system had succeeded well; in him Dickens portrayed the ultimate end of current policies of starving the poor.

Sikes represents the necessary consequence of England's institutions and ideology. Malthus disinterestedly predicted victims among the poor; of greater interest to his class is the notion, as Dickens showed, that killers are quite as likely to appear. Dickens eventually worked out ways—with Headstone (OMF), the Defarges (TTC), and others—to show that the rich had a right to be concerned about killers. Comic though it is, the theme of English cannibalism is brought home when Mr. Bumble brings Oliver "a basin of gruel, and the holiday allowance of two ounces and a quarter of bread." Oliver begins to cry, "thinking, not unnaturally, that the board must have determined to kill him for some useful purpose, or they never would have begun to fatten him up in that way" (3). No cannibal feast do they have in mind, however—only the intention of getting him off the poor rolls. The chimney sweep, Gamfield, has a use for his emaciated form. But Oliver manages to go instead "upon liking" to Mr. Sowerberry—"a phrase which means, in the case of a parish apprentice, that if the master find, upon a short trial, that he can get enough work out of a boy without putting too much food into him, he shall have him for a term of years, to do what he likes with" (4). In English cannibalism, the poor are treated like Jingle's umbrella: they are lived upon—and consumed indirectly. In English cannibalism, the poor are not eaten but, rather, starved.

Almost every human relationship in *Oliver Twist* is reduced to the matter of food or its lack. Sowerberry and Bumble discuss matter-of-factly a reduced tradesman who has died "from exposure to the cold, and want of the common necessities of life" (5).

2: THE PRESENCE OF HUNGER 79

Oliver's first experience as an undertaker's assistant involves the death of the mother of a destitute family who died of neglect and starvation. The fear of worse rigors in the workhouse had prevented the family from making application for help to the parochial committee; finally, a neighbor thought to ask the parish "to send the parochial surgeon to see [the] woman as was very bad. He had gone out to dinner"—-where else? we by now know to ask—"but his 'prentice (which is a very clever lad) sent 'em some medicine in a blacking-bottle, offhand" (5). Remembering Dickens's unhappy time in the blacking factory, we realize how charged with significance this black comedy is. Even if it had been in a less repugnant container, it was not medicine that the woman needed: "I say she was starved to death," says her husband. Dickens has exploited the hideousness of the scene by having the dead woman's mother think immediately of the customary wine and cake—or, at least, bread—that the funeral will bring to them. This macabre vision of incestuous cannibalism at one remove has enough comedy to hold us until the horror is complete.

Against this thoroughly indicted background of utter privation and systematic famine, we follow Oliver's fortunes. After Mrs. Sowerberry remarks that Oliver is small—and Mr. Sowerberry allows that he will grow—she retorts, with the petulance of the Malthusian generation, "On our victuals and drink." Oliver is first given the broken bits of meat put aside for the dog. Oliver, "whose eyes had glistened at the mention of meat" and who is "trembling with eagerness to devour it," (4) is certainly not too dainty to eat the bits. At this point, the narrator wishes that the "well-fed philosopher" could see "the horrible avidity with which Oliver tore the bits asunder with all the ferocity of famine" (4). The narrator implies that if the Philosophical Radicals had experienced hunger, perhaps the official toleration of famine would end. But until the Radicals do experience hunger, the policy enunciated by Bumble—in which he diagnoses the cause of Oliver's rebellion against the persecution of Noah Claypole—will continue:

> You've over-fed him, ma'am. You've raised a artificial soul and spirit in him, ma'am, unbecoming a person of his condition: as the board . . . who are practical philosophers, will tell you. What have paupers to do with soul and spirit? It's quite enough that we let 'em have live bodies. If you had kept the boy on gruel, ma'am, this would never have happened. (7)

Bumble merely makes explicit the principles of English political economy as Dickens saw them. In comparison to Mrs. Sowerberry's natural selfishness, Bumble's notion has the imprint of scientific materialism and the authority of public practice. His only error is to think that hunger always makes for docility.

Naive materialism such as Bumble's, exaggerated as it is, yielded wonderful spoofs by Dickens, Carlyle, and others. With his thunderous irony, Carlyle exposed the ultimate desecration of life that such materialism achieves:

> If man's *Soul* is indeed, as in the Finnish Language, and Utilitarian Philosophy, a kind of *stomach*, what else is the true meaning of Spiritual Union but an Eating together? Thus we, instead of Friends, are Dinner-guests; and here as elsewhere have cast away chimeras.[19]

Since spirit is a product of the digestion, the chimera of mutuality has no logical foundation in philosophical materialism.

It has been as much his soul as his stomach that prompts Oliver to run away. For at Sowerberry's he is fed but is alienated and starved of community. Upon reaching Barnet, Oliver comes upon the flashy young gentleman known as the Artful Dodger. The Dodger's purchase of "a sufficiency of ready-dressed ham and a half-quartern loaf" (8) and a pot of beer has a strong effect on Oliver and, perhaps, the reader. The appearance of a provider is so welcome, the reader does not go behind the act itself. In our experience of the world of this novel—as in Oliver's own experience—generosity and meat are too rare to evoke a critical attitude. Nor is it an accident that the first time that Fagin appears he is manning a frying pan in which sausages are cooking for his boys. Whether or not Fagin's good fellowship is only a semblance, the sausages are real; and after the workhouse and Mrs. Sowerberry's, Fagin's den seems like the land of Cockaigne. Although Oliver does not succumb to these incentives to crime (Dickens wished to make the point against Bulwer's *Paul Clifford* that the true incentives to crime are real but wholly unromantic)—and although Dickens meant through the melodramatic plot to demonstrate the vitality of the spirit in the human being—nevertheless, the reader cannot avoid seeing that a life of crime is made attractive merely by contrast to its alternative, a life of poverty, as that alternative was constituted in England by the Poor Law of 1834 (itself brought into being in order to lay the spectre of universal starvation as depicted by Malthus).

In *Nicholas Nickleby,* we see a carryover of the primary concerns of *Oliver.* We immediately recognize the significance of the fact that Ralph Nickleby renders his "zealous assistance towards despatching the lunch, with all the promptitude and energy which are among the most important qualities that men of business can possess" (3). Ralph is a model of bourgeois voracity; as we learn, even close relatives do not stand beyond the scope of his desire to eat up others. Similarly, the first view we have of Mr. Squeers is at breakfast at the Saracen's Head—eating cold roast beef, hot toast, and coffee—while providing but milk and water for his students. "A shocking thing hunger is, isn't it, Mr. Nickleby?" he asks Nicholas (5). In Dickens's most outrageous humor, this fake Puritan does not mean that it is shocking that people go hungry but that people have "live bodies" to feel hunger. Dickens's humor brings to exquisite focus this hypocritical otherworldliness, which forms part of Malthusian piety.

We cannot be surprised to find that the inmates of Dotheboys Hall have "pale and haggard faces, lank and bony figures." Victims of "cruelty and neglect," they are likely to perpetuate the tradition of Dotheboys: "With every vengeful passion . . . eating its evil way . . . what an incipient Hell was breeding here!" (8). Starvation and voracity, deprivation and aggression: the first inevitably leads to the second. In this respect, the "internal economy" (8) of Dotheboys Hall is symbolic of that of the nation. It is no wonder that the internal economy of a private institution is an index of the political economy of the nation: the same ideology dominates both. Dotheboys operates on the same inhumane principles—and produces the same results—as the larger system.

In *Nicholas Nickleby,* one almost comes to doubt that there are any alternatives to hypocrisy, alienation, deprivation, and voracity. The ideals of public generosity and personal moderation seem almost fictitious in the world of Ralph Nickleby. To create an opening for the spirit in this world, Dickens called up some interpolated tales. In the tale "The Baron of Grogzwig" (whose name—like that of his wife's family, Swillenhausen—is comically pertinent), we see that the idea of moderation in drink makes the Genius of Despair and Suicide shudder, for moderation "breeds cheerfulness" (6). Cheerfulness, comfort, and moderation are closely related terms and constitute an alternative to the Malthusian cosmos of excess and insufficiency. Thus, Dickens was able to insist not only upon the nexus of voracity and deprivation (obvious in Squeers) but also upon an alternative combination. Dickens knew that the Malthusian scheme for society depended on the conviction that voracity in the rich cannot be stemmed. Since the rich showed no restraint, the poor must. Dickens used the device of a spectre in "The Baron of Grogzwig," a device which was to become essential a few years later in the *Christmas Books*. By means of this device, Dickens was able to demonstrate that moderation is viable and, indeed, attractive: he showed that principles other than Malthusian may operate in—and make sense of—the world.

In his first three novels, Dickens amply illustrated the presence of hunger. Pickwick, Oliver, and Nicholas all encounter or experience hunger at first hand. In the latter two novels, at least, this hunger is displayed in close connection with gourmandise. Dickens was drawing the etiology of hunger in England more and more precisely. If Oliver is thin, it is because Bumble and the board members are fat. If Smike and the other boys are emaciated, it is because Squeers devours too much. At this stage of his career, therefore, Dickens saw maldistribution and the voracity of a few as the causes of hunger. If paupers and children were underfed, it was due to the greed of individuals—like Bumble and Squeers—who, unfortunately, had the power to pervert institutions to their own selfish interests.

In *The Old Curiosity Shop,* Dickens used parallel sets of characters to elaborate on the reality of hunger and of Hunger more fully than he had before. In this novel, Nell's spiritual starvation is implicitly compared to the Marchioness's physical deprivations. Thus, while providing a ground-tone of physical hunger and its satisfaction, Dickens developed in more detail his vision of innate spiritual hunger and its satisfaction. For Nell, "separation from her grandfather was the greatest evil she could dread" (24). When the old man alienates himself from her—however much for her sake—he is quite clearly starving Nell, as is evident from the events of the narrative. Indeed, the cause of her death can only be described as malnutrition of the heart. Dickens's tactic here was to reverse Carlyle's ironic stomach to soul transformation: in Nell's economy, it is the demands of the soul that prevail over those of the stomach. Mere food cannot keep her alive; she must have the company of loved ones in order to survive. Perhaps too emphatically for many twentieth-century readers, she is a symbol of the human need for a loving community.

In the alimentary imagery employed by Dickens, the Marchioness lives in the "bowels" of the Brass establishment. She is alone there: "Nobody ever came to see her, nobody spoke of her, nobody cared about her" (36). Her spiritual privations equal her physical ones. But Dick Swiveller (whose name epitomizes the flexibility that Dickens's imagery serves to anoint as the highest human priority) soon comes to care about her: "I don't believe that small servant ever has anything to eat" (36). For one with Dick's personality, such a condition was enough to raise sympathy. Naturally, then, he follows Sally Brass down the servant's stairs, thinking, "By Jove . . . she's going to feed the small servant" (36). No such idea has invaded Miss Brass's head, however; Miss Brass, "bearing in her hand a cold leg of mutton," directly leaves the basement. This demesne is described as follows:

> Everything was locked up; the coal-cellar, the candle-box, the salt-box, the meat-safe, were all padlocked. There was nothing that a beetle could have lunched upon. The pinched and meagre aspect of the place would have killed a chameleon: he would have known, at the first mouthful, that the air was not eatable, and must have given up the ghost in despair. (36)

Although Sally eventually provides a scrap for her, the impression of the small servant's neglect and deprivation is fully established.

Perhaps in no other book did Dickens make more explicit his concerns for a community of love—or what Dick Swiveller calls "social harmony"—for it is evident in both Nell's and in the Marchioness's stories. The need for company brings Dick and the Marchioness together. Dickens's comedy is thematically focused when it shows that Dick is initially offended by her deprived condition—a response whose humorous absurdity does not make it less representative to the temper of the times.

> "Why, how thin you are! What do you mean by it?"
> "It an't my fault."
> "Could you eat any bread and meat?" said Dick, taking down his hat. "Yes? Ah! I thought so. Did you ever taste beer?"
> "I had a sip of it once," said the small servant.
> "Here's a state of things!" cried Mr. Swiveller, raising his eyes to the ceiling. "She *never* tasted it—it can't be tasted in a sip! Why, how old are you?" (57)

The statement "it can't be tasted in a sip!" symbolizes Dick's expansive, generous character. Dick instantly heads to the public house and returns with bread, beef, and a great pot of choice purl. Garrett Steward has characterized Dick as the epitome of the healthy imagination.[20] It is undoubtedly Dick's imagination that rescues him from the influence of bad company early in the novel. Dick's verbal fancy is often called forth by—and expressed in terms of—dining and drinking. Food is the primary stimulus for him to act. Dick's exceptionality among the characters in the novel is as much due to his generosity with food as to other forms of imagination.

When it comes to food, Dick, like all of Dickens's positive characters, is a practicing egalitarian. If Dick happens to believe that "man wants little here below . . . after dinner," (8) he by no means intends to keep all the dinner for himself. After providing the Marchioness with preliminary pulls at the purl, Dick settles down to play cards with her, thus adding to her palatal adventure those of an imaginative and social nature. He gives her food to "squench" her hunger and a taste of his private stock of *joie de vivre*. His words at another time to the Marchioness are typical of him: "Do have a mug of beer. It will do me as much good to see you take it as if I might drink it myself" (65). In the Marchioness, Dick finally has what he has so long needed—a *companion* (in the original sense of the word, *com-pan-ion,* someone with whom to break bread). In their relationship, Dickens has shown the necessity of satisfying spiritual hunger as well as physical hunger.

The Garlands, like the single gentleman, stand as contrasting figures to Quilp—balancing that voracious monster as neatly as the Marchioness-Swiveller tandem balances that of Nell and her grandfather. It is noteworthy, I think, that the Garlands' form of providing is more distinctly culinary than that of the Cheerybles in the *Nicholas Nickleby*. The single gentleman, Brass's lodger, is a hearty man, who is charmed by Dick's impudent wit (35). He invites Dick into the room, where Dick witnesses the lodger removing from his trunk "a kind of temple, shining as of polished silver."[21]

This "temple" is a portable gas stove of marvelous ingenuity, and it duly impresses a mind as imaginative and capable of wonder as Dick's. Of the lodger and his stove, we are told that "into one little chamber of this temple, he dropped an egg; into another some coffee; into a third a compact piece of raw steak from a neat tin case; into a fourth, he poured some water" (35). When the stove is thus filled, the lodger lights it, closes the chamber—and soon an entire breakfast is cooked, including hot water for Dick's drink. All of this food the lodger shares with Dick.

The single gentleman's stove displays man's enduring desire for freedom from the fear of hunger. It is perhaps Dickens's intuition of the technological response to Malthus's dread predictions. Other signs of the repudiation of Hunger appear in every succeeding novel, and we will trace many of these in the fifth chapter. Notwithstanding these hopeful signs, hunger was not soon renounced in England. As we shall see in the succeeding novels, hunger not only continued to cause suffering among the poor but resulted in spiritual deprivation at all social levels. This spiritual deprivation is alienation from others, the loss of community; it is exemplified by Quilp.

The growing estrangement between Nell and her grandfather, which her grandfather inadvertently creates, Quilp sets out to produce. Dickens has left no doubt about the prototype of Quilp. "Having dined off a beefsteak, which he cooked himself in somewhat of a savage and cannibal-like manner" (67), Quilp is joined by his wife, whom he asks, "How dare you approach the ogre's castle, eh?" The dwarf takes every opportunity to play the ogre, achieving in his world the social alienation that has been synonymous with cannibals since Polyphemus in *The Odyssey*. But Quilp, for all of his fairy-tale provenance, manifests the current malformation that Dickens saw resulting from Malthusian theology, laissez-faire ethics, and the unnatural appetites they foster. Quilp is simply the "economic man" revealed in all his voracity: "Where I hate, I bite" (67). He hates all living creation.

As yet in Dickens's works—despite the social ambitions of sharks like the Brasses—the indubitable ogres have been kept beyond the pale of respectable society. Monks (OT) and Squeers (NN)—as their names indicate—are, like Quilp, aberrations from the social norm. But as Dickens elaborated upon the methods of English cannibalism, this assumption of aberrancy was readdressed. Ultimately, Dickens was to reveal that the most dangerous cannibalism lurked behind the common mask of respectability.[22]

Although *Barnaby Rudge* is filled with intemperate license, its primary setting—the Maypole Inn—seems to impose the opposite feeling. The old inn expresses what a harmonious community ought to be, by "blending into one rich stream of brightness, fire and candle, meat, drink, and company" (33). Such, at least, the Maypole seems; but old John Willet's obtuseness and lack of imagination (the failing he prefers to attribute to others) prevent the inn from achieving its promised level of humane satisfaction. When the Gordon rioters invade it—drinking, gorging, and wasting—we see the result of such imaginative and social intemperance as Willet's, whose name types him. Similarly, we witness the result of intemperance when the liquid lead pours off the roof and melts the skull of a besotted rioter. In the cases of the Maypole (in particular) and of London (in general), the intemperate license of the rioters can be traced directly to the equally intemperate withholding of independence, on the one hand, and of sustenance and care, on the other—that is, the license can be traced to spiritual deprivation. Therefore, it is not Simon Tappertit, the resentful apprentice, who was of primary concern to Dickens—although "among the other fancies upon which his aforementioned soul was for ever feasting and regaling itself" was the notion that he could "kill a man . . . and eat him too if needful" (8). Rather, it is the respectable John Willet and John Chester who are truly dangerous to society: Chester is dangerous because he wishes to depend on one son (or anyone else), while ignoring the needs of another son, Hugh; and Willet is dangerous for exactly the opposite reason—because he has no intention of allowing his son to achieve social and psychological independence. Dickens's essentially dialectical constructiveness is clearly shown by these two family groups. Although opposites, both fathers are unnatural: both would reverse the natural course of human and social development. Each father, in his own way, is a metaphoric cannibal—Chester economically and Willet psychologically. Between them, the rising generation in England could not find support for the sanctity of either body or spirit.

Barnaby Rudge is a novel with remarkable structural balance. The rebellions in the first half of the novel are private—against the fathers Willet and Chester. Hugh, the unacknowledged son of Chester, symbolizes the human consequences of England's laissez-faire approach to the problem of the dispossessed. Hugh epitomizes the intemperance that the "disinterested" approach both conceals and produces. The rebellions in the second half of the novel are public; but they enlarge the significance of those earlier, private ones. Persons who are starved physically, socially, and spiritually will devour indiscriminately. Therefore, intemperance reproduces itself. In this novel, Dickens was refining his vision of the interconnection between deprivation and intemperance—and between public and private actions.

In *Martin Chuzzlewit*, the Blue Dragon inn is not as memorable as the Maypole; but Mrs. Lupin, the proprietress, has a sounder notion of the value of hospitality than John Willet could ever have. Her very face "bore testimony to her hearty participation in the good things of the larder and cellar and to their thriving and healthful influences" (3). Like Dick Swiveller, she knows that a good table can refresh the spirit quite as much as the body.

The idea of the healthful influence of good food and cheer is scarcely a new one, but it is an idea that gathered more and more importance over the course of Dickens's career. Dickens's version is more discriminating than the received idea; and unable to let any idea pass him without his reaction, he mocked the crude materialist ideas, which only sound similar to the authentic testimony that Mrs. Lupin bore. A case in point is the doctor whom Montague Tigg hires for the Anglo-Bengalee Disinterested Loan and Life Assurance Company. He speaks professionally of the salubrious institution of lunch: "The true Life Assurance, Mr. Montague. The best policy in the world, my dear sir. We should be provident and eat and drink whenever we can." (27) Appropriately, the last words of this chapter's long title are "biters may be bitten." The doctor is probably speaking facetiously, as when he said to Montague, "If you don't make a point of taking lunch, you'll very soon come under my hands" (27). He believes his advice is a truism. But in the world of *Martin Chuzzlewit* (which is the world of Hunger), such encouragements to eat, especially at the expense of others, are redundant—and biters bite to repletion.

The first half of *Martin Chuzzlewit* depicts a spectrum of characters who, to borrow Mrs. Bailey's words to Mercy Pecksniff, "*Do consume the per-vishuns*" (11). Until Martin and Mark Tapley return from America, only Tom Pinch has truly pleasant, companionable meals—first with John Westlock and then with his own sister, Ruth. The rest—from Sairey Gamp to the lodgers at Todgers, from Montague Tigg to Betsey Prig—eat as their reason for living, but gain little satisfaction from all their "per-vishuns."

In the first chapter of *Martin Chuzzlewit*, the narrator suggests that not only monkeys but also swine are likely candidates as descendants of Adam, for swine are animals "remarkable for taking uncommon good care of themselves." The Chuzzlewits are thus doubly scored, for the point is made that they trace their lineage practically to Adam; they are also well known to be particularly adept at taking care of themselves. As the Chuzzlewit clan gathers around the supposed deathbed of Martin Chuzzlewit the Elder, the family members show that they know each others' characters. One female says, "I beg him to speak out like a man, and not look at me and my daughters as if he could eat us" (4). But the man in question, Mr. George, responds that if he were in fact a cannibal he would find "a lady who had outlived three husbands, and suffered so very little from their losses . . . most uncommon tough" (4). When George goes on, he points out the vulture-like qualities of the family (an image cultivated by Dickens until it culminated in the birds of prey in *Our Mutual Friend*). Obviously, the image of predators is a variation of the cannibal image that was beginning to dominate Dickens's imagination. And the connection to capitalism is pointed, for, as Tigg says, "We companies are all birds of prey: mere birds of prey" (27).

Seth Pecksniff is especially important as an index of the gradual synthesis of respectability and cannibalism in Dickens's work. The wonderful grace he pronounces at the dinner table at Todgers epitomizes the Malthusian cosmology behind which such indirect and impenitent anthropophagists practice: the grace, it is said, was "a short and pious grace invoking a blessing on the appetites of those persons present and committing all persons who had nothing to eat to the care of Providence, whose business (so said the grace in effect) it was to look after them" (9). A blessing on appetites and, as an afterthought, an invocation of Providence to succour the hungry: the self-incrimination is so sudden, so brilliant. Pecksniff, who always seems to appear near a table of food, joins Malthus in the hagiology of hunger. (To slander Malthus the man in this way might be unjust; but it is Malthus the perceived ideologue that Dickens is attacking.) Pecksniff drinks and eats himself into a state of illness. It is one of those strokes of cosmic irony that Dickens's comic genius often achieves when Pecksniff describes his illness as "chron-ic," one which "is carrying me to my grave" (9). Nothing is more chronic than Pecksniff's tendency to overeat; and nothing, given the state of Hunger, is more universal. If we call Pecksniff's malady galloping consumption, we are making a spiritual and not a medical diagnosis.

The lack of "companions"—the absence of what Dick Swiveller called social harmony—is visible in most of the characters in *Martin Chuzzlewit*. For example, Sairey Gamp and Betsey Prig do not so much dine together as eat simultaneously. They dine off each other rather than with each other. "You don't mind dining expensively at another man's expense, I hope?" (28) asks Montague Tigg of Jonas Chuzzlewit, in words that might well serve as the motto for the displaced cannibalism described here by Dickens. The desire of these two to dine wastefully entails the desire to dine at each other's expense—financial, psychological, or physical. Dickens increasingly came to see that just as unappeasable hunger was the common response to the ideology of hunger, so likewise was the Tigg doctrine—or displaced cannibalism—the policy of the England of his day.

By bringing Americans into the narrative, however, Dickens showed that voracity was not a local problem. Even before Martin gets to the shores of the United States he witnesses the editors of several New York papers, *The Rowdy Journal, The New York Stabber*, and *The New York Sewer*, "lunching expensively," each "drinking himself into a state of blind madness" (16). As if such lampoons are not a sufficient indication of the "natur" of Americans—corrupted as their pronunciation—Dickens would very soon give us an instructive scene of dinnertime at the boarding house: "All the knives and forks were working away at a rate that was quite alarming; very few words were spoken; and everyone seemed to eat his utmost, as if a famine were expected . . . and it had become high time to assert the first law of nature" (16). It is a hilarious scene that discloses a number of dyspeptic individuals "feeding, not themselves, but broods of nightmares" (16). In America, dinner has become not a time for communion but an extension of competition. Dickens reiterated this point about Americans. On the riverboat at dinner time, "a perfect rebellion among the hungry passengers" is caused when they are accidentally barred from the dining room while, it is said, "several virtuous citizens at the table were in deadly peril of choking themselves in their unnatural efforts to get rid of all the meat before these others came" (34).

Exaggerated far beyond the law of the jungle—owing to belief in the ideologies of hunger—such voracity is not natural but, rather, unnatural. Martin, in appropriate terms, sums up Dickens's feelings about this flaw in the American character: "A man deliberately makes a hog of himself, and *that's* an institution" (34). The Americans glorified voracity. They made swinishness a model for social behavior, thus "losing the natural politeness of a savage" (34). In a word, the Americans had, by institutionalizing voracity, sanctioned metaphoric cannibalism. With great insight, Mrs. Lupin says of Mark's visit to America, "Why didn't he go to some of those countries where the savages eat each other fairly and give an equal chance to everyone?" What we have called English cannibalism exported well.

Despite the power of the priests of Hunger, there are always characters in Dickens who recognize that the value of a dinner depends on whether the primary mission of the diners is to consume or to take part. When Tom and Ruth Pinch set up their independence for the first time, a major concern is what they will eat on their first night at large in the world. Ruth, formerly a governess, has had little culinary experience; but she has care and intelligence, and she believes that she "could make a beef-steak pudding" (39). Tom exclaims that in "the whole catalogue of cookery there is nothing I should like so much as a beef-steak pudding" (39). Every ingredient is the best; and all is heightened by the pleasure of sharing, of having a companion. Sharing—the giving of the self—is the essential ingredient for harmonious dinners. Dickens avoided banality by concentrating his descriptions on the sensations of the participants; but the message is clear.

Most dinners in the novel, however, offer as their chief pleasure the English cannibal's sensations. For example, it is satisfactory to feel, says Pecksniff, "in keen weather, that many other people are not as warm as you are." This is quite normal: "For," as Pecksniff observes," "if everyone were warm and well fed, we should lose the satisfaction of admiring the fortitude with which certain conditions of men bear cold and hunger" (8). A more succinct critique of the ideology of hunger could scarcely be presented. Without inequities, there would be no pleasure. Ironically, intimate dinners are not the exclusive ones: Tom immediately invites John Westlock to share that first beefsteak pudding of independence. It is public dinners and social dinner-givings that only appear to be inclusive—and, thus, celebrations of community. This realization, underlined by his own childhood experiences, was to remain a consistent part of Dickens's criticism of society.

The different perspectives on hunger and voracity that I have garnered from *Martin Chuzzlewit* show that Dickens's thinking had continued to develop. He seems to have begun asking himself whether there was not enough food for all; hence, if England should prove not to be foredoomed to Malthusian scarcity, would the present voracity of individuals disappear? Because voracity is born of fear, it would seem conceivable. But because fear could not be dissolved until the ideology of hunger was repudiated, the answer Dickens came up with was no.

England in the Victorian era did not provide a sufficiency for all for several reasons. The primary reason was that food is more than sustenance—it is a symbol. As sustenance, food is necessary for the health and even survival of the individual—that is, it translates into very life. Especially for materialists like Bumble (OT), meat is quite literally taken to be soul or spirit. Since there is no other source of soul, can one consume too much meat? If one must grow old, one may at least grow fat.

Because all value lies in matter, Bumble and the other voracious materialists were inevitably tempted not only to seize more than their share but to withhold another's share. Food thus became more than sustenance—it became the measure of social worth. Since the earth's chief evil was lack of food, an adequate—or, indeed, excessive—diet was proof to some of God's grace, or of providential favor; for others, it was proof of superior willpower or of other natural talent. Thus was Malthus transmuted by the apologetics of capitalism and social conservatism. Whether justified by the theory of natural competition or by lapsarian theology, voracity and its sibling, deprivation, are prior even to the universal scarcity that Malthus predicted. Hunger has more than demographic causes; it is more than a fact of nature. It, like sufficiency and excess, is a sign.

Therefore, sufficiency for all will not be achieved because, as a sign, food becomes negotiable currency in the larger economy of human desires—that is, human beings will often attempt to satisfy by food consumption even those desires that one might call spiritual or psychological. Thus, Malthus's theory is not, as Carlyle thought, undermined by social organization. Just the opposite. Since eating proves that one deserves to eat, society is organized to emphasize the disparity in consumption. The doctrine of Montague Tigg supplants the Sermon on the Mount.

With the *Christmas Books,* Dickens brought to the surface several themes that had heretofore been subordinate, especially the themes concerning the past. But in the *A Christmas Carol* and *The Chimes*—as well as in *The Cricket on the Hearth* and *The Haunted Man*—hunger and meals continue to signify the present.

In *A Christmas Carol,* as is well known, the opening of "shut-up hearts" is effected or displayed by the sharing of food. When Scrooge's nephew invites Scrooge to dinner on Christmas day, Scrooge's Malthusian response is just what we expect: "Every idiot who goes about with Merry Christmas on his lips should be boiled with his own pudding" (1). The cannibalistic implication is obvious and reflects Dickens's intuitive certainty that the ideologies of hunger lead to cannibalism—that is, the severest public alienation leads to the severest personal alienation: alienation between body and soul. Scrooge's point is clear: in Malthus's world a fool and his pudding are soon parted. Consistent also with the materialistic strand in Scrooge's ideology is his diagnosis of the apparition of Marley's Ghost as "an undigested bit of beef, a blot of mustard, a crumb of cheese, a fragment of an underdone potato. There's more of gravy than of grave about you, whatever you are!" (1). Thoroughgoing materialist that he is, Scrooge denies the validity of the imagination; moreover, he knows of no function for dining but to fuel his organ of acquisitiveness. Thus, when fancies or memories rise to consciousness, he simply attributes them to physiological causes.

The Ghost of Christmas Past shows to Scrooge the party long ago at Fezziwig's—with its cake, negus, cold roast, cold boiled, mince-pies, and plenty of beer. The Ghost of Christmas Present is a "jolly Giant" (3) sitting amidst "turkeys, geese, game, poultry, brawn, great joints of meat, sucking-pigs, long wreaths of sausages," and so on. Dickens's remonstrance to the ideologies of hunger is nowhere clearer. This Ghost shows Scrooge how merrily even the poor prepare for their Christmas feasts. And what people make of the present determines the future. The Ghost of Christmas Yet to Come shows that the curses implicit in Scrooge's policies come home to roost. This Ghost takes Scrooge to a pawnbroker's shop where the charwoman, laundress, and undertaker's man have come to dispose of items stolen from Scrooge's body and room. *Cannibalism,* the term currently used for the plundering of broken-down machinery, is exactly appropriate to describe what would have happened to the dead materialist—who, after all, held that a man is an economic machine. Scrooge would have been cannibalized. But such was life in the world of Hunger predicated by Malthus.

Food is also a major motif in the second of the *Christmas Books, The Chimes.* But Dickens rather too glibly has Meg attribute her father's fearful Malthusian nightmare to indigestion (4). From my perspective, Dickens has carelessly aligned her with Scrooge the materialist. The indigestion is supposedly caused by the very tripe that had earlier been such a focus of Aldermanic attention, being anatomized (both verbally and physiologically) by Mr. Filer and Alderman Cute. In both *Christmas Books,* for the first time since *Oliver Twist,* the problem of nourishment is translated from a local, personal experience into explicit politico-economic terms. But unlike *Oliver*—where the concern is with the official, institutional treatment of the needy—the first two *Christmas Books* insist on the responsibility of the individual to share the fruits of his labors with others. It is as if, at this stage of his development, Dickens could admit the responsibility of individuals to feed the less fortunate but could not as yet admit the responsibility of ordinary individuals for the system that starved the poor in the first place. Although Dickens's notions were undergoing change, ogres were still aberrations. Dickens had not yet fully expressed his gathering intuition that just below the surface of most ordinary, respectable Victorian ladies and gentlemen beat the hearts of cannibals— hearts formed by ideals and assumptions that the English often took such national pride in. It is the rational ideology rendered so obviously inane by Dostoevsky in *Notes from the Underground.*[23]

In *Dombey and Son,* again, we find the spiritual emptiness of several characters distinctly framed by their voracity. Major Bagstock is summed up as follows: "It may be doubted whether there ever was a more entirely selfish person at heart; or at stomach is perhaps a better expression, seeing that he was more decidedly endowed with that latter organ than with the former" (7). Mrs. Pipchin, likewise, is constantly feeding herself while depriving her boarders; and Little Paul tells her that it is not polite "to eat all the muttonchops and toast" (8). For Paul, the question of nourishment is one of life and death; he is at the point of death when the "apple-faced" Polly Toodle is hired to nurse him. After Polly is dismissed by the possessive Mr. Dombey, Paul's life is a slow dying. Theories of birth trauma and of the oral stages of psychosexual development were unknown to Dickens. Nevertheless, in *Dombey and Son,* Dickens has made plain the effect on Paul not only of being prematurely deprived of Polly's breast but of being permanently deprived—if not of a surrogate at least of what Dickens conceived to be equally important—parental warmth and undesigning love. Polly offered both physical and spiritual nourishment. By contrast, Mr. Dombey can only feed on his son. Dickens achieved in Dombey the full expression of his new vision that the social ideal—the person who best manifested in practice the rationalizations and values of his society—was a "cannibal." Such persons also evoke cannibals: losing Paul, Dombey acquires Carker.

Carker's teeth are the appropriate emblem, designed by Dickens, for cannibalistic England. The teeth represent the *consummatory* behavior naturalized in Dombey's world. In the suggestiveness of name and in dental characteristic, Carker is the very type of man that commercial civilization produces. Filled with resentment, he can never find satisfaction for his hunger. It is significant that the steam engine—a symbol of material progress in most contexts—did not merely kill Carker but, like a raging beast, "licked his stream of life up with its fiery heat, and cast his mutilated fragments in the air" (55). To be dismembered and devoured by a machine turned beast is terribly fitting for a character who— as a Hobbesian utilitarian knowing no duty—has become a beast, excusing himself as a "pleasure machine." Like other ogres in Dickens's works, Carker is destroyed in a fashion that reflects his own disposition and thus represents poetic justice.

Malthus did not specify the ultimate consequences of universal hunger, but Carlyle filled in the omission by proclaiming the vision of Heuschrecke, an apostle of Saint Malthus: "Nowhere, in that quarter of the world, is there light; nothing but a grim shadow of Hunger; open mouths opening wider and wider; a world to terminate by the frightfulest consummation; by its too dense inhabitants, famished into delirium, universally eating one another."[24] As horrible as such an eventuality would seem to Victorians, there was a grim, fatal logic to it.

When the struggle for survival becomes too severe, what else will people have to eat but each other? This question was answered by Douglas Jerrold, friend and a major influence of Dickens, in his *Handbook of Swindling*: "What then is to be done with the superabundant population? . . . [T]hey must swindle."[25] Swindling is only cannibalism by the indirect method—the consumption of property rather than of the individual proper. This type of cannibalism is embodied by Dickens in the person of Vholes, the lawyer in *Bleak House* who, wrote Dickens's narrator, "gave me that slowly devouring look of his" and then "gave one gasp as if he had swallowed the last morsel of his client" (65). The intertwined themes of hunger, cannibalism, and financial rapacity permeate Jerrold's work just as they do Dickens's, proving that the concern was not peculiar to Dickens. In Jerrold's *Chronicle of Clovernook*, England is referred to as "the cannibal country."[26] Even though both Jerrold and Dickens mustered some humor about overpopulation and its personal causes and social consequences, the ideas of Malthus could not be shaken off. V. S. Pritchett was most likely right in arguing that overpopulation is "thought to be funny because the idea of pain and poverty—more mouths to feed—is intolerable."[27] Douglas Jerrold wrote that "philanthropists and philosophers" (meaning, especially, Philosophical Radicals)

> have come to the comfortable conclusion that there are in England too many Englishmen. John Bull has played the Sultan, and has an alarmingly numerous family. . . . He cannot feed all his sons and daughters; he must not choke or drown them. . . . What then is to become of the family of Bull? Shall they tear each other piece-meal?[28]

Despite the comic props and proper names—and despite the play on the word *piece-meal*—Jerrold has born witness here to what the narrator in Dickens's "The Wreck of the *Golden Mary*" called the "one momentous point often in my thoughts" (CS, p. 151)—to wit, will the survivors come to devour each other? For Carlyle, Jerrold, and Dickens, cannibalism was the chief eventuality entailed by the prophet Malthus and his laissez-faire theology. Such an eventuality would be the utter negation of all civilization.

Some contemporary writers have recently argued that the humanistic concept of man has had a stop. To Dickens, English cannibalism showed that the time of the human being never had a start. Thwarted from proper satisfactions for the spirit, men struggle against one another and achieve a false semblance of satisfaction by gaining power over others. This power is displayed by food. In *Sartor Resartus*, Carlyle called this fruitless activity the "clay-given mandate, *Eat thou and be filled.*"[29] Ultimately, this expression of power can have but one result. In *The French Revolution*, Carlyle has written: "The lowest, least blessed fact one knows of, on which necessitous mortals have ever based themselves seems to be the primitive one of Cannibalism: That *I* can devour *Thee.*"[30] To this "fact" had England nearly sunk. Although the cannibalism is hardly literal in Dickens, we see developed in Dickens's work many modes of English (or displaced) cannibalism. His work is an increasingly deliberate exploitation of the twin themes of voracity and cannibalism.

It is evident that for Dickens the present signified not only hunger but also that last resort of the hungry—cannibalism. Both physical and spiritual hunger were reflected in the universal voracity afflicting England. This overriding compulsion to consume threatened to result in the English madly consuming everything that may be legally consumed of another, both goods and spirit. The essence of the Victorian present was, therefore, a displaced cannibalism.

As we have seen, the ogres who first appear in Dickens's fiction seem adventitious; although their voracity may be vaguely disturbing, they seem to be spontaneous, archetypal projections whose relation to the ideological structure of society Dickens had not yet fully worked out. But the longer Dickens continued his representation of the present, the more clearly expressed was his realization that the Malthusian ideology and the capitalistic praxis of English society were creating a continuous and inevitable supply of cannibals who—no longer amusing (though, perhaps, contemptible) aberrations—are, in fact, the terrifying type of modern man. Driven by the logic of his own thematic configurations, Dickens was constrained to reveal ever more explicitly his vision that the presence of hunger had turned the England of his day into a Cannibal Island. But being the dialectician that he was, he continued in the last half of his career not only to confront and expose English cannibalism but also to deconstruct fictionally the ideology of hunger—and to build in future readers a trust in what he called the "best of times" and "worst of times" (TTC, 1, 1).

3
Great Expectations: Fixtures of the Future

The future is not only an image, it becomes an ideal.
—Cassirer, *Essay on Man*

While it is sometimes difficult to separate the future from the present in Dickens's works, it is all but impossible to speak of the future without implicating the past. For example, in the case of Mr. Dombey, we could interpret his desire for a son to perpetuate the firm and name either as a fixation on the past or as a fixation on the future. The two tendencies are similar in that both work to deprive the present of its proper integrity and vitality. Nevertheless, it would be a mistake in a study of Dickens to obscure the demarcations between the three dimensions of time. To Dickens, the divisions of time were not only evident but were also essential to his moral and aesthetic reading of the world.

Dickens focused his literary attention upon the past or upon the future at different stages in his career. We have surveyed Dickens's continuous struggle to make peace with his personal past and the public present. It was not until the middle of his career that he recognized that he had misgivings about his expectations and his achievement of respectability. These misgivings culminated in *Great Expectations* and received further elaboration in *Our Mutual Friend*. One could almost draw a graph, upon which Dickens's suffering over the past would be a descending line across time—and his dissatisfaction with the various projects of the future an ascending one. The lines would, perhaps, cross late in his career. Even as he saw his own successes mount, he gradually came to question the idea of predicating human satisfaction upon the definitive future that his successes seemed to promise. Not only was Dickens aware of the social disparities that were still present in England, he also saw that satisfactions in the present could not be neglected without great personal damage. Thus, he came eventually to doubt his subscription to the conventional Victorian reading of the future as progress. The impetus to doubt the validity of the creed of progress was not merely a standard case of disillusionment—of learning that human happiness lies in the attaining and not in the attainment. There were two other personal reasons for his doubting the myth of progress.

First, Dickens's imagination was so thoroughly dialectical that a man who tried as hard as he did to come to terms with the past must eventually come to question the future as well. Second, at some point he had the intuition that the votaries of progress may be as much a fifth column for death as the votaries of the "good old times" were—that is, Dickens came to realize that it was quite as possible to seek changelessness by looking to the future as by looking to the past. By seeking to either fulfill dreams or make destiny manifest, individuals and nations can commit themselves to stasis. Having great expectations—quite as much as accepting the dead hand of the past—is an attempt to fix once and for all the relationship of the individual to experience. Both trajectories lead to sclerosis by leading to a mode of life in which the capacity to care in and for the present has been eliminated.

There were always characters in his fiction who abused the future. But after Dickens's own life bottomed out on mere success, he began to make orientation to the future the primary theme in his work. His separation from Katherine in 1858 (after twenty-two years of marriage) would have repercussive effects on all his established routines—domestic, professional, social, and psychological—and would cause a severe collapse of his own prior expectations. Not only was his family rent, but Dickens's whole sense of community faded—as old associations were severed with Bradbury and Evans, with Mark Lemon of *Punch*, with Thackeray,[1] and with numerous other literary and social acquaintances.

Even before the separation and its damaging publicity, Dickens had thrown himself into public readings—obtaining from them, no doubt, positive proof of the public affection for him at a time when critics were announcing a weariness with his style. As David Masson said in 1859, "The public have caught what is called his mannerism or trick; and hence a certain recoil from his writings among the cultivated and fastidious."[2] Very generally, we can categorize the "cultivated" as those who favored the development of the realistic mode in fiction—and who therefore found Dickens too gothic. And we can categorize as "fastidious" those who believed that the purpose of fiction was either to entertain or to reinforce the conventional vision of the world. They found Dickens too disturbing.

In learning that he could not please every reader, Dickens was brought face to face with his dreams—just as he had been by his ruined marriage and his besmirched public image. Life had not turned out—he had not turned out—as he had expected. It took him awhile to take measure of his dissatisfaction. Hence, it is no wonder that *Great Expectations* (1861)—two years farther than *A Tale of Two Cities* (1859) from the marital crisis of 1857 and 1858—is devoted to assessing the cost of dreams. Perhaps the capacity to dream is itself incorruptible; but in examining the fears, lack of trust, and the needs that drive Pip's dreams, Dickens showed how the contents of even a child's dreams can be corrupted.

Great Expectations is certainly not the first novel in which Dickens assessed stances towards the future. However, the novel is given over to such an assessment in an even greater degree than *David Copperfield* is given over to an assessment of stances towards the past. In the 1861 novel, Dickens brought into literary being his realization that it is as much a folly to attempt to fix the future as it is to attempt, as Pip says, to "bend the past out of its eternal shape" (GE, 56). Dickens had not only planted expectations firmly in the soil of the present and traced out unsuspected root systems, but he had also come to see how a concentration on the future—on deferred but defined fulfillment—can blight the present quite as much as fixing on past woes.

George Ford has remarked of *Great Expectations* that "instead of a fast-paced progress that the title might lead us to expect, the narrative kept hovering over the past, a past of unidentified guilt and of shame and fear."[3] This is a keen observation, for to speak of expectations is to imply an antecedent—and thus, necessarily, to keep "hovering over the past." In fact, the most insistent pattern in the novel is that of the effect on the present of a motive out of the past—namely, revenge.

Revenge is the major motivation of many characters in *Great Expectations*—Miss Havisham, Magwitch, and Orlick. Even Pip wishes explicitly to revenge himself on Trabb's boy—and implicitly, perhaps, on others. The verb *wishes* reflects the imaginative projection of each of these characters—a projection that appears to be forward in time but actually aims to repair the past. Pip, it has been argued, craves a displaced revenge upon Mrs. Joe.

On many occasions, an orientation toward the past is translatable into an orientation toward the future. Revenge is one such motivation. It is not hard to see how revenge fixes the future. If

Havisham and Magwitch, for example, had their ways, future events would quite simply serve as restitution for past events. The sole purpose of the future would simply be to reverse the past. Hence, the future would be deprived of its own integrity—its plasticity, its mystery. Revenge, if successful, would introduce a kind of determinism into the free flow of events. The future would consist of foregone conclusions; and the only response by human beings would be a weary fatalism or a cynical resignation. As Lawrence Frank has pointed out, Pip "encounters the mystery of the past he must imaginatively reconstruct if he is not to be transfixed by it and made into an image of the dead past, be it the past of a Miss Havisham or the past of a Magwitch."[4]

It is also possible to view Pip's desire to rise in station as simply the natural desire of every human to find a life situation in which one enjoys esteem, loving care, and scope for the development of personal potential. Given this natural and even laudable ambition, what goes wrong with Pip's expectations? From my point of view, what corrupts Pip is not his desire to escape an environment dominated by the heavy hand of Mrs. Joe and the heavier sentiments of Pumblechook. Rather, what corrupts him is his willingness to accept the subtler confinements imposed upon him by his great expectations. The most obvious restriction to which he submits is that of class divisions. Pip desires to become a gentleman; and to his understanding—and that of a majority of Victorians—an immense gulf separates a gentleman from a workingman. By Rigaud's (LD) definition, a gentleman is the polar opposite of a workingman. Part of what Pip accepts, then, with his new role, is the convention that he is permanently alienated from people in the lower stations of society. This solitary confinement by class is illustrated by the scene in which Joe visits Pip in London. Registering all the faults in Joe's attire, Pip shows the extent to which he has become a mere snob: "I had neither the good sense nor the good feeling to know that this was all my fault, and that if I had been easier with Joe, Joe would have been easier with me" (27). In order to live with his great expectations, Pip has been willing to obliterate the past—including its most valuable gift, Joe's "companionation" (Joe's wonderful neologism, which implies the active interrelation between friends).

Pip has not been completely corrupted by his new role. His better feelings are revived when he attends his sister's funeral and rather self-consciously cries, "Good-bye, dear Joe! No, don't wipe it off for God's sake, give me your blackened hand!" (35). But, insofar as Pip has accepted the imposed role of a gentleman with great expectations, he has accepted his alienation from Joe—and has accepted, thereby, a diminution in his own freedom. It is significant that Pip had earlier felt "it very sorrowful and strange that this first night of my bright fortunes should be the loneliest I had ever known" (18). The gulf between human beings—which his future requires—has opened in front of him.

In discussing Compeyson and Miss Havisham, Herbert Pocket defines for Pip the true gentleman: "My father most strongly asseverates . . . a principle of his that no man who was not a true gentleman at heart, ever was, since the world began, a true gentleman in manner" (22). Not in the perfunctory externals is a man a true gentleman, but in the heart—in his dynamic and spontaneous responses to life. To learn mere manners—or a manner—is to harden oneself. Hence, Compeyson is no gentleman. To sympathize is to be truly softened, truly gentle. By accepting his great expectations on the conditions they were offered, Pip accepted an incarceration into a hard and fast role in life.

In many ways, Dickens has foreshadowed how great expectations can become great dissatisfactions. It is said that even the new clothes that Pip purchased from Trabb "fell a trifle short of the wearer's expectation" (19). Barnard's Inn, Pip's residence in London, is an even surer emblem of what his great expectations have amounted to. Rather than leading to greater life, his great expectations have brought him to "a melancholy little square that looked to me like a flat burying-ground" (21). The diction leaves no doubt about Pip's new station: "Dismal . . . dismal . . . dismal . . . dismal . . . rot of rat and mouse and bug . . ." (21). Rather than enjoying new freedom, esteem, and love, Pip has traded for the offal of vengeance the concrete richness of life he once had. Not only is Pip willing to accept the fixed class lines implied by the traditional role of gentleman, but he is even willing to accept what appears to be a colossal meddling in his life and destiny by Miss Havisham. He not only believes that Miss Havisham is responsible for rearranging his future, but he also believes that she has chosen Estella to be his future bride. Amy Dorrit in *Little Dorrit*, John Harmon in *Our Mutual Friend*, and Edwin and Rosa in *Edwin Drood* reject such meddling in their lives. But Pip is willing to accept any constraints upon his future in order to escape those of Mrs. Joe.

Certainly, Pip deems it an immeasurable improvement to escape from the regime of the whip Tickler to the regime of the carrot. Pip imagines Miss Havisham to be a fairy godmother. To gain Estella, Pip would submit to anything. The starry imagery around

Estella cues the reader to the idea that to Pip she symbolizes a perfect existence, free from earthly concerns. He confesses as much to Biddy. "The beautiful young lady at Miss Havisham's, and she's more beautiful than anybody ever was, and I admire her dreadfully, and I want to be a gentleman on her account" (17). Biddy asks whether he wishes to be a gentleman to spite Estella or to gain her: "Because, if it is to spite her . . . that might be better and more independently done by caring nothing for her words." Biddy's word "independently" sounds the point I am trying to make. Pip may indeed desire to spite Estella or Mrs. Joe. Ironically, in accepting his great expectations with such motives and on the conditions they were offered, Pip embraced not freedom or life but their opposites.

Discussing Estella, Herbert asks, "Not being bound to her, can you not detach yourself from her?" (30). The question silences Pip. And Herbert continues: "Think of her bringing-up, and think of Miss Havisham. Think of what she is herself . . . . This may lead to miserable things" (30). "I know it," replies Pip, "but I can't help it." Pip cannot detach himself from Estella because she is not a person but a symbol. She symbolizes all that he has come to desire. She, the unreachable star, represents a haven beyond the reach of Tickler and all other earthly contingencies and humiliations. She incarnates an ideal beyond time. Pip can no more detach himself from her than he can from his own imagination, of which she is a product. The imagination can formulate this end; but in doing so, it shows itself abused.

As an inheritor of Romantic psychology and of Combean physiology—or phrenology—Dickens assigned the human experience of the past and the future to two different faculties of the mind. For him, the memory and the fancy had different locations in the brain and different functions. From Hazlitt and Wordsworth, in particular—and from Romantic thought, in general—Dickens learned that the imagination (or the "fancy," as he usually called it) was the faculty that made it possible to project one's interest into the future or, conversely, to interject future possibilities into present consciousness. For such Romantic thinkers as Hazlitt, the faculty of the imagination had an essentially moral function.[5] It could, by its capacity to project a person's interests into the future or onto others, link human beings in sympathy. But by desiring Estella—and the safety from life for which she stood—Pip had severed his links to moral life. He had alienated himself from Biddy and Joe and from his own better nature. Although he was pained by Estella's tone when she said that "our association [was] forced upon us, and we were mere puppets" (33), she had conveyed an obvious truth. Pip had made himself a puppet to his own imagined future—a future corrupted by his excessive desire to attain some perfect security.

Pip, then, had sacrificed his freedom, his natural feelings, and his integrity to this dream of perfection, this escape from time. Accepting the atemporal symbol embodied in Estella had corrupted the uses of the imagination. Pip's error was to locate his peace of mind not in time and spiritual fluidity, but in quietus—in a static haven outside of time and superior to engagement in the present. Pip's desire was to fix the future, to dwell not in a world of activity but of passivity. His great expectations were, therefore, tantamount to a desire for death. To the extent that they were fulfilled he would be abstracted from life and living, from care and caring. Pip had been willing to accept a slavery, a determination by outside forces—in this case, by several forms of revenge. In wanting the future guaranteed, plotted, and laid out as a haven from humiliation and other spiritual exigencies, Pip had enlisted under the standards of revenge and stasis—and thus had enlisted with death.

Pip's ultimate discovery of Estella's heritage is the way in which Dickens has revealed the corruption of Pip's project, the dark ground of his dreams. Pip's expectations have a source lower in station and esteem than the honest people from whom he chooses to alienate himself. Hence, he has been searching in the wrong direction. At first, Pip is repulsed when he discovers that Magwitch is the source of his expectations. Yet, his acceptance of responsibility for helping Magwitch escape England and hanging brings a spiritual renewal to Pip. By his immersion in the flood of Magwitch's human contingency—by his recognition that Magwitch is not without dignity—Pip revives his own compassion and flexibility.

The novel induces us to see that inflexibility—the accepting of hard roles in life or the setting of fixed goals—is to be eschewed. While it is natural to look toward the future, one must somehow keep the future undefined and fluid. For human eventualities are unpredictable. For example, Pip's one act of generosity—getting Herbert started in business—is the only act during the period of his expectations which endures. Above all, the future cannot be divorced from the present and must not be a mere instrument of the past.

Great Expectations is the apogee of Dickens's study of the Victorian versions of the future. But Dickens's struggle to discover a viable stance toward the future is visible in the permutations of the theme of great expectations throughout his works. It might be objected that the theme of great expectations is too broad. After all, the objection might run, plot equals action. Is not all action purposive? Is not purpose necessarily a project in time? If so, one part, the theme, simply dissolves into another part, the plot. Therefore, are not all plots a rendering of greater or lesser expectations? And is not any discussion in principle unlimited?

Let me try to distinguish between expectations of plot and expectations of theme. As we have seen, the dead hand of the past may retard human projects. When someone desires merely more of the same—that is, desires to perpetuate the past—no meaningful demarcations can be made between past, present, and future. Neither *great* nor *expectations* makes sense in such a context. Yet even beyond such retrogression, Dickens's fiction is often devoid of major characters who exercise purposive action. Reviewing *Little Dorrit, Blackwood's* remarked that "Dickens, with all his fertility of invention, has less constructiveness than falls to the lot of five novel-writers out of six, including the worst."[6] The point is generally admitted that in many of Dickens's novels, as Northrop Frye has said, the plot is "creaky."[7] This creakiness may be largely attributed, I believe, to a lack of purpose in the major characters—a lack of a clearly defined goal toward which the characters move. A strong line of interest must often be traced in the apprehensions of the reader rather than in the ambitions of the characters. The interest is often, therefore, the result of the thematic resonances. Thus, the theme of great expectations exists even in novels in which the character's "arrow of Desire"—to use Blake's term—may seem like one of Zeno's arrows.

Pickwick Papers is an example of such a novel. Pickwick's project is the "observations of character and manners" (1). The finite totality of such objects cannot be empirically exhausted by one individual. Therefore, to some commentators, Pickwick's retirement from the world at the close of the novel looks like an admission of defeat. But the retirement signals, I think, not his defeat by the world but a change in Pickwick's outlook. What Pickwick admits by retiring is that the human world is inexhaustible—not because it is a static totality but because it is a living process in which the changes in the observer are as relevant as the changes in the world. Therefore, Pickwick retires not from life but from a naive vision that conceives of life as static, totally knowable, and thus predictable.[8]

The perfect demonstration of Pickwick's original view is presented in Pickwick's archaeology. In Cobham, Pickwick comes upon a stone with unorthodox lettering inscribed on it (11). His instant assumption is that the markings had always been on the stone, that is, that the stone had gone unchanged in human memory. The loathesome Mr. Blotton—the same person who had called Pickwick a "humbug," in the Pickwickian (or static) sense of the word (1)—argues that the inscription on the stone could be deciphered as "BILL STUMPS, HIS MARK." But Pickwick's view prevails, and "seventeen learned societies unanimously voted the presumptuous Blotton an ignorant meddler" (99). If we follow through on Dickens's satire on pedants, we see that, after all, the butt of the comedy is Pickwick's assumption of changelessness, his lack of a sense of diachrony, and his lack of appreciation of the unorthodox forms that self-expression may take.

Pickwick Papers is a novel largely devoid of references to the past and the future. We never learn much about Pickwick's personal past or hopes. However, Pickwick often attempts to fix the contents of things to come. One such occasion is when he is put into jail for refusing to pay the outrageous judgment for Mrs. Bardell in the breach of promise suit. He vows never to pay the unjust costs but to remain in jail until justice prevails. It is a matter of principle. The upshot of his flat refusal to let events, however unjust, take their course is that the present begins to fill up with suffering and injustice. Sam Weller cannot be said to suffer, perhaps; but he is determined to join his suffering master in jail. Mrs. Bardell is placed in jail; and Winkle appears incapable of winning consent to marry Arabella Allen by himself. The future seems paralyzed. In jail, furthermore, Pickwick must mingle with the desolation brought about by the great expectations of all kinds and ranks. One example is the cobbler, who tells Sam, "The fact is, I was ruined by having money left me" (44). Pickwick witnesses all this agony as a direct result of adhering to "principle" (his term for fixing the future).

In Dickens's novels, perhaps the most absurd example of trying to fix the future is Sam's anecdote in *Pickwick Papers* about the patient who ate "four crumpets ev'ry night for fifteen year, on principle." It clearly addresses Pickwick's own false stand toward the future. Told that to continue to eat four crumpets a night would kill him, the patient goes home and "orders three shillings worth o crumpets, toasts 'em all, eats 'em all, and blows his brains out" (44). He would have a future with crumpets in it or no future at all. But Pickwick's "principle" is similar; it succeeds in forestalling the future. But at last, Pickwick is prevailed upon to soften his

3: GREAT EXPECTATIONS: FIXTURES OF THE FUTURE

position; and the future is allowed to come into being—bearing its full flood of consequences. He has learned the Dickensian lesson—iterated in novel after novel—that even persons of principle may be enemies of the spirit.

In the other early novels, there is only occasionally a defined and desired goal; but even in these novels, the goal is usually not something to which the characters are attracted but a situation that they wish to avoid. This is the case with Oliver, Nicholas, Little Nell, Joe Willett, and Martin Chuzzlewit. With due allowance for the breadth of this generalization, one can argue that—with the obvious exception of Pip—the major and approved characters in Dickens's novels are singularly devoid of an orientation toward a set and defined goal to be reached in the future. Even David Copperfield succeeds inadvertently—being shunted into a writing career and backing into marriage with Agnes. What is more, it is generally the unsavory characters who have the clearest object in mind for their actions: Fagin, Ralph Nickleby, Vholes, Carker, and Silas Wegg. Yet, many of the earlier negative characters are also capable of living for the process: this is true of the most salient personalities—such as Jingle, Quilp, and Gamp—all of whom seem to delight in the process of their asocial activity and not in any specific reward such activity might garner them in the future. Hence, in the work of a writer who by all accounts possessed intense willpower, we find ourselves faced with a huge list of characters who have no defined goal toward which to strive in the distant future.

It is not surprising to find, therefore, that those characters who do opt in one way or another to focus on the future contaminate their lives. It scarcely matters whether one conceives of great expectations for oneself or for others. In the novels, there are a number of characters who, from altruistic motives, seek to lay down a concrete future for friends or loved ones. But even armed with good motives, a character who cheats the present for the sake of the future is almost always frustrated (an exception is Marion Jeddler in *The Battle of Life*).

In *The Old Curiosity Shop,* Dickens illustrates numerous ways in which the present joy is sacrificed to good intentions, or great expectations. Even the benevolent Garlands were guilty of "always looking forward to some period . . . and still letting the present time steal on, as it was the habit of men to do, and suffering the Future to melt into the Past" (68). Nell's grandfather begins to gamble, not for himself, but for the sake of Little Nell, because he fears that unless he can win money Nell "would be left to the rough mercies of the world" (9). Quilp responds, "While I thought you were making your fortune (as you said you were) you were making yourself a beggar, eh?" The old man gambles solely for Nell and calls "on heaven to bless the venture—which it never did." As a result, although Nell's "image sanctifies the game" (31), the attempt of the old man to secure Nell's future serves only to deny her peace in the present and abort her future.

In *David Copperfield,* Lil Em'ly sees in Steerforth not an advancement for herself as much as a reward for Mr. Peggotty, to whom (she announced as early as the third chapter) she would give "a sky-blue coat with diamond buttons . . . and a box of money," if she "were ever a lady." Between this desire and her faith in James Steerforth, Lil Em'ly has enough great expectations to ruin anyone. Neither principle nor generosity protects the spirit from the infection of an immutable future.

In *Little Dorrit,* not only is Gowan spoiled by what his mother calls his always being "accustomed to expectations" (2, 8), but the entire society suffers from a similar "moral infection," one symptom of which is financial speculation. All of England joins in Merdle's financial speculations—Cavaletto, Pancks, and Mr. Dorrit included. Arthur Clennam is infected by Pancks, that paragon of the work ethic who, of all people, might be thought to be immune to great expectations. But speculation is the special temptation of capitalism, which holds that in helping oneself one is only extending economic benefits to every member of society. "Be as rich as you honestly can. It's your duty. Not for your sake, but for the sake of others. Take time by the forelock," says Pancks (2, 13). But to *fore-lock* time, as it were, is to lock life out. For instance, Clennam speculates not because he is thinking of himself but because "of the delight it would be to him to see Doyce better off." Although Doyce had earlier deprecated any form of speculation, Clennam speculates with Doyce's money and loses—as much of England loses—when Merdle falls. In *Edwin Drood,* it is the kindly desire of two friends to see their families united—through their children, Rosa and Edwin—that would circumscribe the future. Therefore, it makes no difference that one's great expectations are for others. What matters is the attempt to gain utter security—for it would bring time to a stop.

If even such laudable attempts to *fore-lock* time have no successful issue, we can hardly expect more selfish reasons for fixing the future to show better success in the pages of Dickens. As Badri Raina has pointed out, *Dombey and Son* differs from previous novels because here "the father [is] seeking the sanctioning son"[9]—

that is, the father needs the future to sanction the present, and thus he locks out experience. "This young gentleman has to accomplish a destiny," says Dombey. In *Dombey and Son,* it is not only Dombey who would enslave the present to the future. Both Mrs. Brown and Mrs. Skewton sell their children's futures for "money, always money!" (46). All misers forfeit activity of the spirit in the present for an idea of security in the future. The Smallweeds, in *Bleak House,* are prime examples: the premature age of the young and the immobility of the old reflect the cost of sacrificing the present for financial security in the future. As with Scrooge, greed deprives the present of its satisfactions. In *Our Mutual Friend,* both Bradley Headstone and Charley Hexam make as their desideratum a static respectability, yielding up all current joys to that absentee God. But as we have seen, the sacrifice proves too great for Bradley; Lizzie's presence utterly destroys his commitment to the future. As happens so often in Dickens's works, characters who invest the present in the future—as Headstone had long been doing—lose both the present and the future.

Disappointment with the future when it turns out to be contrary to expectations is an occasional motif in Dickens—and is usually treated in a comic mode. Disappointed that David Copperfield is not a girl, Betsey Trotwood abruptly rejects what has come to pass. Her failed marriage had given her a bitter taste of imperfect masculinity, and she wishes to run no more risks. Mr. Murdstone, on the other hand, finding David's mother sadly wanting in the sterner virtues, devotes himself to her improvement in the future—and thus to her and David's misery in the present. But it is Tommy Traddles, in *David Copperfield,* who most succinctly summarizes this sub-theme. The uncle who raised Tommy had certain expectations of him: "It was an unfortunate thing, but he didn't like me [when I grew up]. He said I wasn't at all what he expected, and so he married his housekeeper" (27). And Tommy lost his expectations. The future is acceptable for many characters only at a distance; close up it can lose its charm—as for Pickwick, Pip, and Traddles's uncle. Such disappointment is another and comic version of the theme of great expectations: in this version, the future is rejected when it finally presents itself—just as the present is always denied. In these cases, the future must conform to a prior, static idea—or it is rejected out of hand.

What links all of these tendencies to reject rather than to embrace life is the attempt to fix time, to stay history. Like some of the cultures that Claude Levi-Strauss has analyzed,[10] Victorian society had many methods of concealing diachrony behind synchrony. The passion for neutralizing history is the principle common to both the devotees of the dead hand and those of great expectations. For the former, the present succumbs to the past, which is simply maintained ad infinitum: the "good old times" are to enjoy perpetual restoration. For the latter, the present succumbs to the iron dream of what is to be: the heir apparent prorogues the standing circumstances.

Yet, the present is not so much dismissed as transformed—transformed to resemble the more favored time. What disappear, then, in both these transformations are the changes wrought in time—diachrony. The point of both formulations is that the present does not formally differ from what precedes it, on the one hand, and what succeeds it, on the other. There is no succession—hence, no dynamic. If this analysis of Dickens's projections of Victorian preferences has any merit, it is little wonder that Darwin's evolutionary theories caused such consternation. Evolution insists on the reality of change (thus no dead hand)—but on change without teleology (thus no great expectations). To free up change, to insist on the human ability to adjust to new circumstances, and to thus promote the vitality and energy required for adjustment—these were some of the heuristic intentions behind Dickens's fiction, both for himself and for the reader.

In mid-career, there is an emergence in Dickens's fiction of organized groups who wish to fix the future not only for themselves but for everyone. These attempts at social engineering—whether Utilitarian, Comtean, or trade-unionist—met with little favor from Dickens. In *The Chimes,* Meg and Richard plan to marry, thus raising a groan from Filer the Malthusian: "Married! Married!! The ignorance of the first principles of political economy on the part of these people; their improvidence; their wickedness" (2). Filer believes that, far from marrying, "they have no earthly right or business to be born." In Trotty's dream, the chimes show that it is a blunder to capitalize a tolerable future by selling out the present—to empty the present of all the joys and cares that cause men even to desire a future. This is why Dickens calls the Malthusians and their fellow travelers the "maggots of the time"(3): they eat the heart out of the present.

In *Hard Times,* we observe several types of collective great expectations. None are attractive. In Slackbridge and his unionism, we get a picture of how trade unionism could coerce the future into the shape it desires without a thought being given to the integrity of the individual's present. In Gradgrind, we witness the unforeseen consequences of a well-meaning effort to educate the future into desired shape. Gradgrind believes—as the materialists of the preceding century did and, indeed, many Christians do—that the imagination is a primary source of human error and, therefore, of human sorrow. By eradicating or stunting the imagination, Gradgrind genuinely hopes to benefit all future generations. But if—as Dickens certainly believed—the very ability to project thought for the future is found in the fancy, Gradgrind's purpose is paradoxical. To eradicate the fancy is, necessarily, to render one careless about the future. This is aptly shown in Tom and Louisa Gradgrind. Bitzer, too, may be considered a successful pupil of Gradgrind's: operating on self-interested reason, Bitzer cares only for his own present advantage—and shows no scruples about doing so. As Gradgrind's name suggests, all capacity for joy has been gradually ground out of human nature; and all that will remain are discrete, disorganized monads of utilitarian principles—but nothing like a soul (as Bitzer's name suggests). Like Gradgrind's ideas, Bitzer's name implies a loss of continuum—an artificial separation of experience into distinct units lacking the bond of feelings that gives both past and future, as well as the present, their human value.

Both Slackbridge and Gradgrind are willing to abandon that which makes experience a continuum. Slackbridge requires that the union members repudiate past affection and respect for Steven Blackpool, thus clearly engineering their present behavior by means of their expectations. What Slackbridge's method would deprive them of, however, is the mode of behavior that is for Dickens the very purpose of life: the union members must deny their present feelings. In doing so, they will lose all sense of community—which is one thing, according to Steven's words, that they possessed even in the hungry present. To the extent that Slackbridge is successful, their futures are flawed, whatever the strike's success and the union's ultimate security. Similarly, Gradgrind's insistence that his students and children concentrate on the idea of self-interest obscures for them the proper uses of the present.

Mr. Bounderby makes a very curious and inspired contribution to the thematic structure of *Hard Times*. By his name, and by his description as the "Bully of humility" (1, 4), we read him as an incisive parody of the Victorian idea of the captain of industry. He is not simply a Dickensian original intruding upon a thematic context to which he has little relation. He joins Slackbridge and Gradgrind in a triumvirate in the empire of great expectations. Bounderby would have people believe that he rose out of singularly deprived conditions. Born and raised in a ditch—abandoned by all sensible people who might have had natural feelings for him—he can claim that his education was less than that of most ditchers and delvers. Yet now he is Josiah Bounderby of Coketown! In this way, he can thrust himself forward as a paragon of the self-made man—the primary support for the doctrine of great expectations.

As Bounderby tells his spurious story, its rags-to-riches theme appears to discredit any notion of a connection between a child's present and future. Furthermore, if one can rise from Bounderby's supposedly loveless and disadvantaged origins to his current eminence, what need is there to tinker with current social conditions and regulations? He represents himself as a concrete reason for maintaining the status quo. After Bounderby's narrative, who would dare complain that social mobility is limited in England? For Bounderby is living proof of the discontinuity of present and future, as well as the irrelevance of feelings. But like the other apostles of great expectations in *Hard Times,* Bounderby is totally exposed in the eyes of the reader, who may well leave the novel with a renewed sense that the future need not be permitted to undermine the rights of the present—and must not be thought separate from the present.

Too little credit, I think, is given Dickens for the creation of Bounderby—an archetypal character of capitalistic civilization, and one who knows the value of public relations. But is he modeled on someone from life? Bounderby's humbug about his past privations is his most salient characteristic. Certainly a number of Dickens's friends and colleagues rose out of poverty and no doubt sermonized on the theme. But Dickens also rose out of poverty. Consequently, I cannot help but think that Dickens is, in his dialectic of time, beginning to reevaluate his own self-pity over his past.

At the point in history when an innovative mode of fixing the future—such as that which the Malthusians or utilitarians or positivists would favor—is united with the traditional mode sanctioned by Victorian religion and ethics, we find that cardinal Victorian virtue: duty. Dickens's treatment of duty has provided us with an exceptionally clear example of his dialectical mind. Dickens began with a conventional adoption of the term and concept; but by the last half of his career—although Esther in *Bleak House* often counsels duty to herself—Dickens more often derides an uncritical acceptance of the convention of duty. For under the rubric of duty, the future may be as cut and dried as it is by any other means. Duty can be used as a shibboleth to foster stasis and to stymie spiritual progress.

So long as Dickens chronicled failures in duty—especially when the failure jeopardized the future of children—he did not examine the convention. But gradually there accumulated in his fiction characters who, under the name of duty, do what they desire to do. Bumble and Ralph Nickleby provide early examples of duty that has become a mere word. Duty can also have a false object, as it has with Mrs. Pardiggle, Mrs. Jellyby, Mr. Turveydrop, and Mr. Tulkington in *Bleak House*—to name but one novel. Duty may also go wrong by becoming a mechanical process, as it does with Pancks in *Little Dorrit*. Either way, devotion to duty impairs the fullness of the future. Whereas for Carlyle "the same sense of the Infinite nature of Duty is the central part of all of us, a ray as of Eternity and Immortality"[11]—for Dickens the "ray" was too often social, extrinsic, and mortal in source and effect. Dickens came to see that duty, too, may be made into cant. And far from being a laudable and reliable indicator of selflessness, duty may be wholly unfeeling and uncourageous—becoming a mere refrozen runoff of respectability.

In *Dombey and Son,* Dickens provided many views of how duty was held to be a one-way relationship. When Alice Marwood suggests to her mother, Mrs. Brown, that a child is owed as well as owing duty, "'I!' cried the old woman. 'To my gal! A mother dutiful to her own child!'" (34). It is Alice who expresses Dickens's critism of Victorian duty: "I have heard some talk about duty first and last; but it has always been of my duty to other people. I wondered now and then—to pass the time away—whether no one ever owed any duty to me" (34). To neither Mrs. Brown nor Mr. Dombey nor Mrs. Skewton does it occur that children must be credited as well as debited with duty.

Dombey and Son is quite as much a study of duty as it is of pride. Indeed, Harriet Carker has found them equivalent: "There is a kind of pride . . . which is mere duty" (33). Dombey, like the judge who addressed Alice Marwood, assumes that duty in his relationship with his wife, Edith, is nonreciprocal. He does not ask for trust but enjoins it as her "duty" to receive his friends "with a little more than deference" (36). During a subsequent scene of Dombey with Edith, it is revealing that Dombey requires Carker to remain; Dombey is attempting to enforce obedience to a social convention—that of a wife's duty to a husband. Later, Dombey says, "I place my reliance on your improved sense of duty..." (40). The page heading "Mr. Dombey holds his course" indicates how Dombey hopes to parlay the sense of duty into a fixing of all future relations between him and his wife. Dombey believes that it is his wife's duty to submit to him; but a higher duty—apparently her pride—prevents her. Cousin Feenix puts his finger on the "Eternal and Immortal ray" when he admits that Edith, "my lovely and accomplished relative," had "so far forgotten what was due to—in point of fact, to the world" (51). Dombey could not have agreed more. Dombey, Feenix, and most of the other characters interpret *duty* as if it had a Miltonian etymology—that is, as what is *"due to* the world." In all these cases, duty paralyzes the future.

A comic exaggeration of such duty occurs when Dombey's servants—consulting their own pride and "fiercely protective of their own careers," as we might say today—determine to desert his house en masse after his financial failure. Thus, it seems that even desertion can be considered duty to the world. In the persons of Merdle's butler (LD) and the Analytic Chemist (OMF), one may find in Dickens's works servants whose sole duty is to their own respectability, to their own sense of pride—and not at all to their employers. When Harriet claims that pride is duty, she means only that some pride in one's self is necessary in order to serve others well. It is a comic perversion to make self-pride dependent upon *not* serving others. The comic exposure of duty as a mere name continues when Joey Bagstock says, "And when a duty devolves upon an Englishman, he is bound to get out of it, in my opinion, in the best way he can" (DS, 31). The word *duty* has come to mean nothing—or, what is the same thing, has come to mean everything to everyone.

In *Dombey and Son,* Dickens has anatomized duty, displaying the disingenuous perversion of the term grown common in the Victorian era. Alice Marwood pronounces Dickens's judgment on such distorted duty: "I had heard so much, in my wrongdoing, of my neglected duty, that I took up with the belief that duty had not been done to me, and that as the seed was sown, the harvest grew" (58). To lay out the future of others by means of the T square of duty—without reflection on how one's present obligation to others will affect that future—is simply the imposition of the illusion of synchrony upon the protean face of reality. Situations change—and with them, the nature of duty.

Dickens continued his anatomy of duty in the last half of his career. No one in *Bleak House* does duty more assiduously than Mrs. Pardiggle (though it does no one any good) and the little Pardiggles (to their own great regret and resentment). For Pancks in *Little Dorrit,* "the Whole Duty of Man in a commercial country" is to always keep at it or to "keep somebody else always at it" (1, 13). When Plornish says of Pancks, "He really does, beyond belief" (1, 24), and Pancks says to Amy, "You shall live to see," we note again that Dickens's verbal playfulness is making a metaphor out of the surface structure of the sentence. As is often and pointedly the case with the projects of Pancks's endeavors, the sentence lacks a syntactical object. Thus, the language reflects the lack of object—the pointlessness—of Pancks's doing his duty. Merdle, too, lives for the "duty that he owed society"—which neither he nor society ever fathoms. William Dorrit's opinion about duty changes after he and his children become rich: "We owe it as a duty to them and to ourselves, from this moment, not to let them—hum—not to let them do anything" (1, 35). Examples of the perverted sense of duty could be multiplied, but how Dickens's irony undermined such cant is clear.

George Orwell has suggested of Dickens that "where he appears to disapprove of young men who do not work . . . it is because they are cynical and immoral or because they are a burden on somebody else." Orwell has argued that Dickens's ideal "was a dream of complete idleness."[12] Orwell's reduction not only does not jibe with Dickens's sentiments in his letters, but it also smudges obvious facts about even upper middle-class characters in the novels. Neither Richard Carstone, Arthur Clennam, Charles Darnay, Herbert Pocket, John Harmon, nor even Edwin Drood dream of idleness. As for the working-class characters, Dickens knew that the English working-class was the hardest working under the sun.

Yet Orwell has put his finger on the antinomy in Dickens's attitude toward work. Immensely driven—a producer of an incredible amount of finished work—Dickens came to realize that two of his principles were contradictory. On the one hand, he held, with the Victorian ethos, that "one can only work on, you know—work while it is day."[13] On the other hand, he believed in the necessity for play—for human beings to exercise their imagination; to recreate themselves through art, companionship, or nature; and to take "their rightful share, in what our Great Creator formed them to enjoy" (TC). As he argued in the "Preliminary Word" to *Household Words,* the imagination "burns with an inspiring flame, or sinks into a sullen glare, but which (or woe betide the day!) can never be extinguished."[14] If the imagination was not nurtured aright, it would explode into violence as surely as physical hunger drives men to revolt. Dickens, therefore, found himself caught between the duty to work and the drive to play. The discrepancy is apparent when he emphasized the need for recreation. Indeed, this is part of his thinking at least as early as the writing of *Sunday Under Three Heads* in 1836. Therefore, when he appears at times to be rejecting work, he is, rather, rejecting the exclusive doing of duty (often some kind of work) merely as duty. For human beings must also escape duty—must also play.

In the person of the Uncommercial Traveller, whose pleasure it is to tell his readers of "my day's no-business," Dickens articulated his position: "I travel for the great house of Human Interest Brothers, and have rather a large connection in the fancy goods way" (UT, p. 1). Dickens was simply speaking up for the social value of the goods of fancy that he as a writer purveyed. Nor was he alone in this anti-utilitarian position. The *British Quarterly Review* said of his work:

> In looking over the whole series, we consider Mr. Dickens merits much praise for the tone of healthful morality that pervades all his tales. We have no mawkish striving after something which seems to be considered duty, merely because it is difficult, and involves painful self-sacrifice; that prevailing fault of the French moral tale.[15]

Some Victorians agreed with Dickens that duty has become a fixation and an excuse for keeping the humane judgment and divine spirit of human beings unemployed.

In *Great Expectations,* Dickens made superb fun of duty. When Pip is presented to Miss Havisham, it abruptly becomes his duty to play. To have the duty to play is to transform play into work. This is a marvelous send up of the Victorian tendency to try to render all of life into duty. But it is in *Our Mutual Friend,* in which so many moralistic platitudes are subverted, that the value of duty, especially of the duty to work, was brought thoroughly into question by Dickens. Significantly, it is the irrelevant Lady Tippins who most often uses the word *duty*. For example, she rallies Mortimer Lightwood to gossip: "Miserable! Is that the way you do your duty?" With her, the duty and play issue comes full circle. She means to use duty ironically; she assumes that his social duty to talk to her is a pleasure. But for Lightwood that pleasure is the most burdensome duty he has in life. He replies, "I assure you I have no notion of what my duty is" (1, 10). Perhaps such doubt as his must precede the discovery of true spiritual duty. For Dickens, duty was never to be found in such perfunctory social obligations. It is from the mouth of the simple-minded Mr. Toots that the true nature of duty emerges: "I shall consider it my duty . . . to make the best of myself . . ." (DS, 56).

Contemporaneously with *Our Mutual Friend, All the Year Round* printed an article that summed up Dickens's thinking at the time: "Duty is a grand thing to do, and the duty-doer is an indispensable person in his generation; and yet more than mere duty is needed for the perfectioning of our lives."[16] The phrasing seems to suggest that the content of duty may vary from generation to generation. In Carlyle's words, *"Do the duty which liest nearest thee"*[17]—but do not project that to be tomorrow's required duty as well. Clearly, duty as collectively defined and mouthed is not enough instruction for the specific individual in the specific situation.

As for work, that can be a matter of terminology—of letter and not of spirit—quite as well as duty can. Under the ironic title "A Piece of Work," a chapter of *Our Mutual Friend* details the "going about" and "rallying around" and "keeping up appearances" that constitute the farcical election campaigning of Veneering, Tippins, and others. By and large, both duty and work are subjected to scrutiny in *Our Mutual Friend.* When Boffin is pretending to be a miser, he announces a principle that shows how hollow duty may become: "A man of property owes a duty to other men of property, and must look sharp after his inferiors" (3, 5). Earlier, Boffin had recommended the bees as models for human behavior. But Eugene Wrayburn argues:

> When your friends the bees worry themselves to that highly fluttered extent about their sovereign . . . are we to learn the greatness of tuft-hunting? . . . they work; but don't you think they overdo it? They work so much more than they can eat—they are incessantly boring and buzzing at their one idea till Death comes upon them—that don't you think they overdo it? (1, 8)

Wrayburn leaves even Mr. Boffin in doubt about the value of work for its own sake. We can recognize the development of Dickens's ideas when we remember that Skimpole too had "protested against the overweening assumption of bees" (BH, 8). Reader reaction to Skimpole's protest places a positive light on the work of bees. Like Jemmy's judgment of "overdone" duty in "Mrs. Lirriper's Lodgings" (CS, p. 401), Wrayburn's protest casts a negative light—so far had Dickens travelled.

Not that positive duty ceases to be cited in the late novels. For example, Meagles admonishes the forgiving and forgiven Tattycoram to do her duty (LD, 2, 33), and when Neville Landless worries that Cloisterham is an "uncongenial place" for his sister, Crisparkle corrects him: "There is duty to be done here; and there are womanly feeling, sense and courage wanted here" (ED, 17). The juxtaposition of duty and womanly feeling defines duty in its positive, living sense. Hence Dickens did not absolutely renounce the value of either work or duty. But the terms were more precisely defined. For example, the Boffins are approved for having "a religious sense of duty and desire to do right" (OMF, 1, 19). *Our Mutual Friend* is filled with individuals who recognize common duty and who desire to do genuine work. Dickens has matured enough to insist on the spirit and not the letter of these major constituents of the Victorian ethos: both work and duty must be concrete and personal at all times. For Dickens, duty meant primarily the sacrifice of self-interest to loving kindness. And work was simply a means of doing such duty. The distinction is that genuine duty and work cannot predicate the nature of the future. Consequently, duty is—when it is right in object and is properly functioning—a mode of the imagination, informing life, as Crisparkle makes clear, "with feeling" (ED, 17). Duty connects present to future—enhancing both, depriving neither.

Great expectations—or desiring a static and secure future—is an abuse of the future. But Dickens also made ample illustration of the converse—that is, when a secured future renders the present sclerotic. By separating the individual from others, such confirmed expectations can deprive a character of every motive for action in the present. Mortimer Lightwood speaks for a number of characters throughout the novels: "My own small income (I devoutly wish that my grandfather had left it to the Ocean rather than to me!) has been an effective Something, in the way of preventing me from turning to at Anything. And I think yours has been much the same" (OMF, 4, 16). The ocean is no haphazard allusion. In this novel in which so much of the action takes place beside the filthy Thames, the ocean stands in opposition to the changes of the river, which is clear and peaceful upstream but turgid and turbulent as it flows through London. As happens so often with Dickens's imagery, the river becomes an emblem of time; and Mortimer is implying by his allusion to the ocean that his moderate legacy would have done more good if it had never appeared in time.

Eugene Wrayburn also speaks of his "Family Embarrassments—we call it before company the Family Estate" (1, 12). Each son of the Wrayburn family is assigned a future calling by the father, without consideration of his talents or inclinations. Thus, Wrayburn—like Lightwood and so many others—is debarred from active choices in the present by these very modest expectations.

Alfred Starling, in the 1859 *Christmas Story* entitled "The Haunted House," is another representative of this forlorn set of legatees, for he

> is a young fellow who pretends to be "fast" (another word for loose, as I understand the term), but who is much too good and sensible for that nonsense, and who would have distinguished himself before now, if his father had not unfortunately left him a small independence of two hundred a year, on the strength of which his only occupation in life has been to spend six. (CS, p. 239)

Such an independence is so only in name; paradoxically, it inevitably precludes independent action.

But the genteel are not the only ones who can lose motivation to act. Even the poor can be so optimistic about the future that they do not lift a hand to bring it into being. In *Bleak House*, Jobling says to Guppy, "I trusted to things coming around." The narrator responds: "That very popular trust in flat things 'coming' around! Not in their being beat round, or worked round, but in their 'coming' round! As though a lunatic should trust in the world's coming triangular!" (BH, 20). We see in this mockery of the Micawberian worldview not only evidence of Dickens's own continuing dialectic but also the emphatic repudiation of all those promises of the future that prevent present activity.

Bleak House is a repository of the effects of great expectations. Having great expectations is the condition of the "sickness of hope deferred [that] was raging in so many hearts" (24) in the novel. To sacrifice the present joys of human life to the future—and then to find the future indefinitely postponed—drives the expectant ones to madness. No one displays the effects of the "sickness" of expectations more than Richard Carstone. Esther sees that the court has "engendered or confirmed in him a habit of putting off" (13). He can settle into the profession of neither the Army nor medicine. He puts off living, ultimately, in his expectations of a judgment. Like Miss Flite (the sparseness of whose room reflects the deprivation of the present by waiting on a future judgment), Richard cannot do "anything very definite *now*" (37), not until after he has gained a judgment—any judgment. Because he cannot leave the future to itself, he cannot have the present for himself. He summarizes the upshot of his expectations in words that might serve as a motto for this side of the theme: "Now? There's no now for us suitors" (37). Dickens's precise point.

Dickens, as usual, has given ample comic versions of the theme.

In *Little Dorrit,* there is an exquisite irony when Bob the turnkey wants to leave everything he has to his god-daughter Amy. But in a vain effort to make certain that no one in the future could contest the will—and to insure that even Amy could never give anything away once she received it—he fails to act, dies intestate after all, and Amy gets nothing. Bob's attempt to fix the future is emblematic. Perhaps the most absurd example of the will to fix the future occurs in *Our Mutual Friend,* in which Lavinia Wilfer tells her mother, "I'll not grow after I'm married! . . . Nothing shall induce me" (2, 8). Whether in a comic mode or a serious one, the lesson is clear. The future, like Mrs. Pardiggle's children, should not be "unnaturally constrained" (BH, 8), or it will turn out a crop of evil, as Mrs. Pardiggle's children appear on the way to becoming.

But Dickens's dialectical habit of mind did not cease after he had sketched the ways to ruin the present and future through great expectations. For, conversely, there are modes of behavior that make too little preparation for the future. One could argue that characters like the Marchioness (OCS) or Jo (BH) have no expectations, no future whatsoever. But as pathetic—or potentially pathetic—as such characters are, they cannot be said to have an attitude toward the future. They are, therefore, victims of a form of the dead hand of the past rather than examples of any great expectations. But there are characters in Dickens who take too little cognizance of the future.

Eugne Wrayburn (OMF) is such a character. He is asked to "Look on to the end" (3, 10) of his current pursuit of Lizzie, which Mortimer foresees must end in the seduction and possible corruption of Lizzie. This is an end that Eugene himself does not desire; but his indifference to the present has stunted his ability to look forward, and he can only reply:

> See now! That's exactly what I'm incapable of doing. How acute you are, Mortimer, in finding my weak place! When we were at school together, I got up my lessons at the last moment, day by day and bit by bit; now we are out in life together, I get up my lessons in the same way. (3, 10)

"I don't design anything" (2, 6) he admits. Because he cannot—and never could—join his future to his present in an integral, organic relationship, Eugene simply moves bit by bit, moment to moment, temporal monad by temporal monad. Placed by his father in a position with no real future—thus living purposelessly—

Eugene has a future that is definite in status but without hope of change. It is not informed by the caring that binds time together. The same could be said of his type altogether—Steerforth, Carstone, Gowan, Harthouse, and the unconverted Carton. They have no long term goals, and they hope for nothing in particular.

The epitome of men with such solid but featureless futures is Harold Skimpole in *Bleak House*. Assuming a "guileless inaptitude for worldly affairs" (6), Skimpole is shown thrusting the care for the consequences of his actions upon others. Although friends "helped him, in quicker or slower succession, to several openings in life" (6), Skimpole soon closes them again. He evades the responsibility of holding positions in the present. With "no idea of time" or money, Skimpole is only too willing to be, as he says to another, "utterly incapable of helping myself, and entirely in your hands!" He asks only "to be free." For Dickens, this juxtaposition of statements was wildly comic. With his hatred of patronage, Dickens knew that this was the freedom of the drone—for any freedom placed in the hands of others cannot seriously be called freedom. Self-removed from the chains of time—from antecedents, consequences, and duties—Skimpole is, for all his languid life of pleasures, only half living. He pretends to have no expectations—and he certainly refuses to prepare for the future; but his openness is hypocritical because his future is expected simply to replicate the present.

What is more, Skimpole's refusal to attend to consequences soon shows its nefarious side. By turning Jo over to the police, Skimpole shows that—in his reckless refusal to consider the future—he has lost the capacity to feel an interest in another soul. In other words, as a representative of an aestheticism that seeks only to live in the present, Skimpole's faculty of the imagination has atrophied and is no longer capable of the sympathy that is its precious gift. If Romanticism was at least partly constituted by a belief in the value of emotion that is made moral because it is sympathetic to others, then Skimpole stands as an example of the corruption of Romanticism. For his feelings are never projected into others. He, therefore, evinces the underside of Romanticism—which is the wholesale aestheticizing of experience. He is an apostate who has divided art and morality. Speaking of the slaves on an American plantation, he can opine, "I dare say they are worked hard, I dare say they don't altogether like it, I dare say theirs is an unpleasant existence on the whole; but they people the landscape for me, they give it poetry for me, and perhaps that is one of the pleasanter objects of their existence" (18). Apparently, the slaves are supposed to find pleasure in entertaining him; but he is incapable of feeling for them or of wishing to change their lives in the present. This cynicism—if that word does not designate too thoughtful a position for Skimpole—reveals the moral abyss that is a concomitant of carelessness about the future.

Near the end of *Bleak House,* Miss Flite gives liberty to the birds that she had kept caged until such time as her chancery judgment was given. Because her birds bear negative as well as positive names, there has been some ambivalence among readers about their being caged and finally freed. Miss Flite's gesture seems to me symbolic of the import of the whole novel and, indeed, of the theme of great expectations that runs through so many of Dickens's novels. Present opportunities must not be caged until some future event transpires. Caging all of the potential responses to, and consequences of, life—as Miss Flite, Richard Carstone, and all of the full-fledged suitors to Chancery do—is the error of any stance toward life that seeks perfection. Patrick Creevy has written of Miss Flite that her "eschatological expectations . . . divinely sanctioned . . . are never fulfilled."[18] The very anticlimax of releasing the birds after Richard's death has thematic purpose: perfection comes only with death. To have life at all, we must take the mix that all of her birds signify. As Dickens stated in a letter, "The comfort is, that all the strange and terrible things come uppermost, and that the good and pleasant things are mixed up every moment of our existence so plentifully that we scarcely heed them."[19]

To dictate to Providence is absurd. Bergson felt that "the belief in teleology, in perfect finality à la Leibniz is simply mechanism in reverse. . . . This kind of finalism destroys novelty and annihilates *time.*"[20] As Carlyle proclaimed in "Characteristics," mankind has long been trying to bind the future:

> How often, in former ages, by eternal creeds, eternal Forms of Government and the like, has it been attempted, fiercely enough, and with destructive violence, to chain the Future under the Past; and say to Providence, whose ways with man are mysterious, and through the great deep: Hitherto shalt thou come, but no farther![21]

Yet Dickens seems to have had a profounder belief in the absurdity of this attempt to chain the future than Carlyle, at least in his old age, turned out to have. However, Dickens would have concurred with these early words of Carlyle: "Nevertheless so much has become evident to every one, that this wondrous Mankind is advancing somewhither; that at least all human beings are, have been and forever will be, in Movement and Change."[22]

Dickens's conviction was that living fully in the present was essential to keeping the future open. This is confirmed by Tommy Traddles's motto, "Wait and Hope" (27). Later, in *Our Mutual Friend,* the identical doctrine is expressed by Lizzie, who admits, "I cannot stop some dreadful things I try to stop, but I go on in the hope and trust that the time will come" (3). As Carlyle wrote, "if Memory have its force and worth, so also has Hope."[23] Hope, trust, and effort are the seeds that, planted in the present, will produce a future worth living. As for the future, John Jarndyce expresses the best approach: "Trust in nothing but in Providence and your own efforts" (13). This is tantamount to saying that the future offers nothing unless the present is lived fully.

If we accept the notion that Dickens realized the importance of keeping the future open, we can see that the second ending that Dickens wrote for *Great Expectations* is more consistent with his dialectic of time than the first. In the first ending, the conclusion is definite and static. Pip, corrected in his great expectations, is chastened and dutiful but has neither trust nor hope in the future. This passivity is the reverse of Pip's first error. But in the second ending, Pip concludes: "I took her hand in mine, and we went out of the ruined place." He could have added "and out of the ruined time." Change, action, and hope are signified by this conclusion, as they are by the conclusions of *Little Dorrit* ("they went quietly down into the roaring streets, inseparable and blessed") and *Our Mutual Friend* ("Mortimer sees Twemlow home, shakes hands with him cordially at parting, and fares to the temple, gaily"). Clearly, Dickens arranged these conclusions to show how great expectations in all its forms may best be overcome by action in the present.

Dickens believed that if the past was to have a use in the present as an exercise of forgiveness, the use of the future in the present was an exercise of hope, concrete effort, and trust in Providence. All in all, it is clear that for Dickens the truth of life was change— and that whatever would block change must be obviated before it cursed both present and future. The worst blockage would be the belief that the contents of time are, like the words in a positivist's sentence, static and non-commutative in nature. Human beings, therefore, should not look to the guaranteed future any more than they should look to the determined past for their meaning in life. They should look, instead, to *durée* or "real time," which, Bergson described as "concrete and indivisible." Dickens, like

Bergson, refused to let the categories of time become objects—and, thus, possessions. Bergson argued that the intellect does "not *think* real time. But we live it." Mechanistic thought assumes that "the same causes produce the same effects." Consequently, the "essence of mechanical explanation, in fact, is to regard the future and the past as calculable functions of the present, and thus to claim that *all* is given." But Dickens would have agreed with Bergson's rebuttal: "If the future is bound to succeed the present instead of being given alongside it, it is because the future is not altogether determined by the present moment." Not a mere effect, the future is vital. Dickens showed that this is true of past, present, and future.

Part Two
The Uses of Time

4
The Battle of Life

> Boehme is a man of the modern age. He no longer conceives of the world as an eternally static order nor as a hierarchical and unmoving system. The life of the world is a battle, a becoming, a vast process, all fire and dynamism.
> —Nicolas Berdyaev, "Introduction," to Jacob Boehme's *Six Theosophic Points*

Pip's project toward his future—that is, his great expectations—appears, at first sight, to present a view of life in contrast to that of Bradley Headstone in *Our Mutual Friend*. Whereas Bradley has worked hard enough to achieve his social position as a teacher, Pip has seemingly only wished hard enough. Yet, in both cases, their grasp, to modify Browning's phrase, exceeds their reach; neither finds satisfaction in the future that he has created for himself. Therefore, although their approaches to the future are diametric opposites, they suffer similar fates. The reason is that their intentions are identical. In essence, both desire a future place in society that is not only static—marking a terminus ad quem for the trajectory of their desires—but that is somehow not conditioned by the qualities and circumstances of the desirer.

What Headstone and Pip have in common with each other and with so many of Dickens's other characters is their willingness to forfeit their essential freedom for a position of safety. In this way, they would exist beyond threat and need. But such fairy-tale conclusions are antipathetic to the view that Dickens had that time—the future included—was for use.

For Dickens, the faculty of the imagination—so essential to Romantic psychology and political theory—was the solution to corrupted ideas about the future. Indeed, Dickens's fear was that educational practice would grind away this faculty in children. Dickens's frequent allusions to fairy tales, children's riddles, chapbooks, and pantomime are evidence of Dirk den Hartog's point that Dickens considered it vitally important to keep the adult imagination in touch with the character of childhood.[1] The function of the imagination, however, is not retrospective; it is proleptic, enabling man to look to the future. Imagination is, according to Romantic theorists like Hazlitt, the sine qua non of moral behavior.[2] The theory states that by projecting one's sympathies forward in time one learns to project sympathies presently, ambiently, onto other individuals. Imagination is the true use of the future. Because so much has been written on imagination elsewhere,[3] I will focus only on the means that the imagination uses to bring the virtues of the future into use for the present.

The tendency to great expectations is fostered rather than obviated by capitalistic society, which, despite its loud trumpetings in favor of endeavor, seems to contain a secret hankering after a safe and effortless position, as in Carker's desire for a retreat beyond the skirmishes of workaday life (DS). The doctrines of hunger, as I have argued, and the dread of being eaten are the causes that Dickens has indicated for this secret hankering. Against this abuse of the future, Dickens mobilized a number of themes and narrative techniques. What all of these have in common is an emphasis on the continuity between present and future. In Dickens's view, what corrupts the future is an artificial crevasse between the future and the present. This crevasse is made possible by the false assumptions about the nature of time and the nature of the world.

The false assumption about the world is that it can be fully known and reduced to some discrete, definitive form. When characters create and adapt to this partial world—constituted, as Steven Marcus has said, "of mutually exclusive groups"[4]—they become "worldly," in quite a Christian sense of the word. These partial and amoral versions of the world disgust some characters so much that they are tempted to abandon life. All too often this temptation leads to great expectations—to the assumption that there can be opened between the world and some better life a defensive hiatus, a moat protecting the individual from the contingencies of life, including the necessity of difficult moral choices. Everything Dickens wrote militated against such assumptions; but he recognized their attraction. He therefore works both to undermine this atomization of time and its world and to restore the world to the full stream of past, present, and future that is the real world.

Nicholas Nickleby is perhaps the fullest working out in Dickens of the many temptations to abandon the world. One of the subtlest temptations is the result of mere definition. Early in the novel, the narrator warns of this form of temptation—of "what is called the world—a conventional phrase which, being interpreted, often signifieth all the rascals in it" (3). To thus define the world, Dickens showed, is the first step toward the desertion of life. Such a definition of the world has different effects on rascals and on innocents. On the innocents, this definition seems to press a choice: become worldly or abandon the world. But, obviously, this choice is no choice. Either decision effectively abandons the real world, for even to become worldly is only to replace the open world with a word—to replace the world by the rascally part of it. The irony is that the rascals, having accepted this definition—and thus having drastically limited their world—view those who yet possess a broader definition as fools, that is, unworldly. For example, Ralph Nickleby assumes that because Kate is "virtuously and well brought up" (26) she is ignorant of the ways of the world. But Kate recognizes the possibility of both good and evil in the world, and she therefore will never become worldly. Kate intuits what Ralph ignores—that the very constitution of the world is a mixture of good and evil that dictates to the individual the need for continuous effort to differentiate between the moral and immoral.

What Ralph does know, however, is the appeal that the reputation of being worldly has for fools. Fools dote on knavery. On this tack, he attempts to get around Mrs. Nickleby: "I'll address your mother, sir, who knows the world" (20). Mrs. Nickleby—who does not even know so much of the real world as the part that is herself—is nevertheless boastful of her worldliness. "The good lady, then, with the preliminary observation that she might be fairly supposed not to have lived in the world so long without knowing its way" (28), delivers her foolish precepts unabashedly. Yet, despite her foolishness, she cannot sink to Ralph's worldview. She remains optimistic—that is to say, the future remains open to her, as it remains closed to Ralph. Therefore, although Mrs. Nickleby desires to be known as a woman of the world, she cannot abandon the world—as Ralph has—for the "world."

One man of the world, Mr. Bray, will sell his daughter to Gride, the usurer. Ralph incites him to the commission of this deed—which Bray feels is cruel—by making the act seem natural and inevitable: "You are too much a man of the world not to see that in its true light" (47). This is a cruel world, Ralph implies; therefore, "a hundred fathers within the circuit of five miles" (47) would do the same thing. Ralph's *argumentum ad populum* also gives the act the semblance of nature. By accepting Ralph's definition of the nature of the world, Bray translates unnatural cruelty into natural behavior: "I couldn't do anything better for her than advise her to accept those proposals, could I? Now, I ask you, Nickleby, as a man of the world, could I?" (54). As a man of Ralph's world, surely not. "This is a kind of upholding of faith above works," comments the narrator, "and is very comfortable" (54).

Bray, who is a hypocrite, has qualms; Miss Knag, who is not a hypocrite, has no qualms. When Kate fails to take Mantilini as "a fine man," Miss Knag asks, "How can you possibly pronounce an opinion about a gentleman—hem—if you don't see him as he turns out altogether?" (17). This mistaking of sartorial appearance for reality is another version of Ralph's substitution of a part of the world for the whole. "There was," the narrator continues, "so much of the world—even of the little world of the country girl—in this idea of the old milliner"—that Kate avoids further discussion. The "little world" of Miss Knag precludes moral considerations in character judgments.

Squeers is yet another version of the man of the world. Grossly stupid, he does not even comprehend that he continually defeats his own purposes by making the boys under his care desire to die, thereby spoiling his future as well as theirs. He thinks they die merely to spite him. His greed is so petty that it serves to make him contemptible, not awful like Ralph. Squeers takes so much pain for so little profit—his effort is so disproportionate to his results—that he inevitably becomes a comic butt, a parody of rascality. Nevertheless—although Squeers is less formidable than Ralph, less unnatural than Bray, and less deluded than Knag—he represents the common denominator of all their tendencies. Moreover, as a headmaster, he has scope for the exercise of his vices that makes him truly terrifying. Although his "shop for morals" (4) in Yorkshire is a gross imposture, it has an awful consequence. It succeeds in deluding the boys about the real nature of the world. This is the horror: it instills the boys with a desire to, as the Genius of Despair and Suicide puts it, "[q]uit this dreary world at once" (6). Not knowing the full world, they are made sick unto death by the idea and effects of Squeers's world.

Dickens was careful to display the complete world as well. This world exists for those whose imagination has not been sacrificed to fear. It finds representation in the minds of characters like Kate Nickleby. No doubt, Kate is remarkably free of vanity. But she understands that she is the reason for the visits of Hawk and Verisopht, whereas the hypocritically unworldly Mrs. Wititterly does not. It is through Nicholas that the reader gains the fullest view of the nature of the world. Although his youthful spirits get him into difficulty with Fanny Squeers, they nevertheless preserve him from despair. All but crushed at Dotheboy's Hall, Nicholas's spirits rise when he suddenly realizes that Squeers's world is not the whole world. Smike asks him if he will escape:

> "Oh, do tell me, will you go—*will* you?"
> "I shall be driven to that at last!" said Nicholas. "The world is before me, after all."
> "Tell me," urged Smike, "is the world as bad and dismal as this place?"
> "Heaven forbid," replied Nicholas, pursuing the train of his own thoughts, "its hardest, coarsest toil were happiness to this." (12)

Possessed of this knowledge that the whole world is before him, Nicholas refuses to abandon himself to despair over a mere part of the world.

Nicholas has rejected the amoral world that leads people to despair and suicide. Far from denying that rascals exist, he has only refused to give up the world to them. Nicholas reiterates his faith that the world is moral when, speaking to Madeline Bray about Gride, he says that "the most abject poverty, the most wretched condition of human life, with a pure and upright mind, would be happiness to that which you must undergo as the wife of such a man as this" (53). It is the moral grounding of the universe that makes the world a tolerable place.

Understandably, Nicholas has a personal motive for persuading Madeline to his view of the world. For him, her beauty has a moral purpose: it helps to reconcile one to the world. He has, he says, "thought of that sweet face which came upon me in my bitterest distress like a glimpse of some better world" (40). She symbolizes the full, moral world—which is the better world. Significantly, by contrast, Ralph admits, "I have no taste for beauty" (47). This admission is one more example (in the accumulation of evidence throughout the novel) that Ralph perceives little of the real world. Early in the novel, he was slightly moved by Kate's presence; but he is able to suppress even this powerful incitement to realize his better self. Hence, it is no wonder that he is also immune to Madeline's plight: "It would have moved a very hard and wordly heart to see the young and beautiful creature, whose certain misery they had been contriving but a minute before, throw her arms about her father's neck, and pour forth words of tender sympathy and love. . . . But Ralph looked coldly on" (47). He is as blind to Madeline's virtue as he is to her beauty.

Ralph's most characteristic statement is "I know the world, and the world knows me (44)." But, as his machinations are foiled, his knowledge of the world appears ever more dubious. For instance, when Hawk elects not to seek revenge on Nicholas, Ralph says, "There is some spell about the boy. . . . Circumstances conspire to help him. Talk of fortune's favours! What is even money to such Devil's luck as this!" (44). From "spell" to "circumstances" to "fortune's favours" to "Devil's luck," Ralph uses any phrase to avoid admitting that Hawk is too much a man of the world to be foolish enough to tangle with Nicholas again. What Nicholas has is better than money!—quite an admission for one who "always wound up these mental soliloquies by arriving at the conclusion that there was nothing like money" (11). This admission marks the limits of Ralph's world. Later, he replies to his accusers, "I tell you plainly, gentlemen, that little as I care for the opinion of the world (as the slang goes), I don't choose to submit quietly to slander and malice" (59). Ralph is trying to preclude the idea of ethical judgment by calling it slander. Indeed, the opinion of his world *ought* to leave him cold, for he knows well that his world contains only cynicism and hypocrisy. But his heat here reveals his suspicion that the world may possess other than amoral, hypocritical, or stupid persons. Thus, the full world begins to encroach upon Ralph's "cursed world" (62).

Dickens had not yet fully developed his mature capacity to integrate narrative, trope, and theme; he therefore resorted here to underscoring the view of the full world by means of the interpolated tales. As Nicholas is travelling by coach to Dotheboys Hall, he listens to two tales. The first is "The Five Sisters of York." In this tale, a monk counsels the five beautiful sisters to "shun all such thoughts and chances" of life "in the peaceful shelter of the church" (6). But Alice, the youngest of the five—and, therefore, most divinely fresh—prefers "the freshness of the earth and all the beautiful things which breathe upon it." She says that "nature's own blessings are the proper goods of life." And, though, she says, "to die is our heavy portion . . . let us die with life about us; when our cold hearts cease to beat, let warm hearts be beating near" (6).

The monk retorts that "memory of earthly things is charged, in after life, with bitter disappointment, affliction, death." This creed is later put to awful proof by Alice's death. Despite the monk's behest that the remaining sisters bury the frames of embroidery that had once delighted Alice, they refuse. Instead, by causing "to be executed, in five large compartments of richly stained glass, a faithful copy of their old embroidery work" (6), they vindicate Alice's view of the beauty of the world—and, thus, they choose not to abandon the world.

With Nicholas listening, a gentleman with a merry face discusses this tale with the grey-headed gentleman, giving an opinion that "the good in this state of existence preponderates over the bad" and that if "our affections be tried, our affections are our consolation and comfort; and memory, however sad, is the best and purest link between this world and a better" (6).[5] We note the insistence on the link between this world—the world of memory—and the better world. The gentleman then goes on to tell the tale of "The Baron of Grogzwig."

The baron, demoralized by the loss of his bachelor pleasures, the exhaustion of his coffers, and the advent of his thirteenth child, decides to commit suicide. Again, the temptation here is to abandon the world and the future. In preparation for his suicide, the baron takes a pipe and a bottle to a private room, where he is visited by the Genius of Despair and Suicide. When the baron cracks a joke, his plan to give the future its ultimate form is upset. For the Genius admits that a "joke, without any figure of speech, *is* the death of me" (6). Humor is alien to the all-or-nothing attitude that Dickens found to be the norm of modern life and that disposes men to great expectations or to despair. Both attitudes preclude an open future. "Come! Quit this dreary world at once" (6), the Genius counsels. The baron answers, "It's a dreary one certainly, but I don't think yours is much better." Thus, the baron is reconciled to this world, with his future open. And thus Dickens, one of the great comic artists of all time, has made the obvious point that humor does reconcile us to this world. It is a point, however, that was not frequently a theme in Dickens's dialectic of time. In any case, "The Baron of Grogzwig" corroborates the moral of "The Five Sisters of York": the temptation to abandon the world, whatever its source, is based on a shallow understanding of the nature of the world.

Nicholas's return to Yorkshire at the end of the novel is significant. We are pointedly told that he passed "by the little alehouse where he had heard the story of the bold Baron of Grogzwig" (64). Upon his arrival, he learns that Dotheboys Hall has been broken up. The collapse of this last worldly bastion in the novel completes the victory of the moral, active forces. Hence, the novel completes the pattern begun by the interpolated stories. Alice, her four sisters, and the Baron of Grogzwig are vindicated and upheld: the world is not abandoned. "Cloister'd virtue" rated no higher with Dickens than it did with Milton. In fact, it is not possible, in Dickens's view, to abandon the world, for the world is not something discrete or exterior—something that may be left behind at will. Human individuality is itself participation in the world. This conviction is evident twenty years later when Dickens wrote to Wilkie Collins about a story for the Christmas number for 1858:

> Do you see your way to our making a Christmas number of this idea that I am going very briefly to hint? Some disappointed person, man or woman, prematurely disgusted with the world, for some reason or no reason (the person should be young, I think) retires to an old lonely house, or an old lonely mill, or anything you like, with one attendant, resolved to shut out the world, and hold no communion with it. The one attendant sees the absurdity of the idea, pretends to humour it, but really thus to slaughter it. Everything that happens, everybody that comes near, every breath of human interest that floats into the old place from the village, or the heath, or the four crossroads near which it stands, and from which belated travellers stray into it, shows beyond any mistake that you can't shut out the world; that you are in, to be of it; that you get into a false position the moment you try to sever yourself from it; and that you must mingle with it, and make the best of it, and make the best of yourself into the bargain.[6]

Disengagement from the world is, therefore, as much an illusion as determination by the world.

The Baron of Grogzwig and the Sisters, like Nicholas and his sister, keep faith with the world and its future; but Ralph finds his future and his world in ruins. When he learns that he "has persecuted and hunted down his own child to death" (60), Smike—the child of the marriage that he feared to avow out of cowardly and worldly considerations—the final irruption of reality into his narrow world has occurred.

At last, Ralph is forced to see his behavior against the horizon of the full, moral world. When Ralph arrives home for the last time, he hesitates before going into his house. The house is a symbol of its owner's psyche: "When he reached his own door, he could hardly make up his mind to turn the key and open it. When he had done that, and gone into the passage, he felt as though to shut it again would be to shut out the world. But he let it go, and it closed with a loud noise. There was no light. How very dreary, cold, and still it was" (62). Though his own world was always so "very dreary, cold, and still," Ralph had long since "shut out" the moral world and can now do nothing but "quit this dreary world" of his own making.[7] But if trying to escape from the world is wrong, so is its apparent opposite—fighting the world.

The future was intolerable for Ralph because the only relationship he could conceive of having with the world was a fight. He often gives tongue to the phrase. But, here again, he commits the error of false analysis. By hypostatizing the world as an opponent, Ralph has falsely separated himself from it. In his determination to overcome the rascals in the world, he cannot see the rascality in himself. In contrast to Ralph's notion is a trope that Dickens used elsewhere—and it was later to become the title of a *Christmas Book*—*The Battle of Life*.

It is a common enough phrase—"battle of life." Certainly, Carlyle's diction frequently portrays life as a fight. And in 1847, Douglas Jerrold wrote: "The blood quickens and glows as it beholds the daily battle. There are the poor fighting with the world."[8] Charlotte Brontë uses the phrase almost obsessively in *Villette* (1853).[9] What is significant in Dickens's use of the trope is the fine distinction he made between this trope and several related ones. For example, the trope means something quite different from "life is a grind," which also suggests tribulation. When Mantilini says that his "life is one demd horrid grind" (NN, 64), he implies that his spirit is being ground away by the exigencies of life. Found in *Isaiah* (III, 15), the trope "battle of life" was used everywhere by Dickens—from Rob in Grinder (DS) and Gradgrind (HT) to Jasper's description of himself as a "grinder of music" (ED). In all of its uses, this trope of the human soul being put to the grindstone connotes the domination of the human spirit by worldly or material forces. The grey-haired gentleman begins the tale of "The Five Sisters of York" by using this image:

> If, while our bodies grow old and withered, our hearts could but retain their early youth and freshness, of what avail would be our sorrows and sufferings! But, the faint image of Eden which is stamped upon them in childhood, chafes and rubs in our *rough struggles with the world* [italics mine], and soon wears away: too often to leave nothing but a mournful blank remaining. (NN, 6)

The trope of struggle or fight with the world is transmuted here into that grinding that wears away the divine, Wordsworthian freshness with which the heart is born. But a distinction must be made between a struggle *with* the world and the battle *of* life. The trope of the battle of life connotes, at least in the mouths of the uncorrupted characters, the continuing struggle in life to preserve the human spirit against worldly onslaughts.

Dickens employed the "battle" trope not only in his fiction but in his correspondence. He wrote Forster, "How often it is with all of us, that in our several spheres we have to do violence to our feelings, and to hide our hearts in carrying on the fight of life, if we would bravely discharge in it our duties and responsibilities."[10] We note that life is not the opponent. Another letter of his used the battlefield image to emphasize the literal deaths of friends: "It is a tremendous consideration that friends should fall around us in such awful numbers when we attain middle life. What a field of battle it is."[11] As in the first example, the battle is internal, spiritual. Again, Dickens wrote: "Life is a fight and must be fought out. Not new, but true, and I don't complain of it."[12] His duty as a man as well as a writer was not to complain. To complain was to concede defeat in the battle.

Samuel Smiles believed that victory is possible for human beings, but that it should not be too easy: "The battle of life is, in most cases, fought uphill; and to win it without a struggle were perhaps to win it without honor."[13] While winning the battle is possible with Smiles, for Dickens victory was, precisely, to continue to struggle. The victory in the battle of life is only survival but it is the essential survival—that of the human heart.

To understand what the cry "battle of life" means in Dickens's fiction we need to glance at what it does *not* mean, for example, in Murdstone's admonition to David Copperfield, "What is before you is a fight with the world" (10). It does not mean what Murdstone means when he says, "David, to the young this is a world of action" (10). In the first place, the young cannot fairly be expected to act. But what is at least as nefarious is Murdstone's implication that sustenance must be won by raping it from society—that life is a desperate fight with others, a fight to the death, no holds barred, and no quarter given or asked. Murdstone's world resembles that of Malthus, where life is a struggle for external power, for mastery over sources of food (and we note that Miss Murdstone takes, as one of her first acts after being introduced into the Copperfield home, the keys to the provision storage rooms). For Dickens, on the contrary, the battle of life is the struggle to retain the internal life of the spirit. A Murdstonean victory in the fight with the world is tantamount to a defeat in the battle of life—which is precisely the battle to keep open to the world and to keep the future open. Because the future derives from our approach to the world, it is not possible to program a future by turning our backs upon the present.

Since the battle of life is inevitable in the world, only the result is in question. Instructions for beginning it is given by John Jarndyce to Richard Carstone: "Rick, the world is before you; and it is most probable that as you enter it, so it will receive you. Trust in nothing but in Providence and your own efforts. Never separate the two" (13). Jarndyce's words insist upon the continuity of present and future. But Rick, in trying to finish off Jarndyce and Jarndyce before getting on with life, has accepted the idea of a crevasse between present and future. Only what Esther calls "application" (17), only the commitment to living this present life is a, literally, viable choice for Rick. To possess great expectations, even Rick's expectations of justice—or, at least, a judgment in the case—is a form of abandoning the world in the present.

To enter the world, then, one must settle oneself into the present—one must sow oneself, as Dickens indicated with the ultimate expression of that motif in the *Memoranda Book*:

> "There is some virtue in him too."
> "Virtue! Yes. So there is in any grain of seed in a seedsman shop—but you must put it in the ground before you can get any good out of it."
> "Do you mean that *he* must be put in the ground before any good comes of him?"
> "Indeed I do. You may call it burying him, or you may call it sowing him as you like. You must set him in the earth, before you can get any good of him."[14]

The human being, like any seed, must be planted in the ground (or in the river, as we see with Wrayburn in OMF) of the present before there can be any hope of a future from him or her. Neither by having great expectations nor by exercising a spurious choice between a total triumph in, or abandonment of, the world—but by a conscious acceptance of one's relationship with the present, with the given—is the future saved, alive. This is the consistent thought of all the novels, from *Pickwick Papers* to *Edwin Drood*.

The literary problem for Dickens was, how do you sell the seditious idea of forgoing great expectations? How, given the conditions of England between 1830 and 1870, do you gain a commitment to the present, to the given world? Is it possible to glamorize the present environment enough to induce others to enlist in the battle of life? It was one thing to reveal the errors and unhappiness entailed in great expectations, but it was quite another for Dickens to find in the England of his day a locus of affection or a general source of happiness. It was one thing to realize, as Dickens also recorded in the *Memoranda Book*, that happiness must "surely" be found "everywhere" but it was another thing to convince himself and others that the here, the ongoing now, can offer sufficient charm or sufficient moral authority to call forth complete commitment and energy from an individual. In the next chapter, I shall discuss what Dickens did to make the present presentable. In terms of the future, Dickens's whole artistic endeavor was bent upon convincing readers that the only way to the future was through an engagement with the present.

The three themes that we will look at belong under the rubric of the battle of life because they emphasize the concrete methods of engaging in the moral battle—methods that quite transparently connect the present with the creative future. The first theme is work.

Work is one of the ways in which the present and future are fused. Upon this idea, Carlyle built his prophecy. However, Dickens deprecated work if it usurped all the other potentially human uses of time—as it does in Pancks (LD). Comfort, imaginative pursuits, and companionship must never be excluded from life by a preoccupation with work. Unlike Carlyle, Dickens did not conceive of work as a means so absolute that it could be translated into the very end of life. However, work was more to Dickens than just a means to an end, because the willingness to work signified a continuous commitment to this life. Like Dr. Johnson, Dickens's commitment was reflected in his frequent paraphrase of the gospel of John, "One can only work, you know—while it is day."[15]

For Dickens, work was not a value in itself but was both a viable means to the future and a sign of commitment to life. But Dickens made the distinction between activity that makes use of the sign and that which is a commitment. Work is a commitment to life only when it is subordinated to life itself. Dombey, Krook, Pancks, and Headstone are examples of characters who improperly subordinate living to working. There are many characters in Dickens's who fritter away their lives in a profitless but busy evasion of real work. Mrs. Pardiggle, for example, stirs indefatigably at "improving" the brickmakers, without doing a speck of real work. At this point, we realize that part of the difference between Dickens and Carlyle is that Dickens did not assume that an expense of energy must result in spiritual accomplishment. For Dickens, real work was a transfer of energy. Mrs. Pardiggle promulgates information and distributes leaflets and books, which are in themselves without relevance to the life situation of her unwilling audience; but she avoids the real work of improvement, such as ministering to the illiteracy that keeps the brickmakers from reading her improving literature, or tending to their sanitation, employment, or nutrition. Like the Reverend Mr. Chadband, who preaches in vain at Jo, Mrs. Pardiggle does more declaiming than reclaiming. She stays busy meddling, patronizing, and demanding; but she changes nothing. She is one of dozens of Dickens's characters, the genteel and their servants, who spend their lives failing to effect a transfer of feelings—and who, therefore, fail to engage in life. To effect the transfer of energy that gives life to the future—and brings the future into life in the present—work must be performed with inspiration, not just perspiration.

Work, in the best sense, is a means of creating a dynamic relationship between the present and the future. By working for someone or something, the individual becomes a bridge between the present and the future, thus serving as an active agent in an active cosmos.

Dickens's position on work is summed up when Daniel Doyce discusses what one is obliged to do when a "serviceable" idea—a gift of the imagination, or a gift from God—comes into one's head (again the recalled-to-life and the sowing tropes are brought into play): "It's not put into his head to be buried. It's put into his head to be made useful. You hold your life on the condition that to the last you shall struggle hard for it. Every man holds a discovery on the same terms" (LD, 1, 16). Life, then, is an unremitting struggle to implement, to transfer the idea; it is a battle *of* life and, as Doyce says, "for it." This is real work. In a speech to the Birmingham and Midland Institute on January 6, 1870, Dickens sounds a similar note: "To strive at all involves a victory over sloth, inertness, and indifference."[16] By accepting work as the battle of life, the human being enters what Samuel Beckett called the "perilous zones"[17]; the human being keeps the future (and, thus, himself or herself) free by engaging with the present.

In its demands, education is much like work. To learn requires spiritual action, transfer, and joy. For most educators in Dickens's works, however, learning is conceived as quite the opposite. Knowledge is composed of objects with which, for example, poor Tootles (DS) and Headstone (OMF) are crammed to bursting. Mrs. Pardiggle (BH) shares with Gradgrind and M'Choakumchild (HT) the assumption that learning is passive. For Pardiggle, learning has no worldly purpose; whereas, for the others, it has no spiritual purpose. Neither side, therefore, sees learning as a means of interfusing the concerns of time with those of the soul. None of the characters see education as a tactic in the battle of life.

A great deal has been written about Dickens's notions on education. Arnold Kettle, as usual, has penetrated to the crux of the matter: "To insist that Dickens was keen on education is to miss half the point. What he also recognized was that in a class-divided society education itself has a double tendency, to corrupt as well as to liberate."[18] Assuming that Kettle meant that both sides of the class division are equally liable to corruption through education, I would wholly concur. To Lizzie Hexam (OMF), for example, education brings liberation; to her brother it brings corruption. Corruption occurs precisely when an individual accepts the spiritual confinement—the temporal shackles—that come in the train of great expectations. Too often education stifles the active imagination—which connects—and substitutes memorized knowledge—which alienates. But Dickens also knew that certain corruptions are the result of ignorance, such as the violence of Bill Sikes (OT) and Hugh (BR).

Dickens's ideas on education are attacked from two sides. He is accused, on the one hand, of wishing to overeducate the masses and, on the other, of taking formal higher education too lightly. In fact, his ideas on the usefulness of education in the battle of life changed and developed over the course of his career. Whereas Sam and Tony Weller (PP) seem to take pride in the fact that Sam's education was on the streets of London, with the Artful Dodger (OT) and Jo (BH) we get a sterner view of education in the streets. By 16 September 1843, Dickens was writing to Miss Burdett-Coutts:

> I have very seldom seen, in all the strange and dreadful things I have seen in London and elsewhere, anything so shocking as the dire neglect of soul and body exhibited in these children [in a Ragged School]. And although I know; and am sure as it is possible for one to be of anything which has not happened; that in the prodigious misery and ignorance of the swarming masses of mankind in England, the seeds of certain ruin are sown, I never saw that Truth so staring out in hopeless characters as it does from the walls of this place.[19]

He warned England over and over again—"Side by side with Crime, Disease, and Misery in England, Ignorance is always brooding, and is always certain to be found."[20] Behind each separate, petty crime there lay the menacing capacity for the horrible crime of a revolutionary bloodbath. In *Edwin Drood*, in the strange figure of Deputy viciously pelting Durdles with stones, we can trace Jo's successor as well as the future that will result from England's dehumanizing domestic policies. The failure to educate the masses to care for themselves was, for Dickens, a criminal policy, whose results were certain to be a future social disaster.

Dickens scoffed at those who would keep the masses ignorant for their own good. At a Mechanics Institute meeting, he said:

> Fear of institutions such as these? ... Why, ladies and gentlemen, reflect whether ignorance be not power, and a very dreadful power. Look where we will, do we not find it powerful for every kind of wrong and evil? Powerful to take its enemies to its heart, and strike its best friends down; ... Whereas the power of knowledge, if I understand it, is to bear and forbear; to learn the path of duty and to tread it; to engender that self-respect which does not stop at self, but cherishes the best respect for the best objects; to turn an always enlarging acquaintance with the joys and sorrows, capabilities and imperfections of our race to daily account in mildness of life and gentleness of construction, and humble efforts for the improvement, stone by stone, of the whole social fabric.[21]

True education, for Dickens, meant the moral improvement of the *whole* social fabric. Far from creating distinctions between human beings, education should bind them. Education, like his own concept of the fancy, should bring individuals and classes together by engendering "that self-respect which does not stop at the self."[22] As Dickens wrote in *Household Words:*

> Who, knowing England at this time, would wish to utter with his last breath a more righteous warning than [Talfourd did] that its curse is ignorance, or a miscalled education which is as bad or worse, and a want of unnumberable graces and sympathies among the various orders of society, each hardened unto each and holding itself aloof?[23]

In nineteenth-century England, the policy of education for the privileged and ignorance for the working class alienated class from class and human from human, destroying all hope of community.

Such "miscalled education" is that which has no usefulness in the battle of life. Although sponsored by church groups and such well-meaning individuals as Mr. Kay Shuttleworth, education for the poor too often meant a comfortable conviction that a

> parrot-acquaintance with the church catechism and the ten commandments, is enough shoe-leather for poor pilgrims by the Slough of

Despond, sufficient armour against the great giants, Slay-Good and Despair, and a sort of parliamentary train for third-class passengers to the Beautiful Gate of the City, must be pulled up by the roots, or its growth will overshadow this land.... Schools of industry, schools where the simple knowledge learned from books is made pointedly useful, immediately applicable to the duties and business of life, directly conducive to order, cleanliness, punctuality and economy ... are the only means of removing the scandal and the danger that besets us in this nineteenth century of our Lord.[24]

Scenes of Charley Hexam's education in *Our Mutual Friend* reflect the vanity of trying to teach street urchins by means of middle-class conventions and pious precepts. Dickens believed that education has two essential but apparently opposite goals. One goal is spiritual—to humanize the individual through the development of his or her sympathetic imagination. But the linch-pin for this ideal of learning to care for others is the second, practical goal: learning to take care of the self. It is quite as important to teach a practical skill to children as it is to teach piety, for only when the poor can support themselves can they develop a respect for themselves and for others.

Only this grounding in economic competence and literacy could support the edifice of self-respect in working people, without which England would never become a happy land. Dickens wrote to Miss Burdett-Coutts (11 July 1856),

And I think Shuttleworth and the like, would have gone on to the crack of doom, melting down all the thimbles in Great Britain and Ireland, and making medals of them to be given for the knowledge of Watersheds and Pre-Adamite vegetation (both immensely comfortable to a labouring man with a large family and a small income), if it hadn't been for you.[25]

What Dickens was asserting in this letter to Miss Coutts (for she had provided money as awards in a contest for essays on "Common Things," i.e., useful knowledge) was that to teach facts irrelevant to the exigencies of English economic and cultural life was worse than a mere waste of time. By transferring nothing, such teaching bred despair. But to acquire practical skills would enable the individual to turn to in the world. Dickens's other goal, to learn "unnumberable graces and sympathies" through the imagination, would enable the individual to escape worldliness. Hence, his opposite goals for English education were in keeping with his view of what one needs for the battle of life. They both keep the human being grounded in—but not grounded by—the present. Therefore, both kinds of education serve to keep the future free.

Rather than liberating the individual student, false education corrupts in two ways. First, it gives no means of performing work. Second, it places an unfortunate emphasis on uselessness and idleness as social desiderata. In a word, false education promotes stasis. Such knowledge for its own sake encourages neither thinking nor doing, neither hope in Providence nor in personal efforts. Like the ability to make Latin verses—which was all that Richard Carstone had to show for his years in school—such knowledge unfits individuals of all social classes to engage in the battle of life. It fits people only to fill a station.

For the poor, Dickens desired enough learning to support economic liberation. For the young, he seems to have believed that there should be no forced learning à la Blimber (DS) and that fancy and play and art have important places, if not also stages, in the child's development. Clearly Dickens shared the Romantic ethos, especially on the issues of children and education. But Philip Collins has argued that the "anti-scientific and anti-rational tendency of the Romantics . . . recurs with similar naiveté in Dickens. But he is, besides, a significant figure in the covert alliance between Romantic anti-rationalism and Victorian Philistine anti-intellectualism."[26] Collins has stated further that for Dickens "the rights of childhood included . . . not only freedom from forcing but also freedom from intellectual effort."[26]

I think the summary is unjust, even on the face of things. Specifically, David Copperfield is anxious to excel in Dr Strong's school, even though the former first boy—appropriately named Adams—has been out of school for some time and "has not staggered the world yet, either, for it goes on (as well as I can make out) pretty much the same as if he had never joined it" (18). David still wishes to excel—but out of love for the learning itself, and out of respect for Dr. Strong (fond caricature that he is). Surely, this does not reflect an anti-intellectualism in the author. Redlaw, the Haunted Man, is a chemistry professor; not his profession but his personal decision is put into question. Even Boffin desires to learn Roman history; and Bella acquires knowledge of politics and finance in order to be an equal to her husband. Crisparkle teaches an eager, if difficult, Neville Landless. Furthermore, an "anti-scientific tendency" does not jibe with Dickens's faith in progress nor with the many articles on science published in *Household Words* and *All the Year Round*.[27]

G. H. Lewes may well be the source of this charge of anti-intellectualism against Dickens. Lewes not only found Dickens's library a "shock" but attributed to him, as a consequence, "a marked absence of the reflective tendency" and a lack of interest in the "general relations of things."[28] Dickens's intellect was definitely attuned to the practical; and, as a result, his priorities for reflection differed from those of Lewes. Not the general relations of things, but the practical, moral relations interested him. The issues that Dickens dealt with were not comfortably abstract. With Dickens, first things came first: "Sanitary improvements are the one thing needful to begin with; and until they are thoroughly, efficiently, and uncompromisingly made (and every bestial little prejudice and supposed interest contrariwise crushed underfoot) even Education itself will fall short of its uses."[29] Not formal education—not Manchester or Oxford notions of the general relations of things—but the safety and sanctity of raw, unimproved English life itself was the first priority. Hence, education is not the one thing necessary in the battle of life, but it is another source of openness. To accuse Dickens of anti-intellectualism seems to me to require answers from him to questions he found secondary. Not only does such criticism beg the chief issue with Dickens—that of his art—but it reminds me of the *Westminster Review*'s judgment of him, given in similar terms: "We cannot think he will live as an English classic. He deals too much in accidental manifestations and too little in universal priceples."[30]

Two answers may be made to the charge that Dickens expected no intellectual effort from children in school. First, Esther's understanding "seems to brighten" (BH, 3) when she loves; and David Copperfield naturally wishes to learn when he feels loved. Everyone connected with education knows the importance of self-image to learning. Second, to see the charge retorted on general ground, we have only to notice in Dickens's letters the numerous asseverations that there is nothing gained without effort. Work, or intellectual effort, was the only key to success—to understanding nature, human society, and human consciousness. As Dickens wrote to Wilkie Collins:

> As you know, I was certain from the Basil days that you were the writer who would come ahead of all the Field—being the only one who combined invention and power, both humorous and pathetic, with that invincible determination to work, and that profound conviction that nothing of worth is to be done without work, of which triflers and feigners have no conception.[31]

If one assumes that Dickens believed writing to be intellectual, then he, clearly, thought that intellectual gains required effort. Rumpty Wilfer speaks for Dickens when he says, "There's no royal road to learning; and what is life but learning?" (OMF, 4, 5).

Life is learning, adjusting, adapting, altering one's view, transferring energy and knowledge—all of which is the work of the spirit and the true battle of life, which is never over. If this battle ends, the life of the spirit is lost. Philip Collins was quite right when he pointed out that Dickens's "emphasis is wholly on the dangers, not the benefits of the system."[32] Dickens saw not only that a false sense of superiority could develop among the educated, but also that formal education could well discourage the movement of the spirit—which is the authentic purpose of education. Too often, the systems of formal education lull the individual into believing the battle has been won.

The final theme that serves to prevent the corrupting of the future may be called domesticity. This theme is often manifested in the novels as a call for self-sacrifice (usually, no doubt, by women) in personal relations. Often this strand in Dickens is today considered mere Victorian sentimentality. But it is wrong to judge Dickens from a point of view that measures each event and theme in the novels against a standard of present time that is taken to be universal. Susan Horton has warned that "context is boundless"[33] and no reading is fixed. Moreover, it is dangerous to believe that Dickens ever merely parroted a cultural cliché. Here, especially, I must argue that this modern aversion to Dickens's "sentimentality" ignores the need that fostered the theme of domesticity. It ignores the specific existential question to which the theme sought to supply an answer—however unsatisfactory the answer seems to modern temperaments. The question was something like, How do we get volunteers for the battle of life (in the sense of the trope we have been exploring here)? Or, to put it in other terms, between those who find the medieval period powerfully attractive and those who make the future a guaranteed paradise, how does one hold to the center of time? It is this problem that domesticity sought to solve.

Domesticity was not a Victorian conspiracy to remove adventure and challenge *from* life—to make, as Peter Ackroyd has said, "gentleness and passivity emerge as the great virtues of Dickens's characters."[34] Domesticity was, rather, an effort to uncover adventure and challenge *in* life. This was the simple motive that is sometimes overlooked, even when excellent readers like Taylor Stoehr have discussed Dickens:

> When men are baffled in their desire for meaningful work, for a genuine community, and for a goal in life, they turn to the hearth and home for substitutes or consolation. So in *Our Mutual Friend*, Eugene's boredom is relieved by his interest in Lizzie. But the change supposed to have worked upon Eugene by his marriage is not convincing. A wife like Lizzie might make life tolerable, but how could she make "a good opportunity" . . . for her husband's professional and public needs and responsibilities?[34]

Even without questioning the implication here that work and worthy goals are somehow divorced from home, or that a wife should enhance professional opportunities (how? by making dinner for the boss?), or that Wrayburn evinced any professional or public responsibilities *before* meeting Lizzie—and even before arguing that Lizzie's intelligence and warmth, imagination and diligence, and freedom from class prejudices would give her "infinite variety" (if any character in literature may be said to possess it)—it is possible for us to accept the marriage as a literary gesture implying that Eugene will not be bored. For, in simply crossing the class lines to marry Lizzie, Eugene has joined the battle of life. The reader is given to believe that Eugene may encounter some painful, but few, dull moments thereafter.

Nothing could be more wrongheaded than to mistake domesticity for docility (as the modern temperament is liable to do). Wrayburn's marriage is not a dull act of gratitude for saving his life; it is a risky, daring enlistment in life. As Alfred Heatherfield has said in *The Battle of Life*,

> there are quiet victories and struggles, great sacrifices of self, and noble acts of heroism in it [the battle of life]—even in many of its apparent lightnesses and contradictions—not the less difficult to achieve, because they have no earthly chronicle or audience; done every day in nooks and corners, and in little households, and in men's and women's hearts—any one of which might reconcile the sternest man to such a world, and fill him with belief and hope in it. (1)

When Henry James said of Dickens that "he reconciles us to the commonplace, and he reconciles us to the odd,"[36] he was correct not only in the apparent disjunction but also in the radical conjunction of the terms. In the battle of life the commonplace is precisely the odd.[37] This is part of making "Romance" of "all familiar things."[38] When Wrayburn—who has felt restless among the superficially worldly people, like the Veneerings—sinks "down" to the commonplace, domestic role of husband, he finds something exciting enough to live for, in as literal a sense of the term as a writer could provide. Theretofore, Wrayburn's life had been boring him to—and toward—death. Marriage to the common girl Lizzie is noble, liberating, and adventurous.

Part of the configuration of domesticity is a motif that also fosters commitment to the here and now by making the present attractive—the motif of cleanliness. Often referred to in Dickens's correspondence, habits of orderliness, cleanliness, and cheerfulness are positive qualities demonstrated by those who have committed themselves to the daring activity of accepting this life. In the *Christmas Story* (of 1861) "Tom Tiddler's Ground," Dickens combined his distaste for cloistered virtue and for the carelessness about life that manifests itself in dirtiness. In this story, the Traveller says that Mr. Mopes is a hermit, "a slothful, unsavoury, nasty reversal of the laws of human nature" (CS, p. 290). The Traveller says to Mopes that it is "the miserablest drivelling for a human creature to quarrel with his social nature" (p. 298) and that "according to Eternal Providence . . . we must arise and wash our faces and do our gregarious work and act and re-act on one another, leaving only the idiot and the palsied to sit blinking in the corner" (p. 300). To accept the laws of human nature is to commit oneself to work, that is, to social interaction. Mr. Mopes, by the bye, is of the landed gentry. Because of great expectations, the wealthy tend to lose track of the laws of human nature—and of the style of life demanded by those laws. Indeed, *The Westminster Review* of October, 1864, said of Dickens, "He is so far from thinking a man to be any better because he is rich, that he thinks he can hardly be good except he be poor."[39] This putative superiority of the simple-hearted is at the center of Dickens's radicalism and finds expression in the often quoted remark from a speech, "My faith in the people governing is, on the whole, infinitesimal; my faith in the People governed, is, on the whole, illimitable."[40]

In temporal terms, the simple-heartedness of the "people" can be expressed as the keeping of Christmas present. But this cherishing of the present must not be construed as a recommendation by Dickens of simplemindedness or domesticity in any inferior, passive sense. "The fault of Prince's poem," Dickens wrote to Wills,

> besides its intrinsic meanness as a composition, is, that it goes too glibly with the comfortable idea (of which we have had a great deal too much in England since the Continental commotions) that a man is to sit down and make himself domestic and meek, no matter what

is done to him. It wants a stronger appeal to rulers in general to let men do this, fairly, by governing them thoroughly well.[41]

Until government works better, people ought not to be docile and meek. Dickens knew full well that political and social circumstance affects the choices of people in the battle of life. In his strategy, therefore, domesticity is daring, active, and not meek; it intervenes in the processes of the world. It is the farthest remove from cloistered virtue, to which it is sometimes likened by unsympathetic critics of Dickens. Domesticity is the transference of human energy, or love, binding the present to the future, link by daily link.

These several themes find reinforcement in one of the techniques Dickens assiduously employed. In order to render the present exciting—and to attract commitment away from great expectations—Dickens gothicized the London environs that bulk so large in his novels. In doing so, he created a genre that departed from the gothic novel by finding that all the excitement, mystery, and potential for transcendence there ever had been or would be was *there* in England, *then* in his century.

Dickens deliberately made the most of the alienating aspects of London life, but he did so in an effort to create the "romantic side of familiar things" (BH, Preface). In terms of fiction, the phrase means, roughly, finding interest in ordinary experience and ordinary people rather than in the far away, the far past, or the far-elevated in station. As in Browning's "Fra Lippo Lippi," Dickens believed that "we're made so that we love / First when we see them painted, things we have passed / Perhaps a hundred times nor cared to see; / And so they are better, painted."[42] The de-familiarization effect is created by Dickens's gargoyle-like characters, the tenebrous ambience, the activities drawn so often from below the threshold of respectable consciousness. All of these elements render the ordinary quite unfamiliar—and, therefore, fresh, startling, romantic. I am reminded of what G. K. Chesterton said of the modern detective—that he is a hero who "crosses London with something of the loneliness and liberty of a prince in a tale of elfland, that in the course of that incalculable journey the ... lights of the city begin to glow like innumerable goblin eyes."[43] Chesterton felt, too, that Dickens shows that there is ample excitement in ordinary life, which the de-familiarizing techniques mean to demonstrate.

Dickens was fully conscious of this effort to make romance of the everyday. On 12 December 1855, he wrote to Collins, "Look at said *Boots;* because I think it's an odd idea, and gets something of the effect of a Fairy Story out of the most unlikely materials."[44] The task of his artistic imagination was to draw out the weirdness and "romance" from the most ordinary scenes, without sacrificing their credibility. He noted down the following idea: "Representing London—or Paris, or any other great place—in the new light of being actually unknown to all people in the story, and only taking the color of their fears and fancies and opinions—*so* getting a new aspect, and being unlike itself. An *odd* unlikeness of itself."[45] There are, certainly murderous attacks in most of his novels— just as there are in those of Dostoevsky and in the plays of Shakespeare; but Dickens was speaking here of the bulk of the excitement he meant to impart to his stories—an excitement which derives from the essential conditions of life and not from exceptional or sensational events. Ruskin felt that "the thoroughly trained Londoner can enjoy no other excitement than to which he has been accustomed."[46] But, on the contrary, like Jerrold Dickens knew that most lives had all too little excitement to them; and he knew how difficult it is to make the common seem uncommon in fiction—and to make the mundane flash with exciting possibilities. But he deeply felt the importance of making fiction exciting— and this is likely a contributory cause for his development of the cannibalistic imagery in his novels. Ruskin felt that Dickens excited Londoners by representing death; but Dickens sought to excite them by showing the moral dangers of life.

Dickens's "romance" derives from the everyday difficulty of rising to the challenge issued by existence in urban, mechanized, capitalistic society: the challenge of remaining human, the challenge of the battle of life. Ruskin assumed that Londoners required sensation and morbidity. But, in fact, there is no excitement without the element of hope, no matter how many sensational events or morbid characters are introduced. To render the London of his day exciting, then, Dickens had to place it in a universe full of deadly danger and great hope. If, as he wrote, the world is made "odd" by seeing only an aspect of it, then seeing the whole is seeing the grand moral universe. Dickens was a kind of secularized Puritan, showing horrible and wonderful things in the smallest human action.

It was often possible for Dickens to find both danger and hope in the accomplishments of modern science and engineering. This could be seen in the review of Robert Buchanan's *The Poetry of Fact.*[47] Earlier, Dickens's *All the Year Round* had recommended the accomplishments of science as the stuff of romance: "That triumph of man over tremendous elements is a grand thing, and perhaps to the full as poetical as the victory of our patron saint over the dragon.... Could anything be more romantic than the story of [the] conflicts with the water-spirits and the gas demons down in the underground world of London?"[48] Thus is the very trench warfare of progress invested with glory.

If the future receives its character from a present in which the battle of life continues, it also provides the present with a spiritual element without which neither winning the battle nor the "romance of the everyday" would be possible. The legitimate use of the future (which is itself a gift of the imagination) is to hope. Although the capacity to hope is given equally to all, it is far from a worthless gift; for hope is the human activity by which the future beneficially affects the present. In terms of narrative, the present cannot be made exciting without hope.

Dickens held that every man, woman, and child in England should have some reason to hope that their personal and communal situations would develop favorably. If hope becomes great expectations—if it becomes sclerotic and people show greater interest in a certain product than in the process—Dickens counseled a return to the battle of life. But in *Bleak House*, a lack of hope seems to be a major cause of death. The deaths of Jo, Richard, Tom Jarndyce, Mr. Gridley, and Captain Hawdon result from their complete exhaustion of hope. Dickens fiercely assaulted English bureaucracy precisely because it blighted hope—which, for Dickens, was the weapon of the future used in the battle of life. In "Sketches of a Phenomenology and Metaphysic of Hope," Gabriel Marcel wrote that hope "is the act by which the temptation [to despair] is actually or victoriously overcome"; hope means a refusal to "go to pieces under this sentence, to disarm before the inevitable."[49] Florence Dombey, Lizzie Hexam, and Amy Dorrit have hopes for future changes in the attitudes of their respective fathers. Hope does not, in their cases, have an immediate effect on the other person, but it no doubt aids them in refusing to capitulate to despair. Hope discountenances the fashionable, the logical, and the inevitable—those traditional and mechanistic allies of Hunger, the Malthusian vision of the world as ogre. Hope inoculates humanity against fear—and thus returns the present as freedom to man.

Hope means patience, enabling one to refrain from leaping toward great expectations to escape the battle of life. Marcel has said that "patience seems, then, to suggest a certain temporal pluralism, a certain pluralization of the self in time." To have great expectations does not provide a pluralization. Static in concept, great expectations means different circumstances, not a different self. Projected out of time, such monolithic selves cannot retain vitality. This pluralization is not a "perpetual splitting up of the self in relation to itself";[51] it repairs the very nature of the human being, who is, as Dickens said, the "parting and farewell-taking animal." That is, time keeps grinding pieces of our selves away. But, as Marcel expressed it, hope "aims at reunion, at recollection, at reconciliation: in that way, and in that way alone, it might be called the memory of the future."[52] Scrooge's vow to live in all times at once defies the disintegration of the human being by time. By preserving integrity through the pluralization of the self, hope causes time to coalesce in the individual—who, thus, loses nothing of the self to time.

Besides the romance of the everyday, the other technique that contributes so largely to the defeat of great expectations in Dickens's novels is his plot construction and the very mass of his plot elements. These qualities are not often admired in an era of minimalist prose, nor were they always admired even in Dickens's own era. In 1857, it was said in *Blackwood*'s that "in Dickens's estimation, there is no such thing as insignificance."[53] Although not meant as praise, this remark touches on the quick of Dickens's peculiar excellence. At one level, it is easy to retort that certainly an artist who believes in the romance of the familiar is not going to accept normative versions of what is significant and what insignificant. Indeed, it is often the artist's intention to transform the evaluations of significance and insignificance. But, at a deeper level, behind Dickens's estimation of what ought to be significant, lay his personal and artistic experience that the most trivial incident may be graced with significance, not accidently but by deeper patterns of the world system—patterns which, when experienced, are often called coincidence.

Earle Davis has said that "When Ham [and] Steerforth die in the famous storm scene in *David Copperfield,* the reader usually feels that the climax happens in exact harmony with the novel's design."[54] The climactic coincidence is consistent with the larger design of the book. Coincidences are as numerous in *David Copperfield*—or *Our Mutual Friend,* for that matter—as they are in *Pickwick Papers.* Clearly, for all of the stylistic experimentation over the course of his career, or the improved "constructiveness" in his later novels, or the deepening of his characterizations (especially of women), or the assured development of the mythic or symbolic resonances in his later novels, Dickens did not choose to refine away the coincidence in his plots. What, therefore, did he feel that coincidence gave to his work? Oddly enough, a touch of the full world in place of the partial worlds that Ralph Nickleby and Mrs. Steerforth credit. Coincidence is an annulment of historical mechanics, in which the accumulative power of circumstances dictates the future. As has been amply documented, Dickens found his own life to be full of coincidences and such "odd things . . . (and their name is Legion)."[55] Each coincidence in his own life was for him "a curious little instance of the way in which things fit together."[56] Even Fridays seemed to attract most of the significant actions of his life. The many instances in which the statistically improbable happened proved to him that the supposed chains of consequence or influence were often shallow illusions; and in his fiction, he attempted to create occurrences that reflected this perception of his own experience.

Dickens's fictive world scintillates with coincidence. As Dorothy Van Ghent pointed out years ago, "Dickens's use of physical coincidence in his plots is consistent with his imagination of a thoroughly nervous universe. . . . Coincidence is the violent connection of the unconnected; but there is no discontinuity in the Dickens world, either between persons or things, or between the private and the public act."[57] The very word *coincidence* suggests a depth of temporality that is beyond the preconceptions of historical mechanists. Van Ghent's analysis suggests that coincidence is a revelation of connection that renders the two-dimensional causality of the material and logical necessitarians thin and unconvincing.

Through the use of coincidence in his narratives, Dickens designed arabesques of causality that would serve to thwart great expectations. The idea of "man proposes, God disposes" does not bode well for programming the future. Indeed, we can see that Northrop Frye's hints about Dickens's plotting make sense of this phenomenon in his fiction: "This disregard for plausibility is worth noticing, because everyone realizes that Dickens is a great genius of the absurd in his characterization, and it is possible that his plots are also absurd in the same sense, not from incompetence or bad taste, but from a genuinely creative instinct."[58] The violation of conventions of probability did not please realists—those for whom the world is a product and not a process; but Frye seems right in his assessment that, for Dickens, plot is a thematic element: it is designed to preserve human freedom by undermining the historical mechanics that so temptingly enslaves the future to the present and the present to the past.

What such plots imply about time has much in common with Jung's theory of synchronicity: "One distinguishing quality of Synchronicity . . . is that it includes nonphysical as well as physical phenomena, and that it perceives these in *noncausal but meaningful* relationship to one another."[59] Through his use of coincidence, Dickens, like Jung, had in mind the evoking of patterns of causality whose primary functions were to frustrate belief in a mechanical, two-dimensional relationship between present and future. Hence, his plots ruin the "best-laid schemes," while at the same time reinforcing other forms of continuity between the dimensions of time.

Dickens wanted his plots to strike the reader as if they were the workings of Providence (which does not adhere to strict probability). "I think the business of art," Dickens wrote to Wilkie Collins on 6 October 1859, "is to lay all that ground carefully, not with the care that conceals itself—to show, by a backward light, what everything has been working to—but only to *suggest,* until the fulfillment comes. These are the ways of Providence, of which ways all art is but a little imitation."[60] His fiction constitutes, then, an order that one can be certain of only in a backward light—for only then can it be seen how human effort is coupled with providential aid. We, therefore, do not read Dickens to see, as he wrote Collins, "where all this is leading." The conclusion—the future—is not all-important. And, certainly, in his novels, present incidents exist for themselves and not for the sake of future ones. Rather, from the conclusion, we can look back to see how important were some events that did not seem to point to further consequences. Because there is always room made for surprise, the plotting of Dickens denies us not only a fix on the future but also a fixed future.

The battle of life—living in the world—is filled with spiritual risks. As I have argued, all around the individual there are forces militating against his or her spiritual survival—oppressive forces of the past, the future, and the worldly present. All around stagger the victims of these forces—figures from every class worn down to mere matter by what Dickens called "this grindstone" of an earth and world. Within each individual, consequently, powerful forces rage for security and for the manifold kinds of killing—especially of the self—that supposedly achieve security. Insofar as he could, then, Dickens used his techniques to bring us to a knowledge of the inevitable battle of life—and to warn us to arm against the centrifugal pull of fear, on the one hand, and the centripetal tow of anger, on the other. His fiction urges a commitment to this nucleus of time—a lived nucleus which draws from, but does not draw up, the future.

In his dialectic of time, Dickens countered the powerful, culturally supported demand for stasis—which is synonymous with great expectations—with a challenge: the challenge of the battle of life. He demonstrated repeatedly the gallantry of living openly, free from great expectations and from the dead hand of the past. Esther, Little Dorrit, Estella, Bella, and Lizzie—all walk into the future hand in hand with a man almost as full of faith in Providence and themselves as they are. For them, the future and the present interpenetrate: this is the nature of hope.

Henri Bergson's discussion of "duration" is again helpful in understanding Dickens's intuitions, just discussed. "Duration," or "real time," according to Bergson, "has no parts."[61] But the concepts of time developed by mechanistic or finalistic intelligence are necessarily atomistic because such intelligence can only "perceive itself under the form of discontinuity."[62] Even the convenient terms *past, present,* and *future,* which we must use, are a kind of prevarication—false coins, as it were, that it was Dickens's part to subvert, as Scrooge effectively does. "The more we succeed," argued Bergson, "in making ourselves conscious of our progress in pure duration, the more we feel the different parts of our being enter into each other, and our whole personality concentrate itself in a point, or rather a sharp edge, pressed against the future and cutting into it unceasingly. It is in this that life and action are free."[63] Like Marcel, Bergson sought the reintegration of time for the individual, without which freedom is impossible. Although Dickens was combating specific Victorian proponents of finalistic and mechanistic thought, his strategy was essentially in accord with the ideas of Bergson. His integrated characters accept "the whole of reality as an undivided advance forward to successive creations."[64] As Carlyle's powerful influence impressed upon Dickens, the future was in the making. For both English writers, the cosmos was what Bergson called "a continuity of shooting out." For Bergson, "God thus defined, has nothing of the already made; He is unceasing life, action, freedom."[65] The individual must encounter the future with a similar openness if s/he is to find satisfaction in—or to live in harmony with—self and others. All one can have of the future is, honestly, a presentiment. Thus, one is able to retain the "adaptable" quality that R. Wilfer claimed for his Bella (OMF, 2, 8).

For Dickens, literature's task was "to help make people better."[66] He did not mean that people should be made "better" in any narrow pietistic sense; he meant, rather, that they should be fuller, freer, more integral human beings. His own novels contain both themes and techniques that were meant to help effect this alteration in people's lives. Not only do his novels feature characters engaged in the battle of life, but they were also meant to fortify the readers in their own battles. A novel—making a whole out of many temporal, or narrative, parts—is itself an instance of the mode of hope. The novel was made over by Dickens to be no longer an escape from life à la Melbourne[67] but a direct engagement with—and a paradigm of the passages of—life. The structures of his novels—as well as their themes—feature an integration of disparate foci of time. His novels bring the alienated future back into the nucleus of time—and, in this way, seek to reintegrate a sorely divided people. This nucleus is the only ground upon which the battle of life can be fought.

5
Trust in the Present

> A comfortable house is a great source of happiness. It ranks immediately after health and a good conscience.
> —Sydney Smith

In *Our Mutual Friend,* Noddy Boffin says, "I don't go higher than comfort, and comfort of the sort that I'm equal to the enjoyment of" (1, 5). In Dickens's works, the word "comfortable" is frequently associated with characters and contexts that are shown as secure, charming, and attractive. But, as generated by the ideology of hunger, the Victorian present was portrayed by Dickens as having very little comfort. It was, as Dickens named one novel, "hard times for these times." As I have argued, many social attitudes were based on fear—the fear of starving and, increasingly, the fear of being annihilated. According to Freud, the "dread of being eaten" is one of the primal emotions.[1] Although in England, obviously, law and taboos prevented the literal incorporation of others, figurative acts of incorporation were not only possible but were condoned as natural. Indeed, Manchester economic theory converted the great release of energy in the Victorian era into capitalistic aggression, and Malthus was there to exculpate it as the way of the natural world. The fear of me and mine being consumed by others fostered more fears, which in turn generated unappeasable hunger for safety and retribution. Dickens depicted English society as a vicious circle in which one was eating—or being eaten by—someone. The task that Dickens took on in his fiction was to show to his community of readers that the proper use of time can restore genuine security and comfort to the world.

By the time that *David Copperfield* was written, Dickens had come a long way from the exposition of the largely physical hunger haunting the face of England in *Pickwick, Oliver,* and through the *Christmas Books.* With David Copperfield, as with Little Nell and Paul Dombey, Dickens was engaged with spiritual hunger that—though it has its physical manifestations for dramatic and expressive purposes—requires metaphysical satisfaction. Dickens had moved from an exposition of public and physical hunger to a study of spiritual and personal hunger. From *Bleak House* through *Our Mutual Friend* to *Edwin Drood,* Dickens pursued his inquiry ever more deeply, down to the ideological causes of human hunger. He illuminated how English institutions—presumably created to minimize human voracity and rapacity—served to perpetuate them. Created for the common wealth, English institutions had been corrupted in the age of hunger and instead contributed to the common hunger. These institutions, deflecting men from their natural satisfactions, intensified the circle of voracity.

In most of Dickens's earlier novels, a central character is threatened with annihilation by some individual or institutional ogre. With *David Copperfield,* Dickens's plots go beyond that melodramatic situation to give an extended vision of the complex relationship that exists between an individual and a society founded upon the premise of hunger. The plots begin to show that the victims of aggression perpetuate the dissatisfactions that caused their suffering. Thus, the "dread of being eaten" and the desire to consume are passed on. This is the circle of voracity. To the extent that this infection of cannibalism no longer results in either the disintegration or the rescue of its victims, the later novels are less maudlin—and, perhaps, reveal a less traumatized sensibility in the artist. Indeed, it can be argued that in admitting the individual's infection by and participation in English cannibalism, Dickens had taken a huge step toward personal and artistic maturity. Nevertheless, the vision of the present that he now provided was even more disturbing than the earlier one. Voracity no longer finds even the momentary illusion of satisfaction. If the later novels present fewer distinct ogres, it is only because, by the time of *David Copperfield,* Dickens showed the cannibal to be within each of us. Consequently, as his dialectic moved on, Dickens had to evolve an artistry that was adequate to his comprehension of the convoluted and dynamic nature of the peril.

To depict both peril and response, Dickens still worked by means of tried images and themes. The spiritual deprivations—and consequent hunger—to which David is subjected is represented often by images of food. A notorious example is his mother's surrender of the keys of the household to Miss Murdstone. For Clara to surrender access to the foodcellars and pantries is, in the technique of Dickens that Garrett Stewart called "symbolic synecdoche,"² to open up a gulf between David and his natural sources of human satisfaction. But Clara herself is so dependent—so hungry for affection—that she abandons her natural responsibility for the child who is dependent on her. David's treatment by the Murdstones simply exaggerates his human need for comfort and, therefore, conditions the later deeds of extravagance and intemperance that reveal what Gwendolyn B. Needham, in her ground-breaking study, has called his "undisciplined heart."³

The threat and fact of being deprived of food haunt David's life thereafter. When he is sent to Salem House, we are presented with the comic scene of a waiter systematically devouring all the dinner he has just served David. David's innocence and his insatiable need to be liked prevent him from objecting while the waiter consumes the ale, the chops and potatoes, and finally most of the pudding. The worst part of this treatment, David says, "was that I knew I should be ashamed to eat anything, when the opportunity offered," for fear of being thought a glutton (DC, 5). The waiter does to him physically only what Murdstone has long been doing psychologically. By concentrating our attention on David's physical hunger, Dickens has brought home to us the deeper deprivation of David's character.

Soon after arriving at Salem House, David sees "miserable little white mice . . . looking in all the corners with their red eyes for anything to eat" (5). These mice are proleptic of the many experiences David is to have thereafter. This inauspicious introduction to the physical and spiritual regimen at Salem House is neatly capped by the badge "He bites" that David is made to wear. With two words, "He bites," Dickens has summed up the result of the circle of deprivation and voracity—the unfed bite. The relationship between spiritual hunger and physical aggression is marvelously shown in those two words: spiritual hunger has manifested itself as physical aggression. No longer will the spiritually starved, like Oliver (or, at least, like his proxy in death, Dick) or Nell, merely die: they will give vent to their hunger.

Although David does bite back once, his victimization continues. His struggle, in fact, is to elude the cycle of deprivation and voracity. While at Dover with his aunt, he is safe from the general threat; but he has still to deal with his own hunger. Upon leaving Dover to establish himself in London, David attempts to overawe another waiter. However, the waiter—not he—is served when David ends up eating precisely what the waiter suggests; for, according to David, although the wine was "flat, and it certainly had more English crumbs in it than were to be expected in a foreign wine in anything like a pure state ... I was bashful enough to drink it, and say nothing" (19). In trying to adopt the predatory ways of the world, David proves that he is inexperienced—and he fails to satisfy even his legitimate hunger. Even Mrs. Crupp, his landlady, victimizes him by doing little to aid his extravagant dinner party for Steerforth and by carrying off a considerable share of everything edible and potable. To this type of "terrible mother," David is appropriately "Mr. Copperfull"—that is, someone from whom copper and silver are to be easily had.

David manifests his deep-seated intemperance—or voracity— by drinking and wasting too much at his party for Steerforth. The party itself is a repetition of the method by which David first achieved the dubious honor of Steerforth's protection: on David's first night at Salem House, he had ingratiated himself with Steerforth by giving the latter his entire fortune of seven shillings for— what else?—food; and this "royal spread" of seven shillings won David Steerforth's promise, "I'll take care of you" (6). David— whose childhood was marred by abandonment and insufficient care—responds intensely to Steerforth's casual promise. Since Steerforth's care was the highest boon that the young David could imagine, it is no wonder that David would begin to think extravagance a defense against the predatory world. After all, did not Steerforth get satisfaction from the very waiter that David had failed to impress? Therefore, David's allying himself with Steerforth seemed to be the single way of dealing with what David describes as the "distrust of myself" (19), which his earlier deprivations had inspired.

It is no wonder then that, when David and Steerforth meet again for the first time since Salem House, Steerforth says, "I feel as if you were my property" (20). It is merely Manchester comity. "I am never contented," Steerforth says merrily (22); but it is the bitter truth—for himself, for David, for those at Yarmouth, and, metaphorically, for England. Having no cares in life, Steerforth cannot care for others. In his own graceful way, Steerforth is as careless as Clara or the Murdstones. Not recognizing—through his worshipful haze—that Steerforth is as hungry and dissatisfied as he is, David eventually provides Steerforth with Lil Em'ly. And on that fateful day in Yarmouth Steerforth tells David, "At odd times, nursery tales come into my memory, unrecognized for what they are. I believe I have been confounding myself with the bad boy who didn't care, and became food for lions—a grander kind of going to the dogs, I suppose" (22). The voracity theme is evident in Steerforth's words, as is the suggestion of the ongoing cycle of hunger in his reference to "food for lions." Terminally infected by dissatisfaction—the chronic disease of Cannibal Island—Steerforth is no less voracious a cannibal than Quilp or Tappertit. His diet is only more metaphoric.

As long as David is married to Dora, his original extravagance is perpetuated. In her dependence and ineptitude, David's undisciplined heart continues to bear bitter fruit. Dora's carelessness is only an inverted image of David's own kind of carelessness. Dora is a sign of David's extravagance—of his need and discontent. Dickens made this symbolic function amply clear by showing Dora's beloved dog Gip (short for Gypsy) dancing on—what else?—a cookbook, which Dora never opens. The scene is a perfect emblem for what has gone wrong with middle-class life in England.

David reflects Dickens's growing awareness of the way in which personal carelessness was generating the wholesale carelessness of English society. David tells Dora that "it is very painful to me to think that our want of system and management involves not only ourselves (which we have got used to) but other people" (48). The cook, Mary Anne, never receives direction from Dora. For Dickens—with his intuition of a thoroughly connected world—failure in domestic economy has repercussions upon nothing less than the national economy. David's discontented heart, made ravenous by the deprivation of the Murdstone days, blunders into a marriage that is nearly the ruination of the servants, of Dora, of David himself—and, by implication, of England. David's spiritual hunger—compounded by Dora's wasteful spirit—threatens to lead to more waste and more hunger in an ever-widening circle.

An even worse waste of spirit, however, threatens to result from David's attempt to change Dora. Like Murdstone before him, he attempts to discipline his wife; but his own lack of discipline—his own inner dissatisfaction—is at fault. Through Betsey's advice and Mr. Dick's example, David ultimately learns to be content with the present. He permits Dora to provide the kind of comfort she is able to provide—and demands no more—thus refusing, at the last instant, to perpetuate the reign of hunger, what Marcel calls "spiritual autophage."

Previously in Dickens's fiction, English cannibalism was defeated by the intervention of avuncular characters like the Cheerybles and Brownlows. But in *David Copperfield,* Dickens began to sketch a practical strategy for undoing the circle of voracity. First, there must be self-discipline, or temperance. Just as Steerforth stands at one pole of all-consuming, never-satiated hunger, David's own hungry impetuosity is balanced at the other pole by several characters, including Tommy Traddles. The scene in which Traddles attempts, out of kindness and friendship, to eat unopened oysters and "a plateful of raw meat" is a capital representation of the subordination of physical hunger to the spirit (44). Moreover, Traddles' long and patient wait to marry his beloved Sophy represents the antithesis of David's hasty marriage. Then, just as David is tempted to try to make childish Dora over into a responsible adult, he visits the newly married Traddleses—only to hear them playing in the law office like children. Evidently, there is a middle ground between the discipline of a Murdstone and the irresponsibility of a Clara or a Dora.

The Micawbers are difficult to fit into a neat schema. On the one hand, they seem to display the extreme extravagance and improvidence of the undisciplined (and no doubt undisciplinable) heart; on the other, they share with David some of the few comfortable meals that he is shown having in the novel. The Micawbers are improvident but generous—and, thus, they are in pointed contrast to the bête noire of the novel, Murdstone. Master Wilkins Micawber may have reason to dread losing his milk supply or some other dietary necessities, including even water; but his heart—if we may judge (as we must) by the treatment of David—will never be starved. In contrast to David and Dora, the Micawbers behave with an extravagance that is never truly wasteful to the spirit of any other human. Micawber's anti-Malthusian function is obvious: unlike Steerforth and Murdstone in their different forms of restlessness, Micawber finally locates in Australia a situation that is adequate to his capacity to find satisfaction with life in the present. This is because Micawber never, finally, mistrusts himself—as he proves by turning on Heep; and he never loses for long his trust in "something turning up" in time—which makes him the flagship for the theme of trust in the present.

In *Bleak House,* we are shown that English institutions are not solutions to—but matrices of—the endless dissatisfactions that Englishmen were discovering in their present. The novel contains a sketch of how public policy and institutions—born of dread—create dissatisfactions that serve to fuel, rather than obviate, those dreads. An institution like Chancery Court not only creates in its own right a world of anxiety and dissatisfaction but is itself a model for forms internalized in the psyches of the English. The fog imagery implies that the atmosphere emitted by Chancery Court pervades all of London. Characters like Richard Carstone and Miss Flite pull away but are inevitably drawn back to this heart. The novel thus suggests that English life was moving along an unending circle of voracity.[4]

In *Bleak House,* Chancery Court is the central symbol of cannibalism. It consumes fortunes and the human spirit. It sucks the life force from persons like Tom Jarndyce and drives them to suicide; it picks the bones of the human spirit of Gridley and Richard Carstone. Like a "terrible mother," it gives nothing of what by its nature it was supposed to give. As for those who expect justice from Chancery, they will go hungry. Jarndyce and Jarndyce as a case has been stripped of its human content; it has passed into a sadistic joke that "particularly tickled the maces, bags, and purses" (1). These synecdoches precisely image the effect that the Court has on society as portrayed by Dickens: its action (or inaction) dismembers human beings—its own officers as well as the litigants. Such destruction of human wholeness—frequent in Dickens's works—is a metonym for cannibalism. And Dickens did not miss the chance to connect Chancery and cannibalism explicitly. When voices are raised and ask for the reform of the Chancery Court, the voice of the court points out that if its practices were to be altered, the unthinkable consequence would be that such respectable legal practitioners as Vholes would be harmed: "As though, Mr. Vholes and his relations were minor cannibal chiefs and it being proposed to abolish cannibalism, indignant champions were to put the case thus: Make man-eating unlawful, and you starve the Vholeses!" (39). Not only is the legal profession imaged as a group of cannibals, but its activities are placed by society beyond reform—thus, the hunger that it manifests, causes, and fails to assuage are to go on without end.

By his own proud admission, Krook is a type of Lord Chancellor; just as he deals in the rags and bones of the past, the latter deals in rags and bones of the future. The resemblance is obvious: "And all's fish that comes to my net. And I can't abear to part with anything I once lay hold of (or so my neighbors think, but what do *they* know?) or to alter anything, or to have any sweeping, nor scouring, nor cleaning, nor repairing going on about me" (5). In Dickens's works, the quality of tidiness is always antithetical to the cannibalistic, all-consuming mentality. A mess relieves one, after all, of making the difficult distinctions not only between what is mine and not mine but also between sufficiency and excess; thus, everything is clutched and held on to. In Krook's business "everything seemed to be bought and nothing to be sold" (5). With his piles of bones and sacks of human hair, Krook is obviously the ogre of a child's nightmares. His tigerish cat, Lady Jane, represents the aggression that lies just below the surface of Krook's commercial activity. In the logic of the imagination, Krook's voracity finds its only possible conclusion in his self-combustion. Perhaps the catastrophe was precipitated by the unwonted crisis brought about through Guppy's insistence that Krook give up something that he has incorporated—in this case, the letters of Nemo.

Above Krook's packed and ogreish cave live two starving roomers. Insufficiency always cohabits with excess: this was the law of English cannibalism. In Miss Flite's room, there is no food: "Upon a shelf in an open cupboard were a plate or two, a cup or two, and so forth, but all dry and empty" (5). Even her birds are liable to be consumed by Lady Jane—just as the qualities of human life for which they are named are annihilated by the paralysis of life under the Chancery Court. In Nemo's room, the narrator imagines that the holes in the shutters are "gaunt eyes" with which "famine might be staring in" (10). The very atmosphere is hungry. The physical contrasts are manifest: Nemo and Miss Flite live in bare, deprived rooms, whereas Krook's place is too stuffed with diverse material to be comfortable to a normal human being.

Numerous other characters turn out to be metaphoric cannibals, consuming the substance of others. A prime example is the Smallweeds, who counsel each other always to dine "at his expense as much as you can" (21). What Krook is with documents, bones, and rags, Tulkinghorn is with family secrets. Both are parasites. Old Turveydrop feeds at the expense of others: while he requires, as he says, "my few essentials for the toilet, my frugal morning meal, and my little dinner" (23) at such modest establishments as the French House, his son eats cold mutton or a quick sandwich between jobs. Skimpole, whose very simple needs include a good claret and beefsteak; Mr. Chadband, who expends much of his large dinners in the manufacture of train oil upon his forehead; and even Mrs. Pardiggle and Mrs. Jellyby—all of these characters can be said at some level to feed on others.

The most detailed study of carelessness is of Mrs. Jellyby. The appalling condition of her children is obvious, and the ruin of Mr. Jellyby is imminent. Caddy says that Mr. Jellyby's family "is nothing but bills, dirt, waste, noise, tumbles downstairs, confusion, and wretchedness" (14). The Jellyby's house is as noisy as Krook's place is messy. Where care, order, and comfort should reign, "telescopic philanthropy" (4) is installed. Dickens chose to underline the significance of carelessness by describing a meal at the Jellyby's, where there was "a fine cod-fish, a piece of roast beef, a dish of cutlets, and a pudding; an excellent dinner, if it had had any cooking to speak of, but it was almost raw" (4). Although Mr. Jellyby provides sufficiently, waste negates all his efforts. As the skirmishes between the maid and the cook at that unforgettable dinner indicate (4), Mrs. Jellyby had abandoned her domestic duty—part of which was to direct the help. Like Dora, she has let the servants go undisciplined, thus wronging both her family and her servants. "We never had a servant who don't drink," says Caddy. "Ma's ruinous to everything" (38). Against the voracity of Chancery Court—and those cannibals loosely associated with it—should stand domestic virtues, including care and comfort; but with such undutiful, careless parents as Mrs. Jellyby, the home is almost as certain to deny children their due as the Court is. If institutions are blameworthy, so, too, are many individuals: Dickens's social criticism was now moving in both directions. Hunger of the spirit finds no satisfaction in either direction.

Unfortunately, physical hunger is natural. As the hungry Jobling insists with such hilarious aplomb, "Ill fo manger. That's a French saying, and mangering is as necessary to me as it is to a Frenchman. Or more so" (20). Under the conditions shown in *Bleak House,* this comic notion that the English may need to eat more than the French is not so absurd. If the English are to gain any satisfaction for their hunger, in public and private life, the keys of their houses must be turned over to the Esthers of the land—people who are both caring and competent.

Most readers find *Hard Times* truncated. The brevity of the novel, so the argument goes, prevented Dickens from exercising that mythopoetic faculty from which the longer novels benefited. Certainly out of this mythic stratum had come the vision of the world as a place of eaters and the eaten, of tyrants and victims. But in *Hard Times,* Dickens did not cease to pursue his vision of cannibalism and voracity. The voracity that Dickens exposed in *Hard Times* finds its lineage in the *Christmas Books* rather than in the longer novels. In *the Christmas Books,* Dickens was interested in showing how the hunger predicted by Malthus—and the lovelessness that Malthus recommended as its sole prevention (the hunger traded upon by the capitalistic ideologies and the lovelessness infesting utilitarianism)—dictated the specific conditions of cannibal England.

Most of the food imagery is constellated around Bounderby and the aptly named Mrs. Sparsit. Although she must currently eat the bread (or, rather, the sweetbreads) of dependence (with ample brown sauce), Mrs. Sparsit has an aristocratic background. Her primary function in Bounderby's household is to enhance Bounderby's character by serving as a contrasting background of privilege, against which Bounderby displays his own specious rags-to-riches biography, which begins with the pitiful memory of "the flavour of the ha'porth of stewed eels he had purchased in the streets at eight years old" (2, 2).

Bounderby, the materialist, reduces all moral and social questions to a mere question of food. In the House of Commons, Gradgrind and Bounderby testify that the poor "were a bad lot altogether, gentlemen; that do what you would for them they were never thankful for it, gentlemen; that they were restless, gentlemen; that they never knew what they wanted; that they lived upon the best, and bought fresh butter; and insisted on Mocha coffee, and rejected all but the prime parts of meat" (1, 5). To Bounderby it is obvious that the poor, like the old woman in the nursery rhyme, "lived upon nothing but victuals and drink" and still would not be quiet. Bounderby thus backs up Bumble's theory that meat is bad for paupers because it produces "a artifical spirit" (OT, 7).

In *Hard Times,* however, Dickens illustrated that should the poor have enough to eat—a concession that he was *not* willing to make—then their inquietude would be due to a different kind of deprivation—that of the faculty of the fancy. The working people of Coketown, whatever the truth about their diets, were systematically starved of food for the fancy by people like Bounderby, Gradgrind, and M'Choackumchild. Bounderby translates pleasures of the imagination into a desire "to be fed on turtle soup and venison, with a gold spoon" (1, 11). His own imagination is capable of postulating only physical and material ends for imaginative drives—and he ascribes such ends to all men. Bounderby represents the frank tendency of the Manchester School to translate everything into material terms. With cheap potables—perhaps with the milk "drownded" with water that Wackford Squeers serves his students (NN, 5)—Bounderby would attempt to satisfy the "thirst that from the soul doth rise." Dickens, like Carlyle, was warning that the conflict between men and masters is not merely over bread-and-butter issues: the conflict was over the rights of working men to be treated, not as hands, but as whole men—with hearts and imaginations and souls. Gradgrindian utilitarians and Bounderbyan capitalists had blinded themselves to these larger needs of human life.

By titling the three books of *Hard Times* "Sowing," "Reaping," and "Garnering," Dickens was emphasizing the consequences upon personal lives of the dominant ideology. Reading *Hard Times* makes it possible to trace the effects of ideology upon the souls of the individuals in the novel. Bounderby would have his audience believe that "antecedents" mean nothing (1, 4). But in Tom, Louisa, and Bitzer, Dickens showed the disastrous effects of the current ideological conditioning. The dominant ideology had created an England that failed to satisfy the upper classes and lacked the capacity to provide either functional institutions or moral support for the working classes. In depriving children and adults in all classes of imaginative and spiritual satisfactions, the ideology of hunger had created in England a system that could not satisfy the souls of men.

It is only at Sleary's disreputable circus—where the aptly named Childers and Kidderminster flourish—that the imagination of children and the hunger for the unfamiliar in adults is understood and satisfied. Whatever its aesthetic deficiencies,[5] Sleary's circus stands against the ideology that makes "Ogres" (1, 2) of living men—and thus makes *Hard Times for These Times*. By means of the circus, Dickens pointed to the eternal, individual possibility of breaking the circle of voracity—which sows, reaps, garners, and sows dissatisfaction again. The possibility of breaking the chain arises only with the pleasure and wonder stimulated in every child. In each child, the human race has another opportunity to create a satisfied or dissatisfied individual.

The last installment of *Hard Times* was published in August 1854. Approximately a month later, the news broke that not only seemed to bear out Dickens's hints about a national cannibalism but also smashed the Victorian reticence about discussing the subject[6]—a reticence that Dickens's symbolic art, as we have seen, had allowed him to circumvent. Now there could be no reticence. Nine years earlier, in 1845, Sir John Franklin had led an expedition of 138 men in the ships *Terror* and *Erebus* in search of a Northwest Passage to the Pacific. After three years, rescue expeditions were dispatched; and each year thereafter more ships and overland expeditions sought to save Franklin—or at least garner some information about his fate. No trace of Franklin being found, the Admiralty declared him dead in 1854—which seemed to close the issue, except for a small number of persons who urged further searches. But Dr. John Rae, a factor of the Hudson's Bay Company, had acquired not only some relics of the Franklin expedition (from Eskimo he had encountered) but also "decisive intelligence."[7] He duly wrote to the Secretary of the Company and the Admiralty. In October, 1854, the *London Times* printed his communication: All were lost. The men had died of scurvy and starvation. Rae's motivation was the humane one of desiring to prevent further expeditions to those dangerous regions. One sentence served, instead, to heighten demand for further expeditions: "From the mutilated state of many of the bodies and the contents of the kettles, it is evident that our wretched countrymen had been driven to the last source—cannibalism—as a means of prolonging existence."[8] To Dickens and others, all were not merely lost—they had taken with them the best hopes of English civilization.

Accordingly, Dickens, the man who had long been envisioning ogres and economic cannibalism within England, now rose up to deny that Franklin and his men had resorted to cannibalism. To Rae's uncritical acceptance of the hearsay evidence of the Eskimo, Dickens retorted with a desperate argument by analogy that concluded as follows:

> No statement of cannibalism, whether on the deep or the dry land, is to be admitted suppositiously, or inferentially, or on any but the most direct and positive evidence: no, not even as occurring among savage people, against whom it was in earlier times too often a pretence for cruelty and plunder.[9]

Dickens undoubtedly felt that, as a writer and superb physiognomist, he was a better interpreter of the Eskimo communications (often but gestures) than the arctic expert Rae. Against all apparent authority and facts, then, Dickens refused to believe that Sir John Franklin and the men on the ill-fated expedition committed cannibalism. Franklin, he felt, was too disciplined—too civilized in the best sense of the word—to succumb under any circumstances to the "last dread alternative." Evidently, Dickens was of two minds about English cannibalism. On the one hand, Dickens was driven by his vision to disclose the truth about the hunger at the heart of Victorian ideology; on the other, he wanted quite as much to deny its historical necessity.

Although Dickens had developed the horrible vision of the Victorian present as essentially cannibalistic, he refused to believe that cannibalism was inevitable or even natural. He simply had to argue that in the direst circumstances it was humanly possible *not* to be a cannibal. He worked toward this end in an article titled "The Long Voyage," published in 1853,[10] when the fate of Franklin and his men was still uncertain. With the behavior of a transported English convict who twice turned to cannibalism, Dickens contrasted the behavior of other persons of English birth who—in straits similar to the convict's—did not resort to cannibalism. Having developed a taste for human flesh during a previous escape from prison, the convict lured another convict to escape in order to kill and devour him. For Dickens, this convict's alienation accounted for his monstrousness: "I shall never see that sea-beach on the wall or in the fire, without him, solitary monster, eating as he prowls along, while the sea rages and rises at him." The "solitary monster," therefore, was against nature—and nature was against him. A solitary monster is someone who is outside the community of love, which the novelist would have us inhabit. With this terribly disturbing image, Dickens contrasted the story of the survivors of the *Grosvenor* who voluntarily cared for a helpless orphan until all perished of starvation. Therefore, the narrative implies, it is possible to care, even under the most terrible of circumstances.

In his *Christmas Story* (of 1856), "The Wreck of the *Golden Mary*," Dickens was still fighting the accusation against Franklin. His narrator cites the example of Captain Bligh, who, for all his acknowledged harshness, "had solemnly placed it on record therein that he was sure and certain that under no conceivable circumstances whatever would the emaciated party, who had gone through all the pains of famine, have preyed on one another" (CS, p. 152). Franklin, indeed, had also been through all the pains of famine in his earlier expeditions to the Arctic. If Bligh was no cannibal, it was absurd to think Franklin could be. In 1857, with his important contributions to Wilkie Collins's play *The Frozen Deep*,[11] Dickens continued to defend this hero of civilization, Franklin. The solitary monster is invoked in the prologue that Dickens wrote:

> One savage footprint on the lonely shore
> Where one man listen'd to the surge's roar,
> Not all the winds that stir the mighty sea
> Can ever ruffle in the memory.

The play's hero, Wardour—whose name suggests the ardent warrior that he is—proves that the ability to care survives both physical and psychological suffering. Even sexual jealousy cannot make Wardour forget his heritage. Dickens's motive was clear: if Wardour can maintain a disciplined heart, the mere hunger cannibalism can be denied in Franklin's case; and, therefore, the psychological and spiritual hunger then pervading England has no necessity. It is worth noting that Dickens was right: Franklin was eventually exonerated; for he died in 1847, years before the putative cannibalism.

Dickens's examination of the inevitability of voracity—and, hence, of cannibalism—continues in *Little Dorrit*. Dickens sought to undermine English cannibalism and its constituting ideologies by employing the utilitarian method of examining positive results. The question for Dickens was, Does the present mode of social conduct, under the auspices of Malthus, achieve the greatest good for the greatest number? His study of fictional characters reveals the vanity of the satisfactions that the existing system claimed to offer. In Dickens's novels, no one who chooses to obey the clay-given mandate of "Eat" has a moment of genuine satisfaction or even of respite. Dickens showed repeatedly that the "dread of being eaten" is never abrogated by any amount of consumption. With the vanity of English cannibalism thus thoroughly exposed, he then disclosed modes of genuine satisfaction. If these could be shown and credited, Dickens would have created the means to destroy the ideology—or the fiction—of hunger. While such genuine satisfactions can be found over the length of his fiction, they are put to their most severe test in *Little Dorrit*.

G. B. Shaw called *Little Dorrit* more seditious than *Das Kapital*. Many commentators attributed the novel's bleakness to the personal problems that Dickens was having at the time. Perhaps. But we need to remember that the primary target of the sedition was the ideology of hunger, as it is reflected in the novel by economic voracity and personal alienation. Dickens wrote an apparently despairing novel because he was exposing the failure of the existing system of beliefs to provide genuine human satisfaction. Barely maintained during *Hard Times*, the theme of hunger and the imagery of food flare up again powerfully in *Little Dorrit*. No longer a mere narrative event or sign by which to make practical evaluations of characters, what a character does with food expresses his or her ideological stance—his or her conformity or lack of conformity with the gospel according to Malthus.

In the first chapter of *Little Dorrit*, the reader is presented with the prison in Marseilles—and then with the prisoner Rigaud, who is "waiting to be fed." That phrase epitomizes Rigaud's attitude toward others, toward society, and toward life. Every attitude he displays in the course of the novel is derived from that primary characterization. It is his spiritual jail. Even when Rigaud makes a melodramatic appearance in Arthur Clennam's cell near the conclusion of the novel, he issues a characteristic demand before he is willing to converse: "Give me a bottle of wine" (2, 28). Rigaud is always hungry. When he first arrives in London, he says, "I must change, and eat and drink, and be lodged somewhere" (1, 30). He is then shown, in detail, eating: "His greed at dinner, too, was closely in keeping with the greed of Monsieur Rigaud at breakfast. His avaricious manner of collecting the eatables about him, and devouring some with his eyes while devouring others with his jaws, was the same manner" (1, 30). His utter disregard of other people, except, one might say, insofar as they can serve him—or, indeed, be served to him—is only to be expected. He is, quite simply, a solitary monster adapted to polite society.

Dickens, clearly, linked voracity with the idea of gentility. Standing between the aristocratic and entrenched Barnacles and the entrepreneurial and rising Merdle, Rigaud is the type of man who shares both their attributes—and thus brings to consciousness their secret relation. He is, above all, a gentleman: "You know me for a gentleman?" he asks Cavaletto; his proof is simple: "Have you ever thought of looking to me to do any kind of work?" (1, 1). Since we have seen his literal voracity—and since we know him to intend to consume others, figuratively—he represents Dickens's vision of the Malthusian gentleman. "One must eat," he mutters to himself, "but by Heaven, I must eat at the cost of some other man tomorrow" (1, 11). It is no wonder that "the two young Plornishes . . . partook of the evening meal as if their eating the bread and butter were rendered almost superfluous by the painful probability of the worst of men shortly presenting himself for the purpose of eating them" (2, 13). The fancy of these Plornish children touches upon the truth. Rigaud and all the respectable men and women in the later novels live by eating up the substance of other people. Although Rigaud's expectations are aristocratic, his machinations are aggressive in the worst bourgeois manner; thus, in this way, Rigaud combines the qualities that Dickens hated about both classes.

Rigaud may seem to be a figure from Victorian melodrama, but his function in *Little Dorrit* is complex enough. By claiming that certain qualities of his "character" were present at birth, he again broaches the problem of free will with which Dickens wrestled continually. But more important at the moment is the use that Dickens made of Rigaud not only to illustrate the unsatisfactory role of being a gentleman but also to expose other false elements in the dominant system of belief—such as cruel religious doctrines and savage commercial practices. His role in the melodramatic plot of the missing will is insignificant compared to the fact that—by seizing upon the moral standoff in the Clennam

House and trying to turn it to his own advantage—he illuminates the historical causes of the malaise suffered by Mrs. Clennam, Affery, Flintwinch, Arthur's father, and, especially, Arthur.

"In fine, then, I name it the history of this house," begins Rigaud. The history begins with an uncle of "strong force of character" and his "nephew, habitually timid, repressed, and under restraint." Rigaud puts the characterization in terms we might well anticipate. The nephew (Arthur's father) is "a poor devil who had had everything but his orphan life frightened and famished out of him" (2, 30). In Rigaud's word *famished,* we can hear the reverberations of the age of hunger. In Rigaud's version of this family's history, we have the history of the human family, which Dickens had all along been writing—and which includes an extensive list of figures, from Oliver and the Marchioness to Uriah Heep and the Landlesses. It is a history of spiritual hunger and dissatisfaction as much as of physical deprivation.

Rigaud continues his history: From the heritage of such a father and supposed mother—"without pity, without love, implacable"—comes Arthur Clennam. Mrs. Clennam, admitting that she is not Arthur's mother, contributes to the history: before her marriage, she had been told by her father that her husband-to-be "had lived in a starved house, where rioting and gaiety were unknown" (2, 30). When she discovers that her husband had managed on occasion to escape his joyless life—and had produced an illegitimate son—she feels wronged, saying that she is outraged by his "holding a guilty creature in my place." We recognize in Arthur's father the rhythm that Dickens has described often enough: deprivation first, extravagance afterward. Arthur seems condemned to repeat the pattern in his own way. By way of revenge, Mrs. Clennam strips the unwed mother of the son—justifying this act by her concept of Old Testament rectitude, which she fittingly describes in alimentary terms as "insatiable vengeance and unquenchable fires" (2, 3). Although the objects may differ, the depth of the insatiability that links Mrs. Clennam to Rigaud has similar results—the consumption of others' substance, whether comestible, economic, or psychological.

Dickens continued his analysis of English cannibalism with Flintwinch, who is allied to Rigaud and Mrs. Clennam (the economic and the spiritual cannibals) both in single-mindedness and in voracity. Flintwinch is described as one who "drank all the wine he could get ... and would have stolidly done his companion's part of the wine as well as his own: being, except in the article of palate, a mere cask" (1, 30). The phrase "stolidly done" links

Flintwinch to the joylessness of Mrs. Clennam. Dickens's diction intimates much: Flintwinch would have *done* the wine, not *drunk* it or *tasted* it. Like Uriah Heep, Flintwinch intends to consume the substance of the people for whom he has worked. His antagonism towards Mrs. Clennam derives from a bitter opposition—a long resistance—summed up in this way: "You wanted to make everything go down before you . . . you wanted to swallow up everybody alive, but I wouldn't be swallowed up alive" (2, 30). Here is confessed the struggle between the economic and spiritual cannibal, which lasted for years. But for all of Flintwinch's apparent hardness and social indigestibility, it is no accident that Rigaud calls him "my cabbage." Rigaud says, "I'll draw upon you; have no fear" (1,30); and the reader knows that there is a second level here: Rigaud means to draw upon Flintwinch—the cask—personally, and not merely on the firm's bank account. The affectionate term "my cabbage" from across the channel does not hide Rigaud's rapacious intentions.

Pancks is involved in a series of demystifications in the novel—ultimately unraveling the ideology that has him in its toils. An indefatigable engine of the work ethic, Pancks, it is said, "took in his victuals much as if he were coaling" (1, 13). Pancks's sole purpose in eating is to work. As he says, "What business have I in this present world, except to stick to business?" (1, 23). That one sentence manifests the vicious circle Pancks is caught in. But eventually he sees that all his efforts benefit only Casby, who has taken in everyone with his bland, benign, patriarchal appearance: "The last of the Patriarchs had always been a mighty eater, and he disposed of an immense quantity of solid food with the benignity of a good soul who was feeding someone else" (1, 13). A light eater himself, Dickens ridiculed Casby's voracity. In this novel, Dickens has penetrated even the most innocent-looking disguises of the solitary monster. Pancks, too, finally penetrates it and acts to destroy the patriarchal sham. But until he acts, the motto of Victorian England and the crux of the novel might well be captured in this emblematic contrast: "Everybody was thirsty, and the Patriarch was drinking" (2, 32).

It is said that, like Casby, Mr. Merdle—immensely rich and of prodigious enterprise—"was the most disinterested of men,—did everything for Society, and got as little for himself out of all his gain and care, as a man might" (1, 21). However, the only enterprise the reader is given much detail about is the "dinner giving in the Harley Street establishment." These are such dinners that the guests have no proper names—as if they, too, had submerged their personal desires under their posed functions as public servants of the Treasury, Bar, Admiralty, or Church. Even Mrs. Merdle is rendered an institution through her title of the Bosom. But then, her every action belies this appellation—for she means neither to comfort nor nourish.[12] It is also said that the chief butler "was the next magnificent institution of the day" and that he "was the stateliest man in the company" (1, 21). Under the gaze of these ogres of respectability, no meal at the Merdles can be enjoyed—despite the fact that there is "everything to eat and everything to drink." There is altogether too much evidence of the grinding action of severe class inequalities upon the dinners—for example, in the form of footmen's powder: "Powder! There is so much powder in waiting, that it flavours the dinner. Pulverous particles got in dishes, and Society's meats had a seasoning of first-rate footmen" (1, 21). Dickens was providing a bizarre joke on the theme of cannibalism: it is only fitting that Malthusian society should be fed upon such a diet. How much nearer to literal could Dickens have made the metaphors of grinding the poor and of English cannibalism?

Like Casby—in that he had patriarchal pretensions—William Dorrit is always found in the midst of food and drink, whether he is rich or poor. The Father of the Marshalsea is the passive—as Rigaud is the active—gentleman; but both prey upon society from their assumed positions. How altogether appropriate it is that while crossing the Alps Dorrit should meet that summit of respectable society, Mrs. Merdle, at a time when that "very genteel" woman had appropriated a room that the Dorrits had planned to—what else?—"dine in." Only recently released from debtor's prison and newly reclassed, so to speak, Dorrit is excessively touchy. As in the past, he will punish his providers (the innkeeper in this case) by refusing to eat: "I will leave your house without eating or drinking, or setting foot in it" (2, 3). In Ian Watt's excellent phrase, these are "the psychic politics of the baby."[13] An earlier example of this type of politics occurred when Dorrit tried to play the pander between his daughter Amy and John Chivery. When Amy did not deign to reply to his innuendo, Dorrit began "biting at his bread as if he were offended with it" (1, 19). In these cases, Dorrit's vengeance is to deny others the opportunity to feed him—and it has as its assumption the notion that others exist to serve him. In denying them this opportunity, he is in effect denying them a reason to be. This is part of the Dorrit legacy and is the assumption tacitly made by all of the gentle classes in Dickens's works. It is a foundation of English cannibalism.

Both Amy's "gallant brother" and "dainty sister" are "ready to beg or borrow from the poorest, to eat of anybody's bread, spend anybody's money, drink from anybody's cup and break it afterwards" (1, 20). Like Dickens's other ne'er-do-wells—specifically, Rigaud—they assume a station and expect society to reward them for possessing it. Because Amy supposedly lacks such "becoming pride" in the family, Fanny must compensate for her commonness. In a marvellous inversion of values, Fanny disparages Amy, by saying, "While you have been thinking of the dinner ... I may have been thinking, you know, of the family" (1, 20). Fanny apparently assumes that the universal preoccupation of the human mind is with dinner. In the degree to which she is given over to "amour propre"—which is what she means by "family"—she takes after the Father of the Marshalsea. This thinking Fanny inherits from her father, and it binds her more than the Marshalsea. Thus does the circle of voracity continue.

Dorrit, like any lord, ate well enough off his fellow prisoners. Predictably, the first thing he does when he gains his inheritance is to provide all the prisoners with a huge dinner. Although he "did not in person dine at this public repast," the reader is told that he walked about "like a baron of olden time in rare good humour" (1, 36). As with his treatment of the pauper, Old Nandy, Dorrit intends to pay for his social cannibalism only with food. But after he is made wealthy again, he has trouble convincing Amy to adapt to their new circumstances. He reluctantly admits, "our tastes are evidently not her tastes" (2, 5). In the context of the theme of voracity that we have been following, the dead metaphor comes alive. Amy has no taste for social cannibalism. She cannot temporize, in the sense of conforming with the age of hunger.

Amy Dorrit is the antithesis of all these versions of "respectability" and lordliness. The reader was first introduced to Amy in the Clennam house, where part of her "daily contract included meals." We are told that "she had an extraordinary repugnance to dining in company" (1, 5). In the rest of the paragraph Dickens omitted the "she" or any nominative, the prose becoming—as it so often does with Dickens—self-reflective; by its very structure, the syntax signifies the thought it is expressing: Amy has no aggressive ego. The reader learns along with Arthur the reason for her curious and apparently unsociable trait of eating alone: "She had brought the meat home that she should have eaten herself, and was already warming it on a gridiron over the fire for her father" (1, 8). In contrast to Mrs. Clennam—who starves herself excessively in order to assert her own form of lordliness, or spiritual dominance, over others—Little Dorrit spares her food in order to provide for others: she economizes to enhance life. Above all, she stands for the sufficiency of the present—which is recognized by young Chivery who "honoured and loved her for being simply what she was" (1, 18). "Her sister," though "of infinite accomplishments," Chivery knew "could not forget the past." The recognition of the adequacy of the present—of its worthiness of trust—could not have been better expressed.

The frequent criticism of Little Dorrit is that she is too much the Victorian ideal—pure, sexless, and passive. But in the context of this study of the circle of voracity—of the hunger of the present—the character of Little Dorrit seems simply necessary. Moreover, she is not merely a function of this dialectic; there is truth to her function in terms of the politics of the family. Given the configuration of her family—and the roles adopted by her father, brother, and sister—from the point of view of group dynamics, it is plausible that a younger sister of such a family at such a time would attempt to adopt the role of "Little Mother," to use Maggie's phrase. Little Dorrit—replacing the dead mother—has become the provider, sustainer, and comforter of the family. Whether or not Dickens's disappointment in his own mother or wife is reflected here, Dickens had a great need to believe in the possibility of such women as Amy, Esther, Lizzie Hexam—and, indeed, from his own life, Georgina Hogarth. Little Dorrit functions as Little Mother for Maggie—and, ultimately, for Arthur as well. But while her father lived, he constantly received her service. In prison, he cried, "What does it matter whether I eat or starve?" (1, 19). This is a question that the fate of Franklin had evoked. In the age of hunger, it did not matter which individuals starved. This was the ultimate response to the utilitarians and materialists who sponsored Hunger. Only to the loving Little Dorrit—appropriately named Amy—does it matter whether her father starves or not. Little Dorrit offers a positive escape from the circle of voracity that the Victorian ideologies had engendered. She renounces the eternal round of seeking to make a name—of creating a self for the consumption of society—in order to lord it over others. Her own name, Little Dorrit, expresses this renunciation.

Little Dorrit had been serving the members of family for years. Why was she never able to save them from being engulfed in the vicious circle? Because they had failed to derive any great spiritual sustenance from her service—which is probably due to their failure to recognize that her service was a free gift of love and not, somehow, an imposed duty. Even Frederick Dorrit, at first, claims that Amy only "does her duty" (1, 9).

It is Arthur Clennam—for whom duty is so difficult an idea to grasp, and who never received any such gift of love in his own life—who perceives the value of Amy's gift as well as the inadequate appreciation of it by her family. Ironically, Flora's legacy, Mr. F's aunt, throws toast at Arthur Clennam and accuses him of having "a proud stomach." She cries that he should be given "a meal of chaff" (2, 9). It is an absurd scene, and the old woman is absurdly wrong; for, besides John Chivery, only Arthur has a spirit that is not too proud to admit Amy's value. When Amy's Uncle Frederick speaks nonchalantly of her, the reader is told that "Arthur fancied that he heard in these praises a certain tone of custom, which he had heard from the father last night with an inward protest and feeling of antagonism" (1, 9). And the reader is told that to the members of Amy's family, her free offering of love was "vaguely what they had right to expect, and nothing more" (1, 9). But Arthur knows better. Amy provides sustenance for the spirit, without which it perishes.

The metaphor of spiritual sustenance is an ancient one. In his *Confessions,* St. Augustine makes the important distinction clear:

> My God, you have taught me to distinguish between a gift and its fruit. The gift is the thing itself, a necessity of life given by one man to another. It may be food, drink, clothing, shelter, or help. But the fruit is the good will, the right will, of the giver.[14]

But the Dorrits fail to take the fruit of Amy's gifts. Only the fruit will sever the circle of voracity. However, Arthur Clennam has long been suffering from spiritual inanition; and if he is, at first, no more conscious of the fruit of the spirit deriving from Amy than the Dorrits are, he at last recognizes and accepts it. The loss of his physical appetite while in prison reveals the extent of his spiritual deprivation.

Imprisoned as a result of the Merdle debacle, Clennam cannot eat, although John Chivery has nobly brought his rival for Amy's affection fresh butter, boiled ham, and a "little basket of watercresses and salad herbs" (2, 29)—(the action is already predicted by the name "Chivery," which seems to combine *chivalry* and *chives*). It is said that "Clennam tried to do honour to the meal, but unavailingly. The ham sickened him, the bread seemed to turn to sand in his mouth. He could force nothing upon himself but a cup of tea" (2, 27). But mere food cannot repair the annihilation of his ego that a life without care has effected. His spirit is perishing from inanition. Incarceration is only an external sign for the isolation Clennam already feels. In witnessing his profound spiritual hunger, one might come to the following realization about the point of his name: like "Chivery," it is one of those patent Dickensian transformations—for "Clennam" derives from the dialect word *to clem,* or *to starve.* Starved of love, he finds no point in eating for physical survival. Until Clennam knows what he has to live for, he cannot eat. But John Chivery, to his own self-dramatized sorrow, knows that Clennam has ample reason to keep body and soul together—for he is beloved by Amy.

The imagery of Little Dorrit's rescue of Clennam leaves no doubt about the lines of significance Dickens had been so assiduously drawing in this novel. The reader is told that Clennam, who tries to drink some tea left by the woman who arranged his room, "could not bear the odour of it" (2, 29). But when Little Dorrit arrives, she introduces freshness and love, true; but she also brings a "basket . . . filled with grapes and other fruit" as well as "cooling drink and jelly, and prospective supply of roast chicken and wine and water" (2, 29). More importantly, the foodstuffs bear Augustine's "fruit," which Arthur's spirit so desperately needs. Little Dorrit's love is the sustenance that he hungers for.

By means of multitudinous references to food and appetite, Dickens fully developed in *Little Dorrit* his vision of the circle of voracity. From the circle of voracity—consume or be consumed, take in or be taken in—there is only one escape: conversion, change of heart. Only conversion can alleviate the ego's fear of annihilation that motivates the voracity. I cannot attempt to describe in discursive terms the life lived beyond the circle; the threshold is all that we see of that project. For in so many words that life can only be parodied. The reader might catch a glimpse of what it is *not* in the words with which the novel ends: it is a way of life that is *not* the way of "the noisy and the eager, and the arrogant and the froward and the vain" (2, 34)—*not* the way traversed by those who are consumed by the need to consume.

In portraying Dorrit's rise and fall, Dickens in effect revealed that every rank of English society was caught in the circle of voracity. In Dorrit's fall, his rise, and his fall again, the circle is complete. As R. R. Roopernaraine has written: "This is the final triumph of circularity."[15] From Plornish to Merdle and the aristocratic Barnacles, all of the English were caught in the circle, some as psychological and economic victims, some as cannibals—victims of their own unceasing and unappeasable voracity. Although Little Dorrit and Doyce and Meagles lead Arthur out of the circle, *Little Dorrit*, by and large, portrays a present that was intolerable to Dickens.[16] It was a present that apotheosized hunger and ordained voracity.

As if in response to this dire picture of the present, Dickens seems to have avoided a direct portrayal of the present in his next two novels. First, in *A Tale of Two Cities*, he immersed himself in national pasts; and then, in *Great Expectations*, he immersed himself in a study of the connection between the personal past and the personal future. Nevertheless, the cannibalistic themes emerging from Dickens's vision of the present also dominate these two novels.

A Tale of Two Cities was meant as a warning to Victorian England. Certainly the histories of the St. Evrémondes, of Manette, the revolutionaries, and even Carton have a cautionary intention. But the novel also served Dickens's dialectic of time: in its plot as well as its themes, it discloses once again what Dickens so frequently argued—the past, present, and future are reciprocally influential.

In *A Tale of Two Cities*, Dickens again used a cannibalistic imagery. The initial scene—of wine spilled in the street and lapped up voraciously, except for some wine that is used to spell "BLOOD"—leaves no doubt about where the hunger in France must lead. In such a world as this novel presents, the dread of being eaten is not a paranoid response. But a new consequence emerges as well. J. M. Rignall has seen in the novel "an expression of world-weary resignation" and has held that Carton's self-sacrifice "is as perverse as it is noble, as much a capitulation to the uncontrollable forces that have governed his life as a transcendence of them."[17] These historical forces are portrayed in the novel; but practical antidotes to the circle of voracity are also offered—antidotes to the madness of hunger that leads to the cannibalistic rituals of the guillotine. These practical actions lead to trust.

One practical antidote would be the development of a different attitude in England toward cookery and dining. With the first issues of *Household Words*, Dickens had himself—and through his best writers—been examining the English way with food. Good food, one may learn from reading *Pickwick* and *Martin Chuzzlewit*, goes some distance in not only allaying the spiritual hunger of England but also redressing some of the inequalities in wealth. However, instead of exploiting this capability, English cookery had largely failed. English cookery did nothing to counteract the anxieties of the age of hunger for several reasons: (1) the large-scale waste of edibles by all classes, (2) the dyspepsia too often caused by the professional "good plain cooks"[8] and the wives in humbler homes, and (3) the adoption by the upper classes of the ritual of large dinner parties.

So-called good plain cooks were too rarely good; and in contrast to French cooks who used every scrap to create soups and stews, English cooks often mistook wastefulness for virtuous plainness. Dickens's journals, like his novels, made the point repeatedly that English cookery was characterized by carelessness and inedibility rather than by skill and nutritiousness. *Household Words* was in the forefront of English periodicals in recommending the adoption of French methods—which, for Dickens, merely consisted of applying intelligence, science, and care to cookery. The articles in *Household Words* and, later, in *All the Year Round* point out that managing well and cooking well were impossible without the carefulness that is born of love and self-pride. In the light of the novels, I may add that such carefulness is free of the "dread of being eaten"—and, therefore, it can serve to free men from the fear. Behind this provocation of a culinary revolution was Dickens's intuition that political economy in England was quite directly related to domestic economy—and, perhaps, to animal economy.[19]

In *A Tale of Two Cities*, the conclusions of *Household Words* about culinary satisfaction are given full play. The home of Lucy Darnay is the site of a domestic economy that can alter the political economy. In Lucy's home Sidney Carton is welcomed, fed, and consoled—and Dr. Manette is restored. In Miss Pross, Lucy possesses a faithful companion who—in defeating Mme. Defarge later—symbolically puts an end to the political cannibalism of the revolution. But the strength of Miss Pross's devotion is, if less sensationally, more significantly displayed in another manner: "In the arrangements of the little household, Miss Pross took charge of the lower regions, and always acquitted herself marvellously. Her dinners, of a very modest quality, were so well cooked and so well served, and so neat in their contrivances, half English and half French, that nothing could be better" (2, 6). Miss Pross haunted the quarter of the French émigrés to learn new recipes. The half-English part of Miss Pross's contrivances, no doubt, included loving care as well as solid English foodstuffs. The point is that political economy and history were altered by the intervention of this representative of the force of domesticity and trust.

Great Expectations may be the novel by Dickens that is most completely structured by the themes of voracity and cannibalism—

and by the details of an absence of domesticity and trust. It is more emphatically so than even *A Tale of Two Cities* (for all of its mobs animated by a devouring rage). From the first scene in which Magwitch looks longingly upon Pip's "fat cheeks," *Great Expectations* is pervaded by solitary monsters of every degree. Dickens has perhaps released his own deep-seated fears of annihilation most fully in this novel. Magwitch, Mrs. Joe, Miss Havisham, Estella, Orlick—all seem to threaten Pip's animal or spiritual being.

The "dread of being eaten" finds ample expression in almost every meal represented in the novel. Of all the meals described, only a few are free from the taint of figuring as a cannibal feast. The first such meal is the one that Pip brings to Magwitch on the marshes; in providing it, despite the initial coercion, Pip begins to learn to care for the well-being of another. Joe later expresses Pip's own nascent feelings: "We don't know what you have done, but we wouldn't have you starved to death for it, poor miserable fellow-creatur" (5). The second such meal is the one with which Herbert Pocket wishes to welcome Pip to Barnard's Inn—that desolate home for great expectations. The third is the Walworth dinner, at which Wemmick shares his Walworth sentiments. The fourth is the convalescent meal that Joe provides for Pip after the catastrophe. Otherwise—from the traditional Christmas dinner at which Pip is likened to an ungrateful pig (and entertained continually by the Pumblechookian elbow) to his own later and reluctant feeding of the returned Magwitch—all the meals in the novel are spoiled by cannibalistic intentions or fears, at one remove or another. Estella, Pumblechook, Mrs. Pocket, Miss Havisham, and even Jaggers—all provide food for Pip with the intention of also feeding on him. Orlick reveals himself only as the most literal cannibal when he tells Pip, "I won't have a rag of you, I won't have a bone of you, left on earth" (53). In no other novel by Dickens is the "dread of being eaten" driven home more convincingly. But in Joe, Biddy, Wemmick, and in Herbert Pocket, Pip finds sufficient models for another, more satisfying way of life.[20]

As his career progressed, Dickens saw more and more clearly that savagery was not the antithesis of capitalistic civilization but was, rather, fostered by it. The ideology of hunger had made the teeth in Western civilization justifiable. For examples of human beings who were able to withstand the temptations and coercions of this ideology, Dickens was forced to look more and more to the lower classes. To the disgust of some of his contemporary—and even of his twentieth-century—critics, Dickens found the remedy to rampant voracity, generally speaking, not in academicians, scientists, or the gentle classes but in simple folk—especially, those who had, on occasion, passed over the threshold of physical hunger and those who had permanently settled beyond the pale of social ambition and respectability. Dickens was not sentimental on this: he had no use for the so-called noble savage, and he showed that English cannibals emerged from every rank of society—for lower-class characters like Bill Sikes and Rogue Riderhood prove that Dickens was not blind to the faults of the poor. But one thing is certain by the time that we get to Dickens's last decade: he had no hopes for the salvation of any individual who turned his face solely towards personal advancement. The desire for rank, or class distinction, had become for Dickens a major cause of the age of hunger.

Our Mutual Friend contains, perhaps, the ultimate analysis of the ideological cannibalism that Dickens saw pervading English society. On the very first page, we are introduced to the enterprising small-businessman Gaffer Hexam, who makes his living by dredging up the bodies of the drowned from the Thames. He can be said, with very little metaphoric displacement, to live on human bodies. When his daughter Lizzie expresses her repugnance to scouring the water of the Thames for corpses, he is unable to comprehend: "As if it wasn't your living! As if it wasn't meat and drink to you!" The reader can ask for no clearer explanation of what his way of life means. Several times, Hexam is likened to—or is described as—a "bird of prey." Although "half savage," he is, nevertheless, always "businesslike." There is no contradiction here; both attributes are accounted for by his "hungry look" (1, 1).

By juxtaposing chapters on the river and chapters on what he called Society, Dickens has forced us to see that Society, for all of its gloves and protocol, is quite as cannibalistic as those predators who live down in Limehouse Hole. The Veneerings hope to move upwards in society by feeding anyone whom they conceive it potentially profitable to feed. Again, there is no ambiguity about the purpose of Society dinners: their purpose is not for pleasure, company, or even sustenance but solely for social and financial predation. The Veneerings use Twemlow, a first cousin of the unseen and repugnant Lord Snigsworthy, as their "innocent piece of dinner-furniture," to whom leaves may be added as needed (1, 2). Metaphorically, Twemlow boards them. It is comically appropriate that Veneering first became acquainted with Twemlow at their club when they had occasion to agree on "the nefarious conduct of the committee respecting the cookery of a fillet of veal." Veal, therefore, is the "bond of union between their souls" (1, 2). The echo of Carlyle's raucous irony is evident.

The second chapter of the novel gives the reader such a taste of a Veneering banquet that the reader may be replete for some time afterward. The Veneering dinners—dull, pompous, wholly repellent affairs—are epitomized by the behavior of a butler whom the narrator is soon calling the Analytical Chemist. This august personage can never be wholly satisfied with anything the Veneerings may muster by way of respectable display, especially in the way of wine; and he is eternally expressive of his own sense of being declassed by serving the Veneerings. Respectability may be hired, but not respect. Like Merdle, Veneering cannot hope to be accepted by his own servant.[21] Master and servant dissatisfy each other forever on Cannibal Island called England.

Nevertheless, dinner after dinner is held. The primary topic is shares—for shares are presumed to be the ne plus ultra of human life. The holders of shares conceive of a society full of "smaller vermin" crying out to them, "Relieve us of our money, scatter it for us, buy us and sell us, ruin us, only we beseech ye take rank among the powers of the earth, and fatten on us" (1, 10). Cannibalistic fantasies, Dickens suggested, permeate all layers of society, from Podsnap and Veneering down to Hexam and Riderhood—the latter two merely practicing a less indirect translation of human beings into food.

Among the Veneerings' dinner guests is a menagerie of different kinds of cannibals. Lady Tippins is one of the cannibals who dines at the Veneerings most frequently. She generally makes a "series of experiments on her digestive functions" (1, 2). After gorging herself, she falls asleep. On every possible occasion, she is found "partaking plentifully of the fruits of the earth (including grape juice in the category)" (2, 16). Despite all of her mastication, deglutination, and slumber at the Veneerings' expense, Lady Tippins feels very little obligation to her hosts. She is the parasite even while pretending to help them: "Do come and dine with my Veneerings, my own Veneerings, my exclusive property, the dearest friends I have in the world" (2, 3). The host-parasite relationship is summed up this way: "Lady Tippins lives in a chronic state of inflammation arising from the dinners" (3, 17). There is a certain amount of poetic justice in her suffering so much from gourmandising; but, unfortunately, the ideology she lives by also impairs the health of the body politic. Neither her feeding nor her suffering mitigates the suffering of the hungry.

Another kind of cannibalistic guest is represented by Alfred Lammle and Sophronia Akershem. Each is a bird of matrimonial prey whose intentions are well understood by the others: "Buffers are even overheard to whisper Thir-ty Thou-sand Pou-nds! with a smack and relish suggestive of the very finest oysters" (1, 10). The culinary imagery is fitting. But as their names indicate (akin to the words *lamina* and *sham*), both are frauds and take each other in. The Lammles later try to arrange a marriage between the cad Fascination Fledgby and the young, naive, and disaffected heiress Georgiana Podsnap. Dickens has made certain through his imagery that the reader does not miss the continuing theme: the reader is told that after introducing Fledgby and Georgiana, Lammle "engaged in a deed of violence with a bottle of sodawater, as though he were wringing the neck of some unlucky creature and pouring its blood down his throat" (2, 5). An adjective used by Dickens for Lammle is "ogreish."

Although Mrs. Lammle eventually relents and saves Georgiana—showing by her action, at least, an instinct to renounce the cannibalistic premise of her social existence—her excuse for the activities of her husband and herself sounds familiar to us: "Restraining influence, Mr. Twemlow? We must eat and drink, and dress, and have a roof over our heads" (3, 17). The end excuses the means. In their fear of social annihilation, the Lammles choose to annihilate the spirits of others. Moreover, the annihilation they fear is only the loss of image—of their precarious place in the pecking order of respectability. In other words, they fear to fail as predators.

Dickens did not imply that the world is a Garden of Eden in which every human being need only renounce his allegiance to the ideology of hunger in order to pluck ample sustenance from nature. There are no "lilies of the fields" in the age of hunger. To believe there are is mere "Podsnappery."

Podsnap himself is perhaps most renowned for having parochialized Providence. When a "stray personage of meek demeanour" refers "to the circumstance that some half-dozen people had lately died in the streets of starvation," Podsnap dismisses the subject by announcing, "I don't believe it" (1, 11). Even if the circumstances were true, he is sure that Providence would not have permitted it unless the victims had, by some choice, brought the catastrophe upon themselves. It appears from what Podsnap says that Providence provides the provident with the skills to manage the provender. If one side of Podsnappery seems to coddle, the other snaps. If one is vacuous, the other is voracious—two sides of the same emptiness.

Dickens implied that the "haunch of mutton vapour-bath" at the Podsnaps' and the feasts at the Veneerings' must bear much responsibility for the hunger in the streets. In this way, the bourgeoisie pretend to be feasting at the expense of Providence when they are actually feasting, in this alienated society, at the expense of their fellow human beings. These gatherings prove that everyone is a solitary monster.

A number of readers have faulted Dickens for bringing up merely local and sentimental solutions to hard and general problems. One of the problems is the responsibility of society and the individual for the welfare of orphans. However, the Boffins' adoption of Betty Higden's grandson should not be viewed as a serious solution to the social inequities of Victorian England but as the representation of a practical mind-set diametrically opposed to that of Podsnappery. To ask that the social solutions offered in art be anything but figural is to demand something other than art. It is to refuse to view the action in the context of the novel by the novel's rules of notice. In order to create trust, the actions of Dickens's characters must also be viewed against the deprivation and starvation of children throughout Dickens's novels. In terms of *Our Mutual Friend,* the adoption must be viewed against the "circumstance" of a half-dozen people dying of starvation in the street. To demand a policy paper from Dickens is to deprecate art.

At the beginning of *Our Mutual Friend,* dissatisfaction is so rampant that only Podsnap appears satisfied. By the tenets of Podsnappery, not be be satisfied is impious; thus, he is always satisfied with the present. By and large, however, society is agonized through and through with dissatisfaction. Near the bottom of the social ladder is Wegg, vending song-sheets, inedible sweets, and services for a meager living. In describing these wares, Dickens implied that Wegg's bitter dissatisfaction with his life is bound to be passed on:

> It gives you the face-ache to look at his apples, the stomach-ache to look at his oranges, the tooth-ache to look at his nuts. Of the latter commodity he had always a grim little heap, on which lay a little wooden measure which had no discernible inside, and was considered to represent the penn'orth appointed by Magna Carta.... The only article in which Silas dealt, that was not hard, was gingerbread (1, 5).

In direct contrast to these insalubrious and tooth-breaking wares is the food Boffin offers by way of practical hospitality. Ian Watt has written that Dickens had never before "presented anything so close to the hidden yearnings of the human appetite as the total generosity and openness of Mr. Boffin's Bower."[22]

It is fitting that Wegg gorges himself first on Boffin's comestibles and then attempts to realize financial and physical gain at Boffin's cost. How marvelously consistent it is, too, that Wegg should in his paid reading to Boffin pronounce Vitellius as "Vittle-us." By the same token, his pursuit of his amputated leg is one of those comic symbols in which Dickens excelled. For his part, Boffin is dumbfounded by the waste of food he hears of in ancient Rome. Nothing has escaped Dickens's vision—every detail being a reflection of the circle of voracity. Boffin refers to "some splendid book in a gorging Lord-Mayor's-Show" of volumes—probably, the narrator tells us, "meaning gorgeous, but misled by association of ideas" (1, 5). Even point of view becomes "pint of view." The reflections multiply. When Venus offers tea and muffin to Wegg, "it being one of Mr. Wegg's guiding rules in life always to partake, he says he will" (1, 7). This principle—always to partake—is what links Wegg to Rogue Riderhood, on the one hand, and to the dinner guests of the Veneerings, such as Lady Tippins, on the other. It also links Wegg to Bumble, Pecksniff, Rigaud, and many other characters in previous novels.

Wegg is perhaps the ultimate figure in Dickens's representation of the circle of voracity—for he is a self-consuming cannibal. Whereas Wegg hopes to buy and sell Boffin, his language discloses that such mercantilistic ethics enslave the oppressor as much as the victim: "I am worth my price, and I mean to have it" (4,14). He may as well be a calf. Venus, who has secretly renounced trying to feed on others, serves as a contrast: "And I am blest," exclaims Wegg, "if you ain't getting fat!" (4,14). The physiques of the two characters reflect their different spiritual diets. Wegg, by choosing always to be a partaker—by choosing in his way to be a solitary monster—loses both flesh and soul. He manifests Dickens's insight that Wegg's form of cannibalism is self-consuming. All of English cannibalism is self-consuming, for it never finds satisfaction: to devour only feeds the fear of being devoured—which appears to be stanched only by more devouring. As Tennyson proclaimed, "I will not shut me from my kind, / And, less I stiffen into stone, / I will not eat my heart alone."[23] But English cannibalism—life without community—serves only the "heart alone."

In his principle "always to partake," Wegg typifies all of society.

The idea of temperance—of self-sufficiency—seems alien to most of the characters in the novel. Even Headstone, for all of his self-suppression, has no self-restraint. When he tells Lizzie that she could lead him anywhere—to any good or to the gallows—he is expressing an utter lack of self-control. In his desire to absorb and to be absorbed by Lizzie, he becomes similar to the other anthropophagists in the novel. Resembling Krook's hoarding (BH), his esurient warehousing of a "store of teacher's knowledge" (2, 1) is guided by Wegg's principle—not by the ideas of sufficiency or of natural satisfactions and utility. Charley Hexam appeals to Headstone because the former has a similar instinct: "There was a curious mixture in the boy, of uncompleted savagery, and uncompleted civilization" (1, 3). If the Lammles and Veneerings represent civilization, we cannot be sure which half of Charley is most repugnant. Charley intends to make his voracious way in the world and will sacrifice whomever he must. Whereas Lizzie sees much in "the hollow down by the flare," Charley sees only "the brazier, which had a grisly skeleton look on its long thin legs" (1, 3); where Lizzie sees such amazing life, Charley sees only death. Therefore, it is no surprise when Charley renounces first Lizzie and then Headstone. Charley is simply following the principle of his society. It was the law of the jungle: dog eat dog ad infinitum. English society, which Dickens depicted so thoroughly for us in the ambivalently titled *Our Mutual Friend*, is like a merciless uroboros, the mythic snake swallowing its own tail—a fitting emblem for the circle of voracity. English society appeared to be an unbroken chain of individuals *doing* each other *in*.

Was there no hope of breaking this vicious circle? Was Dickens able to offer us any grounds for optimism in *Our Mutual Friend*, as he managed to do in even the bleakest of his previous novels? At first glance, there seems to be very little hope: the novel seems dominated by dinner guests and other birds of prey. Like the drunken woman in the Police Station (1, 3), every member of this society seems to be shrieking for or stalking some other person's liver. Even Wrayburn, in his languid way, is a sexual predator. But there is evidence, which slowly accumulates, that not everyone is motivated by Wegg's principle of voracity. There is, first of all, Lizzie. She refuses to improve her condition for fear that she would thereby cause her father to "go bad and wild" (1, 3). There is Miss Abby Potterson of the Jolly Fellowship Porters, who does not condone predation (or "swindling," as Douglas Jerrold called it). The name of her pub is significant in this regard.[24] Eugene Wrayburn and Mortimer Lightwood also provide the reader with some hope that the human race need not accede to the rampant ogreism; their very disdain of the dinner guest role that they find themselves in indicates that their souls have not yet been transformed into stomachs. Even without yet knowing a concrete alternative, Wrayburn rejects the circular life he has been offered. Instead, wishing to escape Lady Tippins and cannibalistic wedding breakfasts, he expresses a desire to take a position to keep a lighthouse (2, 12). Its "defined and limited monotony" would be preferable to the "unlimited monotony" (1, 12) he currently endures. What is more monotonous, after all, than the law of the jungle or the unending circle of voracity? Although it is significant that a man named *Wray*burn tells the man named *Light*wood that they should keep a *light*house, Wrayburn's accession to an inner light—to the God-given mandate—is but fitfully and gradually achieved. But the cynical attitude that he has adopted to protect himself from Society cannot keep experience from affecting him. When the burnt sherry that Wrayburn and Lightwood are drinking (while they are waiting to capture Gaffer) begins to taste "like the wash of the river" (1, 13), the reader may well see that Eugene has begun to distaste a mode of existence that is merely a lower-class reflection of his own. Later, when Wrayburn outfits the kitchen in their chambers with a complete set of new culinary equipment, he jokes with Lightwood about the "moral influence of these objects" (2, 6). Despite Wrayburn's parody of materialistic notions of influence, two points seem clear. First, realizing that he lacks the domestic virtues, Wrayburn seems to be reaching toward a positive alternative to cannibalistic society (perhaps he has been reading the culinary articles in *Household Words* or *All the Year Round*). And second, he is admitting that he is susceptible to moral influences; hence, there is a moral connection between people in society that cannot be reduced to eat or be eaten.

Bella's development of alternatives to the ideology of hunger is even more precisely spelled out. Her initial domestic knowledge seems to be exhausted when she tells her mother, "And here's the cutlet! If it isn't done very brown, Ma, I can't eat it, and must have a bit put back to be done precisely" (1, 4). But, ironically, in leaving the pinched household of Mrs. Wilfer for the magnificent establishment of the Boffins, Bella increases rather than decreases in domestic accomplishments. As Eugene too must intuit, it is not the proximity of domestic implements that stimulates the domestic virtues but the live influence of the human beings who form a community. Reacting to Mr. Rokesmith's criticism of her, Bella visits her father to take him to dine. "I have already partaken,"

R. Wilfer says to her, using Wegg's term, "of a Saveloy" (2, 8). He would, he admits, have preferred "Small Germans," but he "can't do better than to bring a contented mind to bear on . . . Saveloys!" (2, 8). His contentment contrasts sharply with the rapacious appetites manifested elsewhere in this novel, as well as with the constant discontent of Bella.

Bella is susceptible to the positive influence of the Boffins even before the trick—so aesthetically controversial—that Mr. Boffin plays on her by pretending to become a miser. Before this, Bella visited home and took over in the kitchen, saying to her mother, "You and Lavvy think magnificent me fit for nothing, but I intend to prove the contrary. I mean to be Cook today" (3, 4). Although her good intentions surpass her culinary execution, Bella demonstrates the notion that one should be fit for something besides eating or being eaten—or being sold in marriage. This fresh notion she must have acquired at the Boffins'. Her mother, by contrast—sitting bolt-upright in a corner—thinks herself really too superior a creature to do the things that life and marriage have called upon her to do. "If I am uncomplaining, if I am silently contented with my lot, let that suffice for my family," she says (3, 4). In comparison to her husband's practical contentment, her discontent is expressed in her every word and gesture; it is generated by her commitment to a social structure based on aristocratic predation. If Mrs. Wilfer cannot actually partake in the general economic feast, she plans—by her charade of the reduced but unconquerable noblewoman—to feed spiritually on others.

Boffin's pretense of turning into a miser is the last impulse that Bella needs in order to free herself of the psychophagous contagion of her society. A miser is the epitome of the Weggian principle in action: he wishes always to partake and never to yield up. As Boffin says during his masquerade, "I have found out that you must either scrunch them, or let them scrunch you" (3, 5). This colorful rendition of the philosophy of eat or be eaten does not fail to stir rebellion in Bella's better nature. Running away from the miser's home, she naturally goes to her father—the paragon of contentment with bare sufficiency. And the meal that she, R. Wilfer, and John Rokesmith (soon to be revealed as Harmon) share symbolizes their ultimate refusal to become cannibals of any kind: "It was, as Bella gaily said, like the supper provided for the three nursery hobgoblins at their house in the forest" (3, 16), consisting simply of cottage loaves and milk. In such company as each had, this was a "fairy feast."

It has bothered many commentators that Bella becomes domestic in the last book of the novel.[25] However, through the theme that has been developing, it would seem that Bella's conversion was deliberately prepared for and dramatically right. Here, again, we must bring to consciousness certain rules of notice and read that event against the context by which Dickens has arranged to light it. Domesticity must be understood in the presence of hunger—not against the twentieth-century ethos of professional self-fulfillment. Her gesture is a symbolic answer to the problems that society and its dominant ideology placed before Dickens. Even at that, Bella cannot be accused of having lost caste as an individual. For, after toiling over—and then becoming critical of—the canonical *Complete British Family Housewife*, Bella proves that she is not slavish even to that revered testament. More importantly, by domesticating herself she is also removing herself from the vicious circle of eat and be eaten. Only against the background of hunger and predation can we make an accurate estimate of the aesthetic value of her efforts. Bella refuses to accept the law of the jungle as it was preached to her by her mother and by the miser Boffin and as implied by the values of society. She refuses to be merely a "doll in a doll's house" (4, 5)—which indicates that she refuses to be a possession that is bought and paid for or that is consumed in any economic, sexual, or spiritual sense. By her rebellion, Bella intends to *take part*—not *partake*. Her household duties call not for an expense of her spirit but for an employment of it. Her learning to cook, then, is a practical denial that Wegg's principle of always partaking is universal.

In *Our Mutual Friend,* Dickens did not, I think it fair to say, blink the dangers of living in the present. The present offered a precarious existence for poor and rich alike: even Mr. Boffin sits in his Bower, "a prey to prosperity" (1, 15). That Boffin came into his property through death enforces the perception that this world is not easily made a satisfactory place for human life. For Boffin believes that young John Harmon, on the way home to collect his inheritance, was "made away with, at the moment when he's lifting (as one may say) the cup and sarser to his lips" (1, 8). Boffin's comic addition to the adage shows his comprehension of the contingencies of life; his experience makes him a benevolent realist. Human satisfaction is hard to come by—which is the theme of this book and the upshot of Dickens's lifelong dialectic of time. Mrs. Boffin may be a "highflyer at Fashion" (1, 5), but there will be no Veneering-like social adventures for Boffin. He knows that fashionable society is composed of birds of prey and that life in it admits of no comfort or satisfaction or trust.

"Is Anything satisfactory, Mr. Boffin?" asked Lightwood (1, 8). The question might well serve as the epigraph for Dickens's works. Although there was little that was satisfactory at the moment when Boffin was queried by Lightwood, Boffin admits that he has known some satisfaction in his work. He is only sorry that Old Harmon made so much money—for Harmon's dissatisfaction grew with his fortune: "It would have been better for him if he hadn't so given himself up to it" (1, 8). Boffin will not allow himself to be swallowed up by the Harmon fortune. For that would be to give himself up to the present so fully that he would be incorporated into it. This is *tempus edax rerum* with a vengeance. In Dickens's vision, human beings must learn to live for the present and not by it or wholly in it.[26]

To live wholly in the present is to be consumed by it. This is Riderhood's fate. Like a vampire, Riderhood's determination is not to be shaken off by Headstone; so, he accepts the iron ring that a human being might elude: to eat and be eaten, to be a parasite or a host. Although Riderhood notices on that fateful morning that Headstone takes no breakfast, he makes nothing of the fact. Determined to consummate their relationship, the unhungry host takes the insatiable parasite to the edge of the lock. Following their progress toward the lock, the reader recalls the edacious terms with which Riderhood had described the effect of a human being caught in the lock: "Suck him down, or swaller him up, he wouldn't get out" (4, 11). Later, when Headstone rings him in and jumps, both men are swallowed by their hungers.

To be swallowed up is the chosen end of more characters than Riderhood or Headstone, from the bottom to the top of society. As Lightwood so explicitly observes in the last chapter, civilization as currently practiced is cannibalism: Indeed, speaking to Lady Tippins, Lightwood says that the savages that he (supposedly) had recently visited "were becoming civilized when I left Juan Fernandez. . . . At least they were eating one another, which looked like it" (4, 17). This rare explicit statement of the theme that dominates the last great novels may be Dickens's conscious mind catching up with his mythopoetic creations.

Through the course of his works, Dickens was developing a very delicately balanced dialectic of the present. He had to show, on the one hand, that physical hunger and spiritual hunger compose present reality and, on the other, that this reality is not a necessity. To do the latter, he had to demonstrate that (1) ideologies and corrupt institutions create the personal intemperance that is hunger; and (2) some questions in the present cannot be solved by even a fair and effective distribution of "beefsteak and porter" (4, 17)—(this is the payment that the Contractor at the Veneerings thinks is appropriate for Wrayburn to give the working girl Lizzie for saving his life; the only reward that she deserves for saving his life is to be repaid the precise amount of fuel that was required to save him). But some human relationships—some debts—are simply not translatable into monetary or alimentary terms.

In *Edwin Drood,* Dickens represented in the person of Jasper a continuation of the hunger and dissatisfaction that results in an intended cannibalism (leaving no substance of Drood left in the lime). But in the person of Crisparkle and his mother—with the symbol of her delicious preserves so carefully detailed (10)—there is a viable alternative. Though hunger was real and dissatisfaction was present everywhere Dickens conceived that a large-scale change of heart was possible. An individual could, through renunciation of the ideology of hunger, affect others. After being made conscious of the momentum towards voracity, one could act to elude it. The circle could be broken. In the Manettes' household—as in Joe and Biddy Gargary's, Bella and John Harmon's, the Boffins', and the Crisparkles'—Dickens displayed a viable present that was free of fear, cannibalism, and dissatisfaction. Crisparkle knows that "trustfulness [is] beneficial to a misshapen young mind" (7). The present must be built on a trust that offers free access to the past and to the future.

It was as if Dickens had come to see that it was not by centrifugal force that one escaped the hungry present but only by centripetal force—by entering into the present. One had to turn one's face resolutely toward the present. Satisfaction could only be snatched from and with the teeth of time. In the last chapter, I argue that in the ideas of the mathematician Charles Babbage Dickens found hope that time does not consume the good. To my mind, Dickens's vision of life in the present is similar to what Bergson called *duration:* "It is into pure duration that we then plunge back, a duration in which the past, always moving on, is swelling unceasingly with a present that is absolutely new . . . a present which [we] create by entering."[27] Dickens felt that the human being must have great courage to (1) enter into the present, (2) emerge from the security of the past, and (3) trust that an acceptable future will freely emerge in its own right. And it takes even greater courage not to live by—and wholly in—the present. It takes courage to live for the present, the past, and the future. But if the human being has this courage, the dread of annihilation should disappear. This courage is no grandiose thing; it can be translated into such a simple word as *comfort* or *trust*—the latter word appearing dozens of times in *Our Mutual Friend,* in which it serves as the theme.

6
Beyond Forgetting: The Uses of the Past

> Let me discern, compare, pronounce at last,
>   "This rage was right i' the main,
>   "That acquiescence vain:
> "The Future I may face now I have proved the Past."
>   —Browning, "Rabbi Ben Ezra"

Dickens, I have argued, was able to make peace with—and thus make use of—the present and the future. But his dialectic of time had its greatest difficulty in transcending the past. There were several problems. On the one hand, the received valuation of time was garbled. Despite the public piety addressed to progress—both political and industrial—the Victorians paid a heavy tribute to the past. On the other hand—as Dickens's effort to establish a stance toward his personal past proves—satisfaction was not easy to come by. Nevertheless, his continual effort also shows that while he felt that the past reached dangerously into the present, he also felt that the past could not simply be expunged—for it contained feelings essential for the health of the spirit. Consequently, over the course of his career, Dickens struggled, first, to confront and expose the attitudes that abused the past—transforming it into the dead hand—and, second, to discover and express the proper uses for the past. He wanted to come to such terms with the past as would vouchsafe the moral power of the past without yielding primacy to it. His effort to do this deepened his art. As George Ford has pointed out, "Dickens was by no means a loyal member of the steam-whistle party, and his mixed feelings, his divided allegiance, enabled him to add a dimension to his writing of extraordinary consequence."[1]

The past is abused when the popular mind is swayed by arguments giving the past an unquestioned authority in the business of life. This authority works through three executive positions:

the aesthetic, the mythic, and the rational. Their common effect is to silence the heart and strip the human being of dignity and freedom. Dickens created a two-fold strategy to dissolve the false authority of the past. First, against the three executive positions, Dickens employed comic exposure, satire, and invective. While satire and comic exposure of the abuse of the past were always a part of Dickens's fiction, his invective became honed with years. Second, Dickens sought to undermine the power of the dead hand by imagining a world in which the operations of historical precedent, physical influence, and logical coercion came to nothing. Because all worldviews are self-fulfilling, Dickens learned to create in his fiction a temporal climate that fostered the interactive over the passive, the playful and spiritual over the slavish and material, and the divinely uncertain over the contemporaneously certain.

Let us first review the ways in which Dickens attacked the abuses of the past. In Dickens's day, the doctrine of the aesthetic and moral superiority of the past involved two contentions. One was that life in the "good old times" was much more beautiful and sensuous in style. The other contention was that the past was far more spiritual and less materialistic than the present age. A whiff of antinomy did not apparently affect the adherents of either contention. To the second contention Dickens's response was powerful:

> It is commonly assumed—much too commonly—that this age is a material age, and that a material age is an irreligious one.... I do not understand this much-used and much abused phrase, a "material age," I cannot comprehend—if any body ... can: which I very much doubt—its logical signification.... Do I make a more material journey to the bedside of my dying parents or my dying child, when I travel there at the rate of sixty miles an hour, than when I traveled thither at the rate of six?[2]

In his fiction, correspondence, and journalism, Dickens was not taken in by the idea that material and social improvements rendered the present materialistic. He continually debunked the notion that the past was more spiritual because it had more suffering or that it was more beautiful because it had more "swaggering fighting men" wandering through the cathedral towns like Cloisterham (ED).

This continual debunking of the superior climate for humane living in the past bulks large in all of Dickens's historical novels. Indeed, his *Child's History of England* seems almost to be an injunction to the children of England to snub the national past—just as Dickens for some time tried to snub his personal past. Certainly, Dickens saw a few characters in English history who deserve to be remembered: besides Alfred, Guilbert the Norman, and Oliver Cromwell, there is Sir Philip Sidney, whose "touching action of a noble heart is perhaps as well known as any incident in history—is as famous far and wide as the bloodstained Tower of London" (31). But English history is fraught with characters like Henry VIII—"a blot of blood and grease upon the history of England" (28)—and Charles I, "his Sowship" (32). *A Child's History of England* is an almost uninterrupted recitation of the victimization of the common people by evil superiors: "there was some fighting, however, in which few suffered but the unhappy common people (who always suffered, whatsoever was the matter)." Far from presenting a tapestry that was beautiful and spiritually enriching, Dickens portrayed the national past as a filthy thing that was best done away with. For Dickens, the past ought to be kept in impotent disgrace, unless the act of debunking it should supply sufficient reason for bringing it to mind: "Ah! Better to be two cottagers in these better times, than king and queen of England in those bad days, though never so fair" (4).

As representatives of this supposedly superior past, the aristocrats had attributed to themselves special qualities—leading to a toadyism that reached its comic apogee in the comments that David Copperfield hears at Mr. Waterford's dinner party: "I'd rather at any time be knocked down by a man who had got Blood in him, then I'd be picked up by a man who hadn't" (25). The reference to "Blood" implies that noble qualities are an inherited substance—a historical residue rather than a spiritual choice in the present. This absurd hypostatization covers all three positions—the aesthetic, the mythic, and the rational—by which the past is given primacy. In order to laugh this primacy out of court, Dickens had to show that the past was in such cases subject to— and derived from—the present. Therefore, in *Martin Chuzzlewit*, Dickens's narrator testifies with heavy irony to "the enormous amount of bravery, wisdom, eloquence, virtue, gentle birth, and true nobility that appears to have come into England with the Norman Invasion"—and that would have thus come into England and been thus recorded, the narrator pretends to believe, "even though William the Conqueror had been William the Conquered—a change of circumstances which it is quite certain would have made no manner of difference in this respect" (MC, 1). In one sentence, Dickens has revealed the truth about rank in nineteenth-century England. It was obvious to Dickens that the qualities listed above would not have been ascribed to the descendants of the Normans had they become the lower classes. Thus, Dickens has illustrated the point that those qualities were predicated on present power and did not underlie that power as causes. If the present power of the aristocrats were negated, so would be the attribution of noble qualities. This is an example of Dickens's strategy of historical revision at work.

Dickens showed that the common emphasis in historical development, upon which so much of the power of circumstances was based, must be demystified—and often inverted—in order to be true. The historic determinism that was supported by the genealogical traditions was shown to be facing the wrong way. Remove the greatness, and the goodness would disappear. Such an insight may seem commonplace in the twentieth century, but it was not so in the nineteenth. This altered perception was the standard technique that Dickens used on all the enemies of the spirit. In Dickens's view, to hold that rank in the past exerts substantial claims in the present blighted not only personal ambition but human freedom in all respects. Such a claim amounted to a belief in predestination, in fatalism.

If present greatness derives not from the past but from the present, what of the claim of the present impotence of the spirit? What of the moral indigence that so many Dickens's characters blame on "circumstances"? More dangerous than hereditary rank—indeed, comprehending it—would be the notion that characters in the present are not free but are merely "victims of circumstances" (a patented phrase—or play on words—of Dickens's). Some of Dickens's characters believe that "circumstances"—always in place before they enter a situation—dominate every lived situation. This false determinism is a rampant abuse of the past. For every character who claims to have been determined, or to have been "submitted" or "called" (LD, 1, 5) or otherwise to be the agent of fate or the "victim of circumstances," Dickens provides an exposé, or self-exposé. For example, in the case of Tip Dorrit, Dickens has implied that a change of local circusmtances in the past would *not* have altered Dorrit's present situation. Thus, according to Dickens, Tip Dorrit would not have been much different had he never seen the inside of the Marshalsea (1, 7). For Dickens, the influences of Dorrit's material circumstances were negligible compared to those of the spiritual ones.

A present benefit is granted to each individual who submits to "circumstances." Among other things, such submission would explain the almost "savage torpor" to which both Wordsworth and Malthus refer. But Dickens always showed that it was possible not to submit: John Jarndyce refuses to grant psychological necessity to the lawsuit, and both Boythorn and Woodcourt refuse to grant necessity to aristocratic privilege. In *Bleak House,* Esther is, no doubt, the primary dismantler of the false authority of the past. She refuses to let any of her past sorrows—birth, upbringing, and, later, smallpox—become the determining factors in her life. A few critics have accused Dickens of making her too passive. On the contrary, she is wholly engaged in making the past passive— not so small a task, as may be seen in the novels. The action of burying her doll symbolizes her spiritual decision to keep her past in its proper place and role. As she says later, "It was not for me to muse over bygones" (6). Esther's gesture prefigures all that Dickens would do.

At first, circumstances seem to rule everywhere in *Bleak House.* In the person of Guppy, however, we have a character who—by transparently manipulating the language of determinism—is a parody of such deterministic beliefs. After Esther contracts smallpox, Guppy attempts to recall his heart and his tentative offer of marriage: he says that he regrets that arrangements in his life, "combined with circumstances over which I have no control" (BH, 38), prevent him from fulfilling his offer. His sorry excuse makes a mockery of the argument that there are circumstances over which no one seems to have control. "I may repeat that the idol is down. I have no purpose to serve now but burial in oblivion. To that I have pledged myself. I owe it to myself, and I owe it to the shattered image, as also to the circumstances over which I have no control" (39). When the image loses its valuable resemblance to the aristocracy, Guppy decides that his duty is to give a "burial in oblivion" for the image. This parodic version of Esther's earlier action of burying her past reveals the truth of the past's connection to the present, the truth of the power of circumstances: it is an arbitrary matter. Guppy is free to withdraw from the circumstances that he chooses to withdraw from.

Later, Guppy is brought forward to use the specious terminology of fatalism one final time. "I find," says Guppy, "that the image which I did suppose had been eradicated from my 'eart is *not* eradicated. Its influence over me is still tremenjous and yielding to it, I am willing to overlook the circumstances over which none of us have any control" (64). His diction is precise in its self-exposure: the influence *is* present—and, in fact, the individual may choose to overlook circumstances. In strong contrast to Guppy is

Boythorn, for whom the time of blighted love "has had its influence on all his later life" (9). Despite the pain, he has a "heart and head full of romance yet." As his name indicates, Boythorn is young in spirit; and his nature is to continue as a thorn to those who wish to embrace the past, whether disguised as traditional values or as names of families "as old as the hills" (2).

The power of the past that was based on sociopolitical tradition was often singled out by Dickens for exposure. Often employing, the magical term *circumstances,* this mythic school of the dead hand held that the social, political, and personal legacies of the past were not to be withstood by the individual. Dickens saw, again, that compliance with tradition—with what was called fetishes— always brings a reward. One of his strategies was to make this kickback evident. In doing so, he demonstrated that the power of the past was derived from present desire for—and the gratification of—power. For example, when Mrs. Merdle says, "Society suppresses and dominates us" (LD, 1, 20), she speaks as if Society were a fierce goddess. But she is merely trying to exculpate herself by pretending to be a "victim of circumstances"—while she gets everything she desires from her compliance. Merdle is absurdly described as "the most disinterested of men, [who] did everything for Society" (1, 21). The Father of the Marshalsea, William Dorrit, is the most obvious receiver of kickbacks from his deference to the past, until his new wealth makes him an apostate to the past— for which the dead hand takes its revenge.

When Mrs. Merdle voices a disingenuous preference for living in nature, she carries to absurd lengths her pretense of unwilling subjugation to social "circumstances." Her advice to Mr. Merdle reveals what she truly believes: "You ought to make yourself fit for it [society] by being more *dégagé,* and less preoccupied.... I simply request you to care about nothing—or seem to care about nothing—as everyone else does" (1, 33). Such is the desideratum of respectable society. Because the aristocracy enjoys a capacity to be careless, the bourgeoisie should pretend to it. Dickens abominated this injunction to be careless—in which a false ideal of the past imposes upon the present.

As an avatar of the past, Society serves to keep people apart rather than to join them together. Typical of his later invective, Dickens savaged "that wretched imposition which occasionally in England is known as society—that gathering of vapidity to each component part of which the laws which guide it prescribe a blank ignorance—an uncaring unquestioning acceptance of things as they stand—a horror of talent as low, and of unconventionality as not correct." Dickens wished himself and England to be rid of that "dreary phantasm sometimes regnant among us."³ The question was, How? The mythological authority granted by the past to Society was a difficult thing to combat, although its results were often enough ridiculous and logically outrageous. There was, perhaps, both personal and social outrage when Dickens wrote angrily to Miss Burdett-Coutts (4 October 1854), "When I think how we all know that we have suffered a system to go on, which blighted generous ambition, and put reward out of the common man's reach—and how our gentry have disarmed our Peasantry—I become Demoniacal."⁴

His native pessimism about the "system" caused him to repudiate the myth of the English middle classes as the bulwark of personal freedoms in England. The creator of Dombey and Bounderby came to doubt even the distinct existence of the middle class:

> What with teaching people to "keep in their stations," what with bringing up the soul and body of the land to be a good child, or to go to the beer-shop, to go a-poaching and go to the devil; what with having no such thing as a middle class (for though we are perpetually bragging of it as our safety, it is nothing but a poor fringe on the mantle of the upper); what with flunkyism, toadyism, letting the most contemptible lords come in for all manner of places, reading the Court Circular for the New Testament, I do reluctantly believe that the English people are habitually consenting parties to the miserable imbecility into which we have fallen, and *never will help themselves out of it.* Who is to do it, if anybody is, God knows. But at present we are on the down hill road to being conquered, and the people WILL be content to bear it, sing "Rule, Brittania," and WILL NOT be saved."⁵

If the middle class is a myth, so are many of the freedoms that it was supposed to guarantee.

Instead, Society desires a perpetuation of the *stationary*. As Lady Bowley recites for the improvement of the poor, "O let us . . . live upon our rations, / And always know our proper stations" (TC, 2). In *Our Mutual Friend,* Lightwood's law clerk, Blight, is asked by Boffin why he does not go in for being a magistrate. The boy, it is said, "virtually replied that as he had the honour to be a Briton who never, never, never [would be a slave], there was nothing to prevent his going in for it. Yet he seemed inclined to suspect that there might be something to prevent his coming out with it" (1, 8). That "something" is the tradition of station. The appropriately named Blight started too low at birth to become a judge; his "generous ambition" is forever "blighted" by his station.

Despite the lesson taught in *Oliver Twist*, Dickens knew that the poor classes, deprived of hope, were in greater danger than others from the infection of circumstances. Like Pip, Dickens himself, while an innocent boy, had been exposed to the danger of moral corruption by the world, as he was when he attended a small theater:

> The greater part of the sailors and others composing the crowd, were of the lowest description, and their conversation was not improving; but I understood little or nothing of what was bad in it then, and it had no depraving influence on me. I have wondered since, how long it would take, by means of such association, to corrupt a child nurtured as I had been, and innocent as I was.[6]

Dickens even as a young boy knew the worst side of London. And although Dickens believed that he had survived largely unblemished, he was far from believing that every child of normal endowment could.

As Will Fern says in *The Chimes*, "Tis harder than you think for, gentlefolks, to grow up decent: commonly decent: in such a place" (3). Dickens devoted a considerable amount of effort to an inventory of ways to help the working classes achieve decency without their freedom being vitiated by patronage; for he felt that, even for the poor and desperate, "circumstances" in the past were not the final arbiter of the present. Besides the exercise of certain kinds of freedom that poverty vouchsafed, the lower classes often had a superior degree of feeling and imagination to aid them. "All people," Dickens wrote in a letter to Miss Burdett-Coutts (15 November 1848), "who had led hazardous and forbidden lives are, in a certain sense, imaginative."[7] While the power of "circumstances" may be great, it was counteracted by other strengths also derived from those "circumstances."

Dickens's most specific retort to a claim for the power of circumstances is found in *Great Expectations*. Pip's phrasing is typical: "What could I become with these surroundings? How could my character fail to be influenced by them?" (12). But unlike many of his contemporaries, Dickens did not ultimately accept the necessity that Pip was trying to read into his experience. For Pip's idea that he could not fail to be influenced is precisely the false determinism—the reading of "will he" as "nill he"—which Dickens repudiated over and over.

Pip's character, in fact, contributes to the influences quite as much as his circumstances do. To be sure, Pip's temptations are very great. But neither he, Steerforth (DC), Rigaud (LD), the Marquis St. Evrémonde (TTC), nor Wrayburn (OMF) can be excused. They all believed in the necessitarianism that served their self-interest best. By accepting the status quo—socially and personally—each has opted for security, each has chosen to close down the portals of the imagination.

At a transitional point between the mythic and the rationalistic positions of the dead hand—and hardly to be distinguished from circumstances—is the problem of material influence. The Victorian era was an age whose true charter of belief was succinctly pronounced by Dickens when he wrote to Angela Burdett-Coutts on 7 July 1846 that in "the generality of the cases, it is almost impossible to produce a penitence which shall stand the wear and tear of the world, without Hope—worldly hope...."[8] Morality or spirituality cannot be expected without the basic physical needs satisfied. But the materialistic science of the period had taken as a tacit principle the notion that all material wholes are comprised of—and, therefore, reducible to—their material constituents. Assuming man to be a materialistic whole, then, writers such as Cabanis defined the whole by the various positive material elements that had gone into the aggregate. For example, on the most notorious level, it was believed possible to trace national character from national diet. According to English materialists, the English were braver than the French because they ate more solid food, like roast beef (and it was likely—but unfortunate from a scientific point of view—that French materialists would have come up with opposite results from similar data). Such notions—which enrolled organisms and ideas under the aegis of a simplistic conservation of matter—did have the shimmer of deductive logic. Moreover, in the Victorian era, people still believed that infections were carried by the air (the discoveries of Lister and Semmelweis had not yet been widely promulgated). It was assumed that the atmosphere had more than a psychological influence on an individual—because it was not merely a subjective sense of a place but a quasi-physical emanation of it. Hence, it is little wonder that Dickens—like Poe, among many others—was in something of a quandary about the extent of physical influence.

Humphry House pointed out many years ago that Dickens was concerned in nearly all his novels with "the influence of environment, especially in childhood, upon habits and character." For Dickens, House argued, "two things are in conflict—the desire to show the immense damage that such an environment and upbringing can do, and the natural desire to demonstrate that the fundamental goodness of human nature can survive almost anything."[9] The second desire may be a result of what Forster called "a passionate resolve, even while he was yielding to circumstances, *not to be* what circumstances were conspiring to make him."[10] Dickens did not blink the truth that there are many situations in which the capacity of an individual to escape the power of circumstances is problematic. There is no escaping the power of Jo's environment in *Bleak House*. But Jo's environment itself could be changed by social changes. Tip Dorrit's and Charley Hexam's environments are influences only—not necessities—as the presence of Amy Dorrit (LD) or Lizzie Hexam (OMF) goes to prove. Dickens inevitably displays a psychological disposition to corruption in the self-designated "victims of circumstances."

It was clear to Dickens that material circumstances were not sufficient causes for corruption: he believed that the tendency to corruption must have been implanted by ideological or mythic forms in the victim's mind. This idea is summed up by a remark about Martin Chuzzlewit at Eden: "There could be little doubt that such a state of mind would powerfully assist the influence of the pestilent climate" (23). Climate and material surroundings coerce; but in England, at least, these coercive forces could be deflected by public and personal action, such as the work to provide sewage disposal, clean public water, and housing regulations. In an article on nocturnal London in *Household Words*, Dickens made clear the urgency of public action: "We had stopped by five ragged mounds, and were quite rooted to the spot by their horrible appearance. Five awful sphinxes by the wayside, crying to every passer-by, Stop and guess! What is to be the end of a state of society that leaves us here!"[11] The conditions that deposited those human "mounds"—that rendered that spirit almost into matter— could be reversed. The past was subject to activity in the present. Material influences could be contravened by public acts that altered the environment and by personal acts of fancy and love that changed the perception of past, present, and future. The danger was that the collusion of the notions of material, social, and national necessity would not only obscure the possibility and methods of efficacious action but would also curtail the scope of action.

An even more treacherous form of the dead hand was that created by the rational models of historical, mechanical, and logical necessity. The line of reasoning of *post hoc ergo propter hoc*— when in strict adherence to rules of verifiability—had proven successful in science, but with the result that the line of reasoning became a cultural talisman, causing many individuals to believe that logical responsibility imposed moral irresponsibility upon them.

Everywhere in Dickens's works, characters give themselves up to factitious priority—to antecedent circumstances. Yielding to the rationalized primacy of the past are Malthusians like Mr. Filer (TC), materialists like Gradgrind (HT), and fatalists like Miss Wade (LD). Miss Wade derives a fatalistic attitude from her early sufferings: "In our course through life we shall meet people who are coming to meet us, from many strange places and by many strange roads," she says composedly, "and what it is set to us to do to them, and what it is set to them to do to us, will all be done" (LD, 1, 2). The displacement that she suffers—and the propulsion that she "is set" to impart to others—is the linear result of antecedent actions, namely, those of her parentage and childhood.

The paradigm of mechanical physics—in its reduction of human choices to physical causes—serves Miss Wade as an explanation of human interaction. But Dickens repudiated this rational office of the dead hand: the analogy from physics could not work for human experience for the obvious reason that human beings are not merely capable of receiving external forces but are also capable of converting and generating forces of their own. Hence, for Dickens, mechanical physics did not supply an adequate paradigm for the nature of human interaction.

Edmund Wilson has pointed out that Miss Wade's "handicap is now simply a thought-pattern, and from that thought-pattern she is never to be liberated."[12] But Dickens left no doubt that, as Freud and Laing have said,[13] the patient derives benefits from an illness. As a description for human interaction, *necessitarianism* (a word coined in 1854) renders quite evident benefits. Above all, moral difficulties are erased. In Miss Wade's belief that "all will be done," we note the assumption that every action is the necessary consequent of antecedents. We cannot fail to note that she also uses the passive voice to abstract even further her personal responsibility for what is to happen. When one does what one has to do—when what is set "will all be done"—the result is *nobody's fault*. All is the fault of the past. *Nobody's Fault*—the original title for *Little Dorrit*—speaks for minor and major characters alike. By denying responsibility, this intellectualized form of the dead hand denies human freedom. But Dickens held that free will is inalienable and indisputable.

No small part of Dickens's comic exposure, satiric irony, and invective was directed at the spurious logic supporting the several offices of the dead hand. Throughout his career—but with a clearer focus later in his life—Dickens undermined the false hypostatizations, the mythic attributions of qualitative superiority, and the rationalized surrenders of moral prerogatives to the dubious legions of circumstance. His fiction is an ongoing deconstruction of these arguments that had abused the past.

These attacks, however, represent but half of his strategy. The other half is the creation in his fiction of a world in which the past is not prioritized and yet is given its due respect, so that humans may use it, as Mary Wollstonecraft might say, to "unfold their faculties" in the most salubrious possible environment. This essential respect for the past is signalized in *Great Expectations* by Pip's admiring statement about Magwitch on his deathbed: "He pondered over the question whether he might have been a better man under better circumstances. But he never justified himself by a hint tending that way, or tried to bend the past out of its eternal shape" (56). By not attempting to bend the past out of shape, Magwitch refuses to avail himself of any of the excuses of the dead hand. Refusing to claim himself a victim of circumstances, he preserves his integrity as a spiritual entity.

For Dickens—as in *A Christmas Carol, The Chimes,* and many other places—the past also turned out to be the primary source of contentment in the present notwithstanding the fact that it may have been experienced as sorrow, pain, or guilt. To have had a full past was to be armed for human enterprise in the present. In *The Chimes* Dickens has asserted the essential use of the past. For Meg, a happy memory will soften hard times to come: "Oh Father dear, how hard to have a heart so full as mine is now, and live to have it slowly drained out every drop, without the recollection of one happy moment of a woman's life, to stay behind and comfort me, and make me better!" (1). Meg intuits the moral power of a happy memory, expressing her creator's agreement with the moral philosophy of his good friend, Rev. Sydney Smith, who had written: "Mankind are always happier for having been happy: so that if you make them happy now, you make them happy twenty years hence by memory of it. No enjoyment, however inconsiderable, is confined the present moment."[14] By adding "and make me better," Meg only makes explicit what Smith implied.

Meg naturally wishes to find some joy in life. But the Malthusians—by recommending celibacy and alienation instead—would have denied her and her loved ones not only the present but also a worthwhile past that would affect further presents. The value of happy memories is demonstrated once more by the next *Christmas Book* titled *The Cricket on the Hearth*. John Peerybingle, the hardworking carrier, is much older than his wife and grows jealous of the Stranger in whom his wife has shown such interest. John would have committed murder one night if the cricket on the hearth had not chirped and reminded him of his past happiness—and thus, "moved and softened him" (3). The cricket is a transparent symbol of the happy past and its "gentle influences and associations." In the contrived fashion of melodrama, the Stranger turns out to be Edward, the lover of another woman. However trite the plot, *The Cricket*—by its insistence on the accumulation of trust through past happiness—adds something to the record of Dickens's effort to come to terms with the past.

For Redlaw in *The Haunted Man*—as for Dickens, personally—what is problematic about the past is the value of painful memories. The creation of Redlaw seems to have been a conscious effort by Dickens to face the pain of his own past. In *The Haunted Man*, Dickens has asked the simple question, Is an individual better off in the present when he is free of the pain of memories? Through the form of the story, Dickens has asserted a bald answer: No, do not seek to eliminate even the pain of the past, for "the intertwisted chain of feelings and associations, each in its turn dependent on, and nourished by . . . recollections" (1) would be lost with those recollections—that is, the feelings or the capacity to care would be lost. Old Philip Swidger is proof of the value of memories: at eighty-seven, he is kept hale and hearty by his memories—by the painful no less than the joyful ones. The numinous quality of such recollections is expressed by the old man in this way: "At last, it seems to me as if the birth-time of our Lord was the birth-time of all I have ever had affection for, or mourned for, or delighted in—and they're a pretty many, for I'm eighty-seven!" (1). In such categories as (1) having affection for, (2) mourning for, or (3) delighting in, Dickens has captured various qualities of the infinitive *to care*. To be without these memories, then, would mean to be without the very springs of caring.

The appearance of the urchin presents Redlaw with what amounts to clinical proof of what happens when a human being has no memories of any kind. Only six years old, the urchin is a "baby savage, a young monster, a child who had never been a child . . . a mere beast" (1). Apparently unreceptive to such plain evidence, Redlaw learns from the Phantom that the boy "is the last, completest illustration of a human creature, utterly bereft of such remembrances as you have yielded up. No softening memory of sorrow, wrong, or trouble enter here" (3). But Redlaw has chosen to extirpate his memory of the past. Because one man cannot act without affecting those around him, everyone who associates with Redlaw loses the "inter-twisted chain of feelings and association" and becomes as hardened—or careless—as the urchin itself. Expressing once more Dickens's constant image, the Phantom says, "There is not one of these—not one—but sows a harvest that mankind MUST REAP. From every seed of evil in this boy, a field of ruin is grown that shall be gathered in, and garnered up, and sown again in many places in the world" (3). But, notably, it is not the past but the very absence of it that breeds evil. Therefore the past, even the painful past, has essential value for the present.

It is not the past itself that Redlaw wishes to abolish—in fact, he argues that "the past is past . . . it dies like brutes" (2); rather, it is the present pain of past "sorrow and wrong" (1) that he wants to eradicate. But the pain of the present is surety that the past does not die like brutes. Only for brutes does memory die when pain disappears. Redlaw, ironically, by choosing to bring the pain to an end, chooses to make himself into a brute. He is forced to discover that suffering is intertwined with other humanizing qualities and cannot be abolished without spiritual loss. Milly, in fact, apprises him of one reason to "remember wrong that has been done us": it is that "we may forgive it" (3). Hence, far from being a dead hand that dries up the springs of life, the contents of memory are here shown by Dickens to be essential to the fully human experience of life. In a letter of 1860, Dickens expressed his mature attitude toward painful memories:

> But we must not think of old times as sad times, or regard them as anything but the fathers and mothers of the present. We must all climb steadily up the mountain after the talking bird, the singing tree, and the yellow water, and must all bear in mind that the previous climbers who were scared into looking back got turned into black stone.[15]

In every novel following the *Christmas Books,* Dickens continued to wrestle with the question of how one should act toward the painful past. The further development of his dialectic of the past is shown in *David Copperfield.* There Dickens has managed to show the reality of the pain and evil in the past, even while he has David ultimately accepting and limiting it: "What I reaped, I had sown" (59). David's great victory over the past is to accept his past decisions and to permit Dora to remain the Dora that he married. David comes to understand that human beings are wholes and that changing a part changes the whole; since positive and negative are interrelated, to obliterate the negative would be to obliterate the positive. This is the same lesson that Redlaw learns about the past. Murdstone never understands this lesson. Consequently, he continues to "improve" the character of others—as is recorded by Dr. Chillip, when he tells David that Murdstone and his sister are presently breaking down a new wife, just as they had broken and killed David's mother. Dickens had not yet learned to intertwine plots and themes as well as he would later do. Therefore, David cannot act to intervene—for any action on behalf of Murdstone's new wife, whom he does not know, would appear to the reader to be revenge, or a stroke of the dead hand. Hence, Dickens had to resort to a form of poetic justice for the Murdstones, who are "very much unliked" and who "undergo a continual punishment, for they are turned inward, to feed upon their own hearts" (59).

So long as the only precedent carried forward is the precedent of caring, the painful past deserves to live as memory. Otherwise, let "any unpleasant bygones," as Meagles in *Little Dorrit* says, be "bygones" (2, 33). "One always begins to forgive a place a soon as it's left behind," says Meagles, who, whatever his faults, carries no craving for revenge. The haunted man learns that you cannot dispose of the pain of the past without also disposing of its lifegiving force. As the *Christmas Books* shows—and as many characters created in the middle of Dickens's career testify—the past is given to us in order that we may make human beings—not brutes—of ourselves. The past permits us to act and to feel. Even those "swaggering fighting men" (ED, 6) of the past can have a use for the present: "Perhaps one of the highest uses of their ever having been there was that there might be left behind them that blessed air of tranquility . . . productive for the most part of pity and forbearance—which is engendered by a sorrowful story that is all told, or a pathetic play that is played out" (ED, 6). The abuse of the past is precisely to create out of it reasons not to feel or act. But for Dickens there are irrefutable facts of human nature that can turn the past—however painful—into supports for the human spirit. Many of Dickens's most noticeable fictional techniques were meant to convey these transformations to the reader.

To keep the past safe for humane uses, Dickens employed his second strategy—which was to create a fictional world that disenfranchised the executive offices of the dead hand. In plot, character, thought, diction, tone, and ambience, Dickens's fiction generates a world in which the logic of necessitarianism is completely short-circuited. A major technique in the creation of this world is the theme of the "mystery" of the individual.

Despite the success that science has enjoyed in predicting the material world, it is impotent before the human spirit. Dickens intuited the distinction that Gabriel Marcel has made between a "problem" and a "mystery."[16] Science is competent to objectify and to solve problems, but once the human factor enters the equation, a "mystery" results: before this "mystery," objective science is self-proscribed. Dickens created in his characters a recognition of (and he finally names this theme) the "mystery" of the individual. For Dickens, there is in the human spirit a quality that need not bend under the force of temporal circumstances. This belief in the "mystery" of human nature is expressed both thematically and through action. Esther puts it this way in *Bleak House:* "I had for a moment an undefinable impression of myself as being something different from what I then was" (31). Without seeking for occult analogues (however numerous and however well exploited by animal magnetism, which Dickens knew well), one might see that Esther has the sense of being no longer subject to the order of time. In her, there is a mysterious "something different from what" she *then* was; she senses that her existence cannot be confined by the narrow limits of linear time. She is always more than an aggregate of effects. She keeps faith with her possibilities: she senses that she is beyond mere material or mechanical causality—that her spirit is of her own making and not the product of "circumstances." As Cassirer has put it, she is free of the fallacy of simple location.[17]

The behavior of many characters in Dickens's works demonstrates the presence of this human mystery. Even Alderman Cute—upon hearing of the suicide of the banker Deedles, who lived in princely circumstances—cannot help but blurt out, "Oh the nerves, the nerves; the mysteries of this machine called Man!" (TC, 3). This allusion to J. O. de LaMettrie's book *Man the Machine* is comically confounded by the antimechanistic notion of man the mystery. Another example of the human mystery is the conversion of Wrayburn—a feature that leaves some readers of *Our Mutual Friend* cold. But Wrayburn's problematic conversion must be seen in the light of Dickens's effort to stress this mysterious, unknowable quality of the individual. All conversions insist on this mystery. We must not forget that Dickens made a point of showing that Wrayburn's behavior toward Lizzie was incomprehensible not only to Headstone but also to Lizzie, Lightwood, Jenny, and to Wrayburn himself. Wrayburn defines his own character accordingly: he is "an embodied conundrum" (2, 6). Wrayburn's antidefinition of his nature could serve as a motto for Dickens's conviction that human nature is not reducible to its nest of conditions, or circumstances.

There are other explicit references in Dickens's novels to the mystery of the human being. While calculations can easily be made of a mill's steampower, its hands elude such calculations: "there is an unfathomable mystery in the meanest of them, for ever" (HT, 1, 11). Thomas Gradgrind is a prime example of one who would make the human mystery a mere problem—and, what is more, a problem to be solved by the felicific calculus of Benthamism. Because Gradgrind thinks that human beings are simple creatures to understand, he cannot see Louisa's unhappiness nor her spiritual deprivation—for "to see it, he must have overleaped at a bound the artificial barriers he had for many years been erecting, between himself and all those subtle essences of humanity which will elude the utmost cunning of algebra until the last trumpet ever to be sounded shall blow even algebra to wreck" (1, 15). Those "subtle essences" escaped Benthamite algebra and defied mechanistic reductions. Gradgrind complains that "it would appear from this unexpected circumstance of today, though in itself a trifling one, as if something had crept into Thomas's and Louisa's minds which is—or rather, which is not— I don't know that I can express myself better than by saying— which has never been intended to be developed and in which their reason has no part" (1, 4). Gradgrind's verbal difficulties are symptomatic of his incapacity to understand the real relation between the human being and time. Furthermore, Dickens has provided him with precise terminology: Dickens's worldview is comprised of unexpected circumstances that are quite appropriate to the "subtle essences of humanity." Gradgrind did not intend it—does not expect it; but something is there—something beyond the quantitative input that one can measure. That is, his children possess something that was not added to them (as if their minds were empty bottles) by his educational program. Michael Goldberg[18] was right to stress that Mrs. Gradgrind, speaking to her children, begins to suspect that "there is something—not an ology at all—that your father has missed" (2, 9). Mr. Gradgrind himself is ultimately "possessed by an idea" that in Sissy Jupe there is something that, in his words, "could hardly be set forth in tabular form" (1, 14). That "something" is prior to mechanical time, material influences, and ideological indoctrination—and, thus, it is beyond the dead hand.

In *A Tale of Two Cities*, Dickens was as specific as he could be: "A wonderful fact to reflect upon, that every human creature is constituted to be that profound secret and mystery to every other." Dickens continued: "every beating heart in the hundreds of thousands of breasts there is, in some of its imaginings, a secret to the heart nearest it! Something of the awfulness, even of Death itself, is referable to this" (TTC, 1, 3). It is possible to read this fact of human mystery as a melancholy fact—as a proof of alienation and, thus, as evidence of Dickens's dark period, but it needs, to be read by the rules of notice that I have been developing—to be read, that is, in the context of Dickens's response to the threats of mechanistic causality and of Benthamite or Manchester reductionism. Read in this context, the mystery is a "natural and not to be aliented inheritance" (1, 3) that makes the messenger equal to the king. No Gradgrindian edification by deprivation, no past suffering, and no material circumstances can make a human being predictable.

For readers who have no doubts about the existence of free will, this whole discussion will seem superfluous. But modern readers must keep in mind, so far as possible, the context in which Dickens's writing had its polemical purpose. In the Victorian era, the weight of evidence seemed to be swinging decidedly to the side of the dead hand.

The delicate problem that Dickens had was to create strategies that would render temporal succession problematic without at the same time seeming to foster a distortion and devaluation of the past that would sacrifice its gifts. He could not overtly "bend the past out of its eternal shape"; and yet, he had to create a climate in his fiction in which the past—as represented in its empirical and rationalistic forms—would not deprive the human spirit of its freedom.

Some few of Dickens's characters are quite conscious of the freedom of others. Mr. Boffin learns from his own human experience that it is, in fact, silly to attempt to bind others to his will. He refuses his lawyer's advice to bind Mrs. Boffin in his own will: "It would be handsome in me to begin to bind Mrs. Boffin at this time of day!" (OMF, 1, 8). His refusal carries an important implication. He has simply said no to the chains that Harmon's fortune and bequest originally created. In this way, Mr. Boffin has severed antecedent and subsequent. By contrast, in *Little Dorrit*, Mrs. Gowan argues that it is futile "for people to get on together who have such extremely different antecedents; who are jumbled together in this accidental, matrimonial sort of way; and who cannot look at the untoward circumstance which has shaken them together in the same light. It never does" (2, 8). It does not dawn on her that such antecedents as she has given her son could free him from the mythic antecedents that she relies on. With Little Dorrit, Dickens showed that antecedents can be disengaged—that it is possible to come after the antecedent and unbind the subsequent. The Boffins, in effect, do this with Old Harmon's will. The opportunity to sever the consequent from antecedent is, in fact, one of the gifts of the past. Esther (BH), Darnay (TTC), Lizzie (OMF), and many other characters avail themselves of the opportunity.

Through his strategies in theme, plot, and characterization, Dickens attempted to dispel the popular tenets of human determinism. He denied the inviolability—the discreteness—of the past, upon which determinism so largely depends. He showed that the human present is not merely stamped out by the past. This is the truth, partly, of the mystery of the human heart. For past events—such as those that cause suffering—may stengthen rather than efface the freedom of the will. As memory, the past's influence is not irreversible—it is commutative. To the operations of the imagination, the pattern of events is not inviolable. The colligation by the individual imagination of the contents of time is not the same as chronological succession—and is not subject to the order of mechanical time.[19] Mind operates on events; and because of this, the human being is able to live in all times at once, as Scrooge proposed to do.

Fiction works by more means than the conscious parry and thrust of exemplum and assertion. When we as readers call up "poetic faith," a worldview, which works on the subconscious, is enjoined on us. Persuaded, for the occasion, by this worldview, readers may find themselves enabled to accept several more of Dickens's techniques—all of which have the tendency to render the supposed chain of cause and effect null and void. One such technique is found in the gradual growth of poetic justice in his plots.

Poetic justice can be defined as the plot eventuality that both is and is not the proposed effect of a character's intention, much in the way that Paul Goodman has described the apparent and the hidden plot lines in tragedy.[20] Poetic justice is usually constituted by a bifurcation of willful antecedent into conscious and cosmic consequences—and it serves to weaken credence in man's control and understanding of causality. Poetic justice—an eruption of cosmic irony in the plot—occurs when characters get what they want and it turns out to be what they deserve, as villains are hoist by their own petards. The major example in English literature is, no doubt, Milton's Satan, who is punished by getting precisely what he, in his alienated intelligence, thought he most desired—an escape from God's presence. His punishment is to have his desire fulfilled. In *A Tale of Two Cities,* Dickens showed Monseigneur regretting the loss of ancient prerogatives, including "the right of life and death" (2, 9) over others. But, ironically, the revolution does not do away with this prerogative but merely alters the possessor. Thus, what Monseigneur sows in France is identical with what he reaps: the Defarges are merely the reverse of the same coin, the back of Monseigneur's own dead hand.

There has always been an element of poetic justice in Dickens, as there is in any author with a degree of irony to his writing. For example, in *The Old Curiosity Shop* no one can save Quilp from drowning because he has, literally, locked everyone out of his life. His closing the gates on that fatal night is in itself merely a symbolic gesture representing the social exclusion he had maintained all his life. Despite such early examples as the fates of Quilp (OCS) and Anthony Chuzzlewit (MC), I believe it is fair to say that in Dickens's final books there is a determined emphasis on poetic justice.

In *Hard Times,* Gradgrind produces precisely what he desires. By rearing his children with unfeeling carefulness, he garners careful unfeelingness. He sows only facts in the minds of his children—but is appalled when facts but no values are produced. In *Little Dorrit,* Rigaud seeks his fortune by felling the House of Clennam—so that, as a gentleman, he need never lift a hand again. When he is caught in the literal fall of the house, he achieves his goal of never lifting his hand again. In *Great Expectations,* Miss Havisham reaps a loveless relationship with Estella, whom she had nurtured to be unloving. Pip ultimately garners Estella—who had symbolized all that was desirable to him in the world—only when she symbolizes nothing but the vanity of his desires. In *Our Mutual Friend* Bella marries the poor John Rokesmith and deservedly garners the rich John Harmon. Gaffer Hexam dies in a river whose drowning victims had given him a livelihood. Rogue Riderhood refuses to leave Bradley Headstone alone, even after the latter's decision to die. So, they die together. Sophronia Akersham and Alfred Lammle are the most obvious examples of poetic justice because they bring nothing to their marriage and get nothing from it. In all of these cases, the results do not reflect a causal, developmental structure but rather poetic justice—the non-serial, self-reflexive structure of events. Poetic justice can be considered the backlash of time when its mysterious nature is taken for granted.

If there is some validity in this argument of an increased incidence and importance of poetic justice in Dickens's later works, it would coincide with the suggestion of atemporality that I noted earlier. When the effect is identical with the cause, there is no sequence and no discernible movement of time; and when the effect shows a mirror reflection of the intention—therefore, disappointing desire—irony rules and determinism is undone. Hence, in poetic justice, there are no determinative antecedents, properly speaking; the past has not passed, it is simply a temporal particular with the same priority as the present. The present is a recurrence or exploitation of, not a derivation from, the past. Poetic justice rebuffs the momentum of mechanical and logical necessity.

The so-called expressive symbol is another technique that Dickens employed to make the past lose its "pastness"—and, thus, its capacity to determine the present. In the representation of the phenomenon of the expressive symbol, Dickens showed how the past is made useful to the spirit in the present through the agency of an unlikely combination of matter and the imagination. The theory of imagination was always central both to Dickens's thought and to his fiction. The term *expressive symbol* comes from one of Dickens's major influences, William Hazlitt, who, writing of the sound of a bell, observed that "a thousand real feelings and incidents hung upon those impressions." Then, Hazlitt asks, "And should we not preserve and cherish this precious link that connects together the finer essence of our past and future being by some expressive symbol?"[21]

Expressive symbols are not created by arbitrary fiat; they are naturally created when a person's interest fixes upon some aspect of the external world. Wordsworth in *Prelude,* Book First, called a similar phenomenon the "presences of Nature"; but for Dickens the "presence"—or the hauntings—derives from human rather than external nature. What happens is that a material object, even a sound—contiguous or contemporaneous with an intense human experience—somehow absorbs some of the excess affectivity of the experience. Whenever an individual finds the object within his or her perception again, it radiates—sometimes quite unexpectedly—the retained affects of that experience. The Romantic upshot of the phenomenon—whether in Hazlitt, Wordsworth, or

Dickens—is that the individual is moved anew by the past experience. The "finer essence" is precisely the capacity to be moved—and to this capacity the expressive symbol appeals again. The phenomenon, therefore, connects man's spirit to the material world—as well as past to present. Since I have explored the workings of the expressive symbol in some detail elsewhere,[22] let me give here only a few examples before summing up how the phenomenon fits into Dickens's strategy against the abuse of the past.

Fittingly, it is in *Bleak House*—a highly conscious exploration of the material and the static upon the minds of the living—that Dickens has most frequently recorded instances of objects becoming expressive symbols. Although instances of the technique can be found earlier, it is as if in *Bleak House* Dickens felt an urgency to exploit the phenomenon. Esther is one of the many sensitives in Dickens's works who can read the future in the fire—for she possesses fancy, the colligatory faculty of the mind that knits together images without reference to their temporal priorities. Hence, the fancy is, by its nature, immune to necessity or other laws of time. The fancy fleshes itself out from the past or the future with equal facility. Those who have fancy, like Esther, are not confined to the present.

When Esther's fancy imagines a lurid sky over London to be "engendered of an unearthly fire," an expressive symbol is developing.

> But I have always remembered since that when we had stopped at the garden-gate to look up at the sky . . . I had for a moment an undefinable impression of myself as being something different from what I then was. I know it was then, and there, that I had it. I have ever since connected the feeling with that spot and time and with everything associated with that spot and time, to the distant voices in town, the barking of a dog, and the sound of wheels coming down the miry hill. (31)

Her "spot and time" resembles Wordsworth's "spots of time" (*Prelude*, Book Twelfth) both aurally and conceptually. Fancy has given Esther access to impressions, however "undefinable," not ordinarily perceived—that is, the fancy has loosened the hold of chronology: the mind is able to flit backward and forward in time. The falsehood of mechanical causality—the idea that man is propelled along an irreversible course of events—stands exposed by this experience. One is not locked into a single dimension of time. What is also evident is that the spirit modifies matter.

Water, like fire, frequently has a mesmeric, sleepwaking effect on the fancy. Dickens's sensitive characters often become clairvoyant. When Esther is with Bucket in search of Lady Dedlock, she records the following: "The river had a fearful look, so overcast and secret, creeping away so fast between the low flat lines of shore—so heavy with indistinct and awful shapes, both of substance and shadow; so death-like and mysterious. I have seen it many times since then, by sunlight and by moonlight, but never free from the impressions of that journey" (57). Thus, the natural world is influenced by the mind—and forever bears the aspect that the mind gives it.

Viewed properly, the expressive symbol is not an instance of the past dominating the present. Nor is it a mere association of ideas. Unlike associative psychology, the mind here is not a passive recipient of impressions linked by contiguity. Rather, Esther's mind is each time excited to a high degree: it is this subjective quality of passion that selects and inspires an object. Random objects serve as vehicles for the spirit, and the accidental mode of their selection negates any idea of material determination.

To believers in the unseen powers of animal magnetism, an object such as a pond could be so charged with magnetic power by Anton Mesmer or the Marquis de Puysegur that individuals ignorant of the original "passes," in which the mesmerist infuses the water with "magnetic" energy, would nevertheless receive a physical shock when they touched it. Dickens did not carry the analogy of the expressive symbol quite that far; yet, we may surmise that he meant the aesthetic effect of his novels to be analogous—that is, he intended that the reader should find some spiritual influence in objects similar to those that Esther inadvertantly invested with spirit. Peter Ackroyd responded to this element in Dickens when he commented on Dickens's taking James and Annie Field on a walk along the Thames: "Yet how strange a picture this is, Dickens pointing out these dwellings as if his characters had been real. As if his novels were now part of the bricks and stones of London."[23] For many readers, moved by Dickens's fiction, the bricks and stones of London may well bear the spirit of Dickens's characters forever.

Expressive symbols conform to this dictum of Carlyle's: "What changes are wrought, not by Time, yet in Time! For not Mankind only, but all that Mankind does or beholds, is in continual growth, regenesis, and self-perfecting vitality."[24] Not by "Time," not by mechanistic causality, but in "Time." The expressive symbol defeats this causality, for to revisit a scene charged with affect is to leap over intervals and to receive a contingent gift of the spirit.

That which funds the belief in mechanical succession—the idea that the perception of one unique event inevitably brings about another, like a linked chain—is everywhere blurred in Dickens's works. By severing—or, perhaps, better said, by looping—so as to disengage the consequent from antecedent in these several ways, Dickens created in his fiction a sense of timelessness. This sense of timelessness is wonderfully represented in the voice of Mrs. Tickit, whose very name suggests a clock:

> As I was saying, I was thinking of one thing and thinking of another, and thinking very much of the family. Not of the family in the present times only, but in the past times too. For when a person does begin thinking of one thing and thinking of another in that manner, as it's getting dark, what I say is, that all times seem to be present, and a person must get out of that state and consider before they can say which is which. (LD, 2, 9)

Her very sentences seem to lose traction, as they begin to eddy or loop; and time ceases to make progress. In "Mrs. Lirriper's Lodgings," one of the *Christmas Stories* (1863), Mrs. Lirriper's sentences also swirl and loop. But in answer to Mrs. Lirriper's sentiment that "life is made of partings" (CS, p. 393), an orphan tells a story—beginning with "Once upon a time, when Pigs drank wine"—that ends with a facetious denial of death, "Nobody ever died" (401). Besides instilling a tranquility born of a past sorrow, stories whose characters remain alive within the memories of readers do defeat time.

Our Mutual Friend contains the ultimate projection of timelessness (although there is evidence that *Edwin Drood* would have depended no less on the effect). In *Our Mutual Friend,* time circles and eddies, actions pile up vertically rather than horizontally, and caesuras punctuate all lines of expected succession. In some scenes, there is an absolute reversal of conventional temporal ordering. For example, Jenny Wren equates life itself with death. For Jenny, to be high above the streets is to have "such a strange good sorrowful happiness" (2, 5) come upon you. Such oxymorons blunt the sense that only one result is to be expected from an action. Jenny pities Riah insofar as he has to be "called back to life" (2, 5). Dickens's dialectic now reverses the significance of the phrase so prominent in *A Tale of Two Cities*. Into such a life above time as Jenny proposes—into this third dimension—the two-dimensional framework of antecedent and consequent cannot reach.

Jenny again reverses the normal order of events when she calls her father the "bad old boy!" (2, 2). More is implied here than Dickens's usual theme of prodigal parents. "If my poor boy," she says, "had been better brought up, he might have done better." She scolded, reasoned, and coaxed; but, she says, "I was obliged to let him go into the streets. And he never did well in the streets" (4, 9). The streets are the channels of time. This curious parody of Wordsworth's "the child is father of the man" reverses succession; it seems to imply that antecedent and consequent are interchangeable. Therefore, Jenny's duty to her father, like Lizzie's duty to her own father, is primarily to try to obliterate the antecedent—to efface all the harmful precedents of which the parent is the guilty cause. This reversal of chronological authority makes the individual responsible for his own antecedents. Moreover, it implies that much human experience is atemporal.

Even old Betty Higden takes "the upward course of the river Thames" in her flight from the expected commitment to the Poor House, thus tacitly reversing chronology (in its representation by the river) by going to "the young river, dimpled like a child . . . unpolluted by the defilements that lie in wait for it on its course" (3, 8). To represent time, Dickens had for a long while consciously employed the universal image of the river. This explicit revision reveals how integrated were his strategies for creating a sense of timelessness in *Our Mutual Friend*.

When Jenny asks Riah, "Is it better to have had a good thing and lost it, or never to have had it?" Riah answers that, at least in the former case, "the happiness was." Jenny's shrill retort reflects her own misery: "You had better change Is into Was and Was into Is, and keep them so" (3, 2). But Riah convinces her otherwise. Not only will "Was" bring into the present greater physical pain for Jenny, but "Is" in some sense contains the "Was" in a way that "Was" can never contain "Is." Determinism implies that the past delimits the scope of the present: Riah's notion, like the other indications of atemporality, suggests just the opposite—namely, that the present is quite able to turn upon and limit the past. Jenny's proposal to change "Is" into "Was" would appear to reverse the flow of time; but, in fact, such a change would merely bring about stasis and—by stopping experience in "Was"—succeed in ossifying the heart. By refusing to let "Was"—the past—swamp time, Riah's measure keeps the heart actively engaged in liberating the past. Giving the present priority, as Riah proposes, defeats the sclerosis entailed in Jenny's desire.

Over and over in *Our Mutual Friend*, the usual flow of causality is reversed. Immediately after inheriting Old Harmon's fortune, the Boffins go to work to amend the past. First, they adopt and name Johnny after the lost boy who should have inherited the fortune; and then, after Johnny's death—unbinding the curse on that name—they take in Sloppy and keep his unrespectable name. Similarly, John Harmon, the lost boy, refuses to accept the consequences of past determinations—and refuses to come alive in order to inherit an enslaving fortune and to take a wife "as a Sultan buys a slave" (2, 13). Representing himself to the world as John Rokesmith, Harmon exists in a kind of timeless realm from which he can test the world. Because the river symbolizes time—and because Riderhood, Wrayburn, and Harmon were saved from it—they all have the opportunity to deny the force of the past and to change the direction of their lives. That Wrayburn and Harmon are able to change proves the existence of spirits capable of freeing themselves from the personal past. Bella and Venus join Wrayburn and Harmon in defying the momentum that their antecedents had given them—thus creating, in *Our Mutual Friend*, multiple examples of how the past is determined by the present.

By reducing all time to one "duration," Dickens had—after long experimentation and a lengthy dialectical exercise—found a solution to his personal question of what one does with a past that carries both pain and humiliation. If we allow it, the past goes on being lived, not as an exterior antecedent forcing present actions upon us—and certainly not as an exterior precedent—but interiorly as a present opportunity. This is the essence of the benefits presented by the past to the human being. The past provides the opportunity for subjective and objective action—that is, for action in accepting, forgiving, and redressing the past.

A Tale of Two Cities contains an important example of the faultiness of keeping the past exterior and discrete. Murray Baumgarten has argued that Dr. Manette "does not imprison the events of history" and, thus, releases himself from the "traumatic past."[25] But there is reason to believe that the doctor did not, in fact, face the past—did not actively internalize and forgive it. Because Dr. Manette keeps his "old pain" external and discrete, he fails to find in it "a power that has brought us through the barrier" (TTC, 3, 2). He cannot save Darnay from execution—as he attempted to—because one cannot wield one's suffering as power in the world; otherwise, it would be possible to use the past without forgiving it or embracing it. For Dickens, the past had to be internalized and made a part of a person in order to soften and heal. The painful past, internalized, augments the spirit living the present.

Absorbed into the horizon of human freedom, the past no longer manifests itself as one of the many forms of the dead hand—but as pure choice. Far from being tied to the past, then, the individual must constantly renew it as an opportunity to continue caring for—or in—the present. The forgiving is never finished. This opportunity to care that the past provides may be its greatest boon for the present. Here, the dialectic begun by Dickens's pain over his own past reaches its quietus.

To continue caring is what Scrooge implies when he utters his promise to "live in the Past, the Present, and the Future" (4). The differentiations of time have lost their mere seriality. The past, present, and future are realigned by the spirit along a simple ethical axis: they become either sclerotic forms or true opportunity. This is the notion behind Lizzie Hexam's refusal to "let bygones be bygones." She is dedicated to repealing Riderhood's smear of her father's name. For her, the past offers the opportunity to "make some amends" (OMF, 2, 1). Whether or not the past turns out to be opportunity depends upon the mystery of the individual. But in any case, mere circumstances have lost their potency. Magwitch's refusal to "bend the past"—his acceptance of all of his antecedents—frees Magwitch, even in death. The past leaves him unscathed and unhardened. The lesson is not lost on Pip. He is able to ignore Pumblechook's final efforts to replace the dead hand of false gratitude upon him by making him accept a gift of bread and butter—his version, apparently, of humble pie. But what is more important, when Pip learns that Estella's parents are a murderess and a convicted thief, he finds that he can accept Estella—as well as all of his own past errors of meanness, vanity, and snobbery that she has witnessed.

Dickens—by continually readdressing the issue of his own, and the national, past—came to the vision and conveyed it in his fiction that the past had powerful spiritual uses. The past gives the human being an opportunity to act and to respond. For memories of every kind have the power to stir or move an individual. To be moved is an act of the spirit—and action is essential to vitality. Therefore, this power must be cherished. Another opportunity offered by the past is the paradoxical chance to move against its own momentum. For Dickens, the past was subject to forthright action in the present. Although he often despaired of it, Dickens was vociferous about government intervention for the improvement of the living and working conditions that were breeding so much evil in England: "Sanitary improvements are the one thing needful to begin with; and until they are thoroughly, efficiently, and uncompromisingly made ... even education itself will fall short of its uses."[26] Despite the impulse toward evil that these conditions created, Dickens believed that present action could intervene between cause and dire effect. Forster has reported Dickens's advice about priorities in the Ragged Schools that he visited: "I [told her], too, that it was of immense importance that they should be *washed.*"[27] When Mr. Dick advises Betsey Trotwood on what to do with her runaway nephew—namely, "wash him" (DC, 13)—he could well be serving as a model for public action on problems that have a long history. One action can undo much neglect, in the person and in the nation.

In *Little Dorrit,* except for the fact that Meagles is a little impressed by the Barnacles, he usually takes a healthy attitude toward the past, especially its painful contents. For example, when one of his twin girls dies, he finds and cares for an orphan, whom he calls Tattycoram (even though the caring may not have been on quite the same—perhaps excessive—level as that for his remaining daughter, Pet). He makes of his suffering an opportunity to act. After Tattycoram runs away and returns, Meagles enunciates another important way in which the power of the past can be nullified: "Duty, Tattycoram. Begin it early, and do it well; and there is no antecedent to it, in any origin or station, that will tell against us with the Almighty, or with ourselves" (LD, 2, 33)—that is, antecedents may be divorced and negated by current action. Even though, as I have pointed out, Dickens had by the time of *Dombey and Son* begun to question this Victorian absolute called duty, the phrasing of Meagles's idea is important: certain kinds of action admit of no precedent, no influence, no circumstance—and, therefore, are always free in the present, safe from any dead hand.

All of these actions tend to sever the line of chronological succession. If critics want a justification, for instance, for the salvation of Wrayburn, it is surely to be found in the principles that enable him to talk Lizzie into accepting his offer of a tutor. He argues that her reluctance to accept the offer would do an injustice to her father. Referring to Lizzie's father, Wrayburn says to Lizzie that her reluctance would keep the dead hand alive by "perpetuating the consequence of his ignorant and blind obstinacy. By resolving not to set right the wrong he did you. By determining that the deprivation to which he condemned you and which he forced upon you shall always rest upon his head" (OMF, 2, 2). Although we cannot alter the past, we can, argues Wrayburn, dissolve the consequences of it by taking action in the present. Wrayburn's notion—exactly the opposite of Miss Wade's desire to alienate agent and event(LD)—is that past events are subject to amelioration by present human action. Similarly, John Harmon's determination that "no ghost should trouble Mr. and Mrs. Boffin's peace" (2, 14) is a present action that lops the evil consequences from Old Harmon's will.

For Dickens, human action altering personal and social history was always possible. Two instances of such human actions are (1) conversions, such as Scrooge's, which derails the train of events, and (2) acts of forgiveness, as expressed by Mrs. Bagnet (BH) in the words "forget and forgive" that Amy Dorrit (LD) must have overheard. Such action places primacy in the present. Therefore, it is possible to reverse the tradition of carelessness that is indigenous to the notions that deify the past as sole creator and arbiter of the present world. In many ways—in character, in theme, and in plot—Dickens revealed that the human experience of time is not that of recording a simple, serial accretion of events. Ever unfinished, the past is an opportunity to care and to act. The past of the human heart is commutable.

The ultimate benefit of the past, however, resides in its very fact: it is the past. The opportunity to withdraw from a present situation is the most basic opportunity offered by the past. For example, Jenny Wren finds joy in the simple escape from the present. Insofar as it escapes determination, being high above the streets is to "come out of [the] grave" (OMF, 2, 5). The past can emancipate us from the present. As a means of evading the determinations of the immediate, memory of the past is similar to creation by the imagination. The ultimate gift of the past, then, is in its very fact. It constitutes difference itself—without which there is no choice and no freedom. Its existence denies that the immediate is all—and, thus, it provides a human resource: an escape from—and a repudiation of—the power of the present. Just as the present can be used to ameliorate the past, so, likewise, can the past be used to ameliorate present circumstances. By being kept discrete—but not external—by being both different and within the same continuum, the dimensions of time can interact to create the moral economy of the world.

Part Three
Conclusion

7
Transcending Time: "Out of the Ruined Place"

> Was there . . .
> No feat which done, would make time break
> And let us pent-up creatures through
> Into eternity, our due?
> —Browning, "Dis Aliter Visum"

It is obvious to me that for Dickens the ideal relationship of the individual to the past or to the future is one of caring, not fixation. The three dimensions of time must—quite like human beings—be given their due independence; yet, like human beings, the dimensions of time gain their integrity only as parts of a continuum. Each has its own value—its own particular gift for life—yet its value depends upon its participation in the whole. To secure that value, the individual must internalize the dimensions of time—making them intermingle in his experience of them. By analogy, then, one can easily argue that for Dickens the contributions of past, present, and future should be, "From each according to his abilities, to each according to his needs"—to gain surplus value from the well-known dictum of Marx.

I have tried to show how important it was to Dickens to transcend each dimension of time. The way to transcend any dimension is by a movement of the spirit toward another dimension—or toward the totality of time. This movement, however, never flees time but resolutely embraces it—affirming its integrity and the human being's responsibility for its contents; that is, one transcends time only by acting in the world in such a way that no dimension of time withers in—and none petrifies—the human heart.

This spiritual movement is supported by the undisclosed assumptions about material reality that lie behind Dickens's world. The spatial imagery in his fiction suggests the transcendence of worldly time. At the end of *Great Expectations,* Pip relates that he and Estella "went out of the ruined place" where Satis House had stood. Most of the worlds of Dickens's novels have been ruined—and, often, ruined by the abuse of one of the dimensions of time. The title originally intended for *Bleak House* was *Tom-All-Alone's: The Ruined House.* As his letters show, Dickens often referred to the Houses of Parliament as the "national dustheap"—a step beyond mere ruins. But in the nature of the world that Dickens envisioned, it was possible to leave the ruins—the evil—and to move on by abandoning the temporal fixations that caused it. I want to conclude this study of Dickens by glancing at his ideas about the physical nature of the world—ideas that make possible the metaphors of movement that bulk so large in his fiction.

From the very outset of his career, Dickens was determined to make his contemporaries aware of the interpenetration of the dimensions of time. On 14 July 1839, he wrote Forster the following:

> Thus the Chapters of Chambers which I have long thought and spoken of, might be very well incorporated with it; and a series of papers has occurred to me containing stories and descriptions of London as it was many years ago, as it is now, and as it will be many years hence, to which I would give some such title as The Relaxations of Gog and Magog dividing them into portions like the Arabian Nights . . . .[1]

Even so early in his career, Dickens planned to prompt his readers to look backward and forward in time. Dickens's lifelong fascination with the *Arabian Nights* no doubt derived in part from its theme of the infinite extendability of the present and the denial of mortal necessity. Even his advice to Charles Knight about an article for *Household Words* bespeaks his consciousness of art's capacity to keep "always a living present before the mind's eye." He argued that it is possible for a writer to see that no phase of a character's "existence passes away, if I choose to bring it to his unsubstantial and delightful life. The only death of which to me, is my death, and thus he is immortal to unnumbered thousands."[2] In art, what was always is; this fluent integration of temporal dimensions experienced in art may serve as a model for experience in life.

Such integration requires that one not be locked in or locked out of any dimension of time: "I have converted Mr. Scrooge by teaching him that a Christian heart cannot be shut up in itself, but must live in the Past, the Present, and the Future, and must be a link of this great human chain, and must have sympathy with everything."[3] The phrase "a link in this great human chain" is scarcely a metaphor; it implies a vision of the universe that underlies and supports the world of Dickens's fiction.

The universe is so constituted that nothing exists that is not related to every other existent by either impulse, gravity, magnetism, participation, organization, effect, or history. The conservation of momentum, matter, and energy are presuppositions of this theory. It is toward this idea of an interlinked universe that Dickens has drawn us in *Bleak House*: "What connexion can there have been between many people in the innumerable histories of this world, who, from opposite sides of great gulfs, have, nevertheless, been very curiously brought together!" (16). In *Little Dorrit*, Dickens worked out in detail his fascination with the idea. Even in *A Tale of Two Cities,* the idea emerges when "Lucie sat in the still house in the tranquilly resounding corner, listening to the echoing footsteps of the years" (2, 21). In discovering the double connection between Estella and himself(GE), Pip discovers that the connection between the links of the human chain may be manifold—and not simple and obvious. Coincidence is, therefore, not imposed but is merely one of the natural connections abruptly exposed.[4]

Dickens's plotting (like the expressive symbol) finds rationalization in the physics of mechanical motion—and in its corollaries of the conservation of momentum and matter. "No motion that is impressed by natural or human agency, is ever obliterated," wrote Charles Babbage.[5] Dickens has appropriated the idea, for it is perfect for his moral universe:

> It was suggested by Mr. Babbage, in his *Ninth Bridgewater Treatise* that a mere spoken word—a mere syllable thrown into the air—may go on reverberating through illimitable space for ever and for ever . . . that human calculation cannot limit the influence of one atom of wholesome knowledge patiently acquired, modestly possessed, and faithfully used.[6]

Thus, the good that an individual does or speaks endures; that is, in all physical acts—in both words and deeds—the future and the present and the past coexist.

To produce an act of goodness is to constitute reality in the present and the future; and the effect links (and so modifies) all actions of the past. By contrast, to suppose that only the present has reality is, in the light of this notion, to deny the facts demonstrated by physics. Babbage has written on the subject with powerful effect:

> Thus considered, what a strange chaos is this wide atmosphere we breathe! Every atom, impressed with good or ill, retains at once the motions which philosophers and sages have imparted to it, mixed and combined in ten thousand ways with all that is worthless and base. The air itself is one vast library, on whose pages are forever written all that man ever said or woman ever whispered.[7]

By retaining an impression, matter gives actions permanence. Babbage has caused this notion—which amounts to materialistic omniscience and reminds one of stories by Borges—to take a strange turn later by suggesting that perhaps punishment after death consists simply of having to make contact with the atoms carrying one's inhumane words and actions from life.

Many poets have expressed the idea that the words or actions of "good" men are as eternal as matter itself. Babbage has merely given a scientific cachet to Shelley's testimony in "Adonais": "And many more, whose names on Earth are dark / But whose transmitted effluence cannot die/ So long as fire outlives the parent spark."[8] In fact, this notion of the perpetual act is so commonplace in the mid-Victorian era that it was given almost comic employment in an advertisement for a laxative called Eno's Fruit Salts in which "Riches, Titles, Honour, Power and Worldly Prospects" were promised as the rewards of regular bowel movement induced by Eno's—for, as the advertisement's absurd aphorism put it, "A Great Act does not Perish with the Life of him who performs it."[9] Although its use in an advertisement for a laxative may astonish, the phrase and concept could well serve as propaganda for the spirit of the Victorian Era. Certainly, it implied a harmony between material reality and human will. With almost as much assurance as Eno's copywriter had of being understood by his contemporaries, Carlyle could say (in "Characteristics") that the "true Past departs not, nothing that was worthy in the Past departs; no Truth or Goodness realized by man ever dies, or can die." Human goodness is in harmony with the ground of the universe.

Babbage's notion of atoms preserving human actions can account for Dickens's ingenuous commentaries that time necessarily exposes criminal actions. In *Martin Chuzzlewit,* for example, Dickens has spoken of "the truth, which nothing would keep down, which blood would not smother and earth would not hide" (51).

He has even used the problematic Nadgett as one of the "phantom forms of this terrific Truth!" (51). Nadgett's investigations presume that all human intentions have taken material forms—and, thus, imply the version of Babbage's universe. Bucket (BH), as his name implies, must go deep into the well of human experience and its physical residue to come up with the truth; since nothing vanishes, there is a presumption in the narrative that he can ultimately do it. Even in *Edwin Drood,* the truth awaits us—despite the probable scheme of John Jasper to dissolve material reality through the action of lime (and time). Justice, therefore, is made possible by the nature of things.

Indeed, the creation of the literary figure of the detective is possible only at that point in history when matter is conceived to bear forever the impress of actions. Like Dickens's detectives, Sherlock Holmes must have his material to analyze, his tobacco ashes and footprints. The detective novel depends upon these scientific conventions: (1) there are no spiritual (i.e., nonmaterial) agencies; (2) matter always remains and always bears the imprint of any action upon it; and (3) a detective can track imprinted matter—that is, clues—so precisely that nothing significant in the chain of events can escape him. Although the methods of the fictive detectives change over the years—from sympathetic imagination in Poe, ratiocinative brilliance in Doyle and Futrelle, empirical knowledge in Collins and Chesterton, to professional loyalty and doggedness in later American detectives—the premise and the effect of the genre remain constant: detection demystifies causality. There are no untraceable acts. Such demystification is the intent and presumption of science as well.

Another corollary of such theories as Babbage's is physiognomy. The logical connection runs like this: Matter is the guardian of truth; the human countenance is matter; it follows that the visage will bear its own imprint of physical and social action. We recall that Mrs. Lupin bore evidence of her cheerful philosophy (MC). Similarly, the evil-doer will bear, like Cain, the marks of his deed. This accounts in part for the melodramatic description of Bill Sikes, Jonas Chuzzlewit, and Quilp. This corollary was affirmed by Babbage:

> If the Almighty stamped on the brow of the earliest murderer,—the indelible and visible mark of his guilt,—he has also established laws by which every succeeding criminal is not less irrevocably chained to the testimony of his crime; for every atom of his mortal frame, through whatever changes its severed particles may migrate, will still

retain, adhering to it through every combination, some movement derived from that very muscular effort, by which the crime itself was perpetrated.[11]

Although Dickens's later killers do not always proffer physical manifestations of their crimes, their propensity is implied in their features, gestures, and words.

Phrenology aspired to a priori certainty, seeking to reveal the marks of Cain (and all others) before the event occurred. Although Dickens claimed to believe in phrenology, "in the main and broadly, as an essential part of the truth of physiognomy,"[12] it seems that what he believed in, as we understand it, was physiognomy. One may recall how, in *Great Expectations,* phrenologists were mocked by Magwitch, when he says, "They measured my head, some on 'em—they had better a-measured my stomach" (42). As Hazlitt pointed out, "It appears to me that the truth of physiognomy (if we allow it) overturns the science of craniology."[13] Physiognomy held that physical features display the actions of men; this is consistent with Babbage and is expounded by Mr. Brownlow, in *Oliver Twist,* when he confronts Monks and refers to him as "you ... in whom all evil passions, vice, profligacy, festered, till they found a vent in a hideous disease which has made your face an index even to your mind" (40). Dickens hedged a little by adding disease as a mediate cause; but he always believed that he had the capacity himself to read that index of the mind—the facial features. Whereas phrenology led to the idea of predestination, physiognomy implied free will—as Hazlitt indicated ("On Personal Character"). Physiognomy was descriptive and not prescriptive. Hence, to Babbage's list—"earth, air, and ocean, are eternal witnesses of the acts we have done"[14]—the human countenance could well be added.

The shadow of determinism does rise from these theories of inertia and conservation of matter. For example, David Copperfield writes, "It is done. Nothing can undo it; nothing can make it otherwise than it was" (31). It would seem that if past actions endure in material permanence, individuals will eventually be trapped in quite palpable patterns of necessity. The imprisoned Charles Darnay espouses the material determinism that was the dark side of Babbage's inspiring physical laws: "Good could never come of such evil, a happier end was not in nature to so unhappy a beginning" (TTC, 3, 11). Although this pessimistic principle of determinism contradicts both Carlyle and the conclusion of *A Tale of Two Cities,* it is hard to conceive—given the paradigm of

Newtonian physics—how the train of consequences set in motion by the Evrémondes' evil acts could be deflected. Motion—and the atoms that receive the impress of evil—must go on. Dr. Manette, who had earlier admitted that "mysteries arise out of close love, as well as out of wide division" (TC, 2, 10), finds that the demand for revenge—that he had set in motion years ago by manuscript—has arrived to enclasp his son-in-law.

Nevertheless, the mystery of the human heart does enter into and dissolve the deterministic equation. Carton (TTC), whose carelessness is another version of the Evrémondes', takes upon himself all the evil consequences that his carelessness sets in motion; in *Little Dorrit,* Amy does the same for her family; and in *Our Mutual Friend,* Wrayburn, willy-nilly, plays the scapegoat. Obviously, then, the motion begun by evil intentions can be converted when it is combined with the proper subjective motion. Although Amy is a scapegoat with a future, neither Carton nor Magwitch are vouchsafed survival. Therefore, although the momentum of the effects was often softened, Dickens did not attempt to disguise the truth of the cost.

The forces of necessity can be diverted, but the problem of evil remains. If good endures, do the consequences of evil acts continue to endure somewhere in the universe? Babbage, out of his materialistic principles, could affirm that "the propagation of an error, although it may be unfavorable or fatal to the temporary interest of the individual, can never be long injurious to the cause of the truth."[15] Eventually, the laws of nature will shed the distortion. The human being can be comforted "knowing that time alone is waiting to complete the triumph of truth."[16] Something of this perspective is provided in *Great Expectations:* "The sun was striking in at the great windows of the court, through the gittering drops of rain upon the glass, and it made a broad shaft of light between the two-and-thirty [offenders] and the judge, linking both together, and perhaps reminding some among the audience how both were passing on, with absolute equality, to the greater Judgment that knoweth all things and cannot err" (56). Even the response of Magwitch to the sentence suggests that greater motion that lies beyond the scope of human laws: "My Lord, I have received my sentence of death from the Almighty, but I bow to yours" (56). We do not have here the bitter equality of death-the-leveler; rather, we have the mystical view that the direction of the cosmos is toward truth and the good, whether man apprehends it or not. The world spirit works beyond the ken of man. Like Carlyle,[17] Babbage tolerated even miracles, "not as deviations from the laws assigned by the Almighty for the government of matter and mind; but as the exact fulfillment of much more extensive laws than those we suppose to exist."[18] Of the human being's words and deeds then, it is necessary to say that, though all are impressed into matter, truth alone propagates; truth alone continues beyond the moment. This is Carlyle's notion *(Past and Present):* "His name is Destiny, is Divine Providence, and his Sermon the inflexible Course of Things."[19]

Evil does not endure. "Out of all Evil, comes Good; and no Good that is possible but shall one day be real," Carlyle wrote.[20] Somehow, the universe aborts evil. Before assuming this to be a notion of a Panglossian cosmologist, I would like to work the idea out. Clearly, it is impossible to deny the present fact of evil; but although evil is perpetrated, it is somehow not retained—not propagated by the fact of things. Thus, the theogony that the human being witnesses and participates in—the universal process—is one in which all evil, or nothingness, is transformed. If the "true Past departs not," evidently the universal process works to convert what is inharmonious and ungrounded into true being. The work goes on, presumably, so long as there is anything left to convert.

I will not attempt to trace the source of this persistent idea of good from evil in Western thought, except to say that, according to Nicolas Berdyaev, such an idea was transmitted to a number of Romantic writers through the works of Jacob Boehme: "Evil, says Schelling, has its roots in that which is the most positive of all things. Evil is the lack of the root of existence, that is, it is linked to the Unground, to potential freedom. All this, of course, is Boehme."[21] In any case, the tendency to think of evil as sickness or unreality or nonbeing is certainly part of the working tradition of Dickens; it goes beyond the influence of Carlyle. One may recall the repetition of the idea of unreality about Monseigneur in *A Tale of Two Cities* (II, 7). The people around Monseigneur are unreal because they are caught in immediacy; incapable of—or uninterested in—acting upon material reality, they must fail to register in the scale of being. For (and it seems to come down to this) evil is freedom that has chosen against being.

How? Here, with the help of Berdyaev, we come full circle. In freedom, the spirits of human beings can be actualized. Acts that foster selfless emulation are fecund and expansive—and, therefore, must be real. Acts that cause contraction, alienation, and entropy become extinct—and, therefore, must be false. Evil is groundless, rootless, and returns to potential freedom. Good is freedom realized: it is human will that is in harmony with the universe. Evil is unrealized freedom. Although this terminology is a long way from Dickensian concreteness, Dickens did work within the premise that the material universe is innately receptive to being formed only by good acts. Good acts move; the universe is in movement; and, therefore, good is not left behind.

A less esoteric heritage than Boehme for this train of thought is the Bible: "I will cause those that love me to inherit SUBSTANCE; and I will fill their treasures" (Prv. 8:20). To love, to sympathize, to be moved or transported is to be filled with divine substance: it is to have being; it is to be real. Characteristically, Dickens works out the idea of the real and the unreal in terms of ordinary themes. One of these themes we may call that of "Nobody, Somebody, and Everybody"—to use the title of a magazine article by Dickens.[22]

According to the *Oxford Dictionary, somebody* means "a person of consequence"—a word that is appropriate in the light of Babbage's physics. But the term is often used ironically—and *somebody* may denote the devil. Dickens did not hesitate to extend the irony, as when in *Sketches By Boz* he pretends to accept the common usage of *somebody*—that is, a person with traditional social status. In *Sketches By Boz*, the character Horatio Sparkins, enters an assembly to great speculation about who he might be: "Was he a surgeon, a contributor to the magazines, a writer of fashionable novels, or an artist?—No; to each and all of these surmises there existed some valid objection. Then, said everybody, he must be *somebody*" (p. 357). Inasmuch as Dickens himself was a contributor to magazines—anxious to write novels and be an artist—there is a double irony that Sparkins can be imagined as "somebody" only if he is not a writer or artist. Obviously, *somebody* connotes gentlemanly birth; and when we remember from King Lear that "the prince of darkness is a gentleman," we apprehend more of the links between Dickens's radicalism and both physical and metaphysical theories of substance.

In *Bleak House*, Dickens used the word *somebody* in a straightforward sense when Esther wrote, "They said there could be no east wind where Somebody was; they said that wherever Dame Durden went, there was sunshine and summer air" (30). After a childhood of being nobody to anybody, Esther is a prime example of how, by active love—paradoxically, by *Selbst-tödtung*, in Carlyle's terminology—an individual gains consequence, or being. Dickens used the word *somebody* in much the same sense when he suggested "reserving Nobody for statues, and stars and garters, and batons, and places and pensions without duties, what if we were to try Somebody for real work?"[23] Part of his radicalism was his simple assumption that consequence should be attributed where consequence is manifest. In the physical nature of things, according to Babbage, consequence is inherent in certain actions, not in others; therefore, the usual attribution of consequence by society in the word *somebody* is absurd.

Dickens discovered that the word *nobody*, also referred to the privileged classes, especially when things go wrong. In the Crimean War, it was "Nobody who made the hospitals more horrible than language can describe, it was Nobody who occasioned all the dire confusion of the fatal Balaklava cavalry charge." With heavy irony, he continues: "We have, it is not to be denied, punished Nobody, with exemplary rigor. We have, as a nation, allowed ourselves to be deluded by no influences or insolences of office or rank, but have dealt with Nobody in a spirit of equal and uncompromising justice that has moved the admiration of the world."[24] The savage irony here—born of the same impulse that made Dickens want to give *Little Dorrit* the title *Nobody's Fault*—is double-layered. For the guilty parties are not merely somebodies who have been whitewashed but, in the universal scheme of things, truly nobodies, creatures without substance for the future.

In "Nobody's Story," Dickens's bitter anger over misgovernment and the oppression of the working people again found vent, as it had ten years earlier in *The Chimes*. The oppressors in this story are the members of the Bigwig family, who, with great noise and uproar, assume the management of the working classes and arrogate all "honour and glory in the highest, to the highest merit" (CS). Statutes were not made of doctors, liberators, or artists "whose skill had filled the working man's world with accumulated wonders." (All three occupations, it should be noted, could be termed liberators of body, mind, and soul.) Statues were made instead of persons "whom he [the worker] knew no good of, and even others whom he knew much ill of." Furthermore,

> when some few voices were faintly heard, proposing to show him the wonders of the world, the greatness of creation, the mighty changes of time, the workings of nature and the beauties of art—to show him these things, that is to say, at any period of his life when he could look upon them—there arose among the Bigwigs such roaring and raving, such pulpiting and petitioning . . . that nothing changed. ("Nobody's Story," CS, p. 63)

The working people get no benefit from government by the Bigwigs. When the Bigwigs wrangle, troubles multiply and "a scourge" appears that carries off both low and high, although "not a man" of the latter "ever admitted, if in the least degree he ever perceived, that he had anything to do with it" (p. 65). Dickens ended the tale with these words: "So Nobody lived and died in the old, old, old way. . . . Has he no name, you ask? Perhaps it is Legion" (p. 66).

Little Dorrit draws much from this theme of the value of action, not inheritance; and Dickens's intention—which had been constant throughout his novels, but was growing more emphatic—was to alter the very fund of cultural presuppositions by altering the accepted meanings of such words as *somebody* and *nobody*. With the writing of *Little Dorrit,* Dickens conceived *somebody* to be a person who does and not a person who is, that is, someone who makes consequences and is not merely of consequence—a person active and not passive. Thus, *somebody* was conceived to be in harmony with the laws of nature as outlined by Charles Babbage. Dickens wrote:

> Where do I, as an Englishman, want Somebody? Before high Heaven, I want him everywhere! I look round the whole dull horizon, and I want Somebody to do work while the Brazen Head, already hoarse with crying "Time is!" passes into the second warning, "Time was!" . . . I want Somebody to be clever in doing the business, not clever in evading it.[25]

In *Little Dorrit,* Doyce, who is never in line for a star or garter, is this type of new Somebody—but no more so than Little Dorrit herself is.

Many of Dickens's characters respond to the question asked of Teufelsdruckh in *Sartor Resartus* "Thou art still Nothing, Nobody: true, but who, then, is Something, Somebody?"[26] Carlyle's diction insists on being—on the translation of action into substance. For both Carlyle and Dickens the answer was that Somebody is one who serves, works, and, thus, puts himself or herself into use; one who does not temporize and does not defer.[27] Carlyle and Dickens would have disagreed to some extent as to what uses are proper and best; but on the general outline, they would have agreed. Teufelsdruckh learns that "for thee the Family of Man has no use; it rejects thee."[28] In the social structure of the ancien régime, Teufelsdruckh is of no use; but in the "Everlasting Yea," he makes himself of use at a universal level. Similarly, Esther Summerson realizes early that she "had brought no joy at any time to anyone's heart" and that, as a result, she was of no consequence to anyone; therefore, she determines to "strive as I grew up to be industrious, contented, and kind-hearted and to do some good to someone, and win some love if I could" (BH, 3). She puts into practice what Dickens had recommended a year earlier in an often quoted letter: "In every human existence, however quiet and monotonous, there is range enough for active sympathy and cheerful usefulness."[29] The "work" in Carlyle's phrase "work thou in welldoing" finds a domestic setting in Dickens. For Dickens, one became Somebody to the extent that one was able to do that which would "win some love." What Teufelsdruckh discovers in *Sartor Resartus* is that he is Somebody—and, thus, has permanence in the eternal order of things—to the extent that he acts to contribute permanently to it. Everybody, therefore, must become Somebody, insofar as he or she turns from the merely social, merely superficial, existence and applies himself or herself to the difficult work of founding the new social organization in which Nobody vanishes. For Dickens, one truly became Somebody simply by choosing to accept the human condition of being connected to Everybody—of being part of the eternal human community. As early as *The Sketches by Boz* (1836), Dickens's notion that human interconnection is in harmony with the universal structure of things was made clear when he wrote that

> all men and women, in couples and otherwise, who fall into exclusive habits of self-indulgence, and forget their natural sympathy and close connexion with everybody and everything in the world around them, not only neglect the first duty of life, but, by a happy retributive justice, deprive themselves of its truest and best enjoyment. (p. 596)

Our term for this "happy retributive justice" is poetic justice. An example of "retributive justice" appears in the imagery of *A Tale of Two Cities*, in which the hard-hearted Marquis, in death, joins his stone statuary—"one stone face too many, up at the château" (2, 9). By denying human connection, the Marquis makes himself into one of the dead stones among which he preferred to live.

From the applause of audiences and critics, Dickens, no doubt, gained a sense that he was Somebody; the visual and aural demonstrations of his affect on others relieved him from an anxiety of non-being. The experience of performing in *The Frozen Deep* gave him "a strange feeling," as of a communion with the audience. This feeling was an enhancement of the sense of belonging to a loving community that he so desperately needed. Hence, it was neither greed nor megalomania that drove him to persist, against his physician's advice, in his public readings; they gave him the same sense of being in company and of winning some love. Dickens could make himself of use, according to Babbage by having his name "pass in after times from mouth to mouth, cherished and admired by those whose applause is won by no personal recollections." Although the desire to be remembered through family ties is mere selfishness, Babbage argued that "the wish for more extended reputation . . . admired by those whose applause is won by no personal recollections . . . these hopes, these longings receive no interpretation from the all-dominant principle of *self!*"[30] By affecting others, a mere novelist—a "Schnüpsel," as Carlyle called him—a Nobody, truly becomes Somebody.

In the living universe, the human ego cannot exist in a reserved, discrete, shut-in, cold, stiff, and wooden state, "like a lone prisoner in a cell" (DS, 3); rather, it must remain warm, comfortable, diffused, and fluid. It is not frozen by fear; it is open in love. Hence, Dickens's novels do not focus on self-assertion—nor upon the uncovering of determinate conditions for the self. Such ideas of a fixed self are antipathetic to Dickens's moral vision. A human being gains substance only insofar as he or she is lent it by the heart of another—only insofar, therefore, as it is communicated, as it is transitive. From the time that Pickwick meets Sam Weller to the time that Bella Wilfer decides to be a companion to—and not a bought slave of—her husband, Dickens's works emphasize the giving of the self as the condition for becoming Somebody. Being is attained only by giving—by the movement of the heart.

Whatever simile that one may employ in attempting to describe Dickens's worldview, one will find the vital fact to be that the relation between message and medium—content and form—remains constant. The lack of personal integration and social interaction is depicted in a hard character and or a "stiff un" (DS, 56) like Mr. Dombey. "Stiff" characters flounder in the fictional stream of events,[31] but imaginative, adaptable characters often contribute to the softening of others. The tale as a whole is designed to move the reader, whether to tears or to laughter. Readers thus affected are likely to look upon others with greater sympathy—and, hence, may begin to repair a society in which class is "hardened unto each, and holding itself aloof."[32] Dickens wrote with the Romantic conviction that art, by moving the individual, can reshape the world. But in order to do so, the artist must take great care to soften the readers—and not to inadvertantly harden them by concentrating on grim realities or alienate them from either the work of fiction or the work of the world. For the poor—"the hardest workers at this whirling wheel of toil"—Dickens would teach "that their lot is not necessarily a moody, brutal fact, excluded from the sympathies and graces of imagination." As for the rich, Dickens's work would, as he wrote in the "Preliminary Word" to *Household Words,* "dispose them to a better acquaintance and a kinder understanding"[33] of the poor. Above all, fixed boundaries between rich and poor are to be expunged, just as are boundaries between the dimensions of time, even "the boundaries between fiction and reality, what is real and what is imagined, seem to disappear."[34]

Behind each critical advisement, each pronouncement of principle, and each literary theme and strategy—constituted as they are by the domesticated Romanticism—is Dickens's belief that moral health is dependent upon fluidity of spirit. This fluidity can be exercised by adapting to the points of view that imaginative literature provides for its readers. This is not to say that Dickens conceived of morality as relative, or flexible. Far from it. Yet, like Carlyle, he saw that the continuous adaptation by human beings in time is a necessary condition for moral life. The nature of society, of the self, and of the physical world encourges entropy and inflexibility. Although the essence of morality does not alter, the forms by which it is apprehended—and, to some degree, achieved—fossilize constantly and eventually come to be a mockery of the abiding truths. But the forms are only intellectual schemata and social institutions. To Dickens, any hardening, any clinging to one point of view, any settling in—any settling on an *unum necessarium,* literal or metaphoric—was to be eschewed. The essence of moral health was mobility—the capacity to move in and out of points of view and dimensions of time. It is no accident that the hero of *Great Expectations* is given not one but two palindromes for a name—Pip and Pirrip—to connote his eventual reflux from the settled position in the future. Even Philip, his given name, is as close to a palindrome as one could ask. The point is that Pip represents the truth of the commutations open to the spirit of the human being. Against entropy and inflexibility, Dickens arrays a constellation of imagery denoting the idea of fluidity, of movement. After all, movement is the manifestation of time in the world of space.

Dickens's every work attempts to counter the tendency towards sclerosis—and does so in every feature, just as every theme extols movement of some kind. From its very beginning, Dickens's works are filled with motion—social, physical, perceptual, and spiritual.

Sketches by Boz is the precipitate of his own passages through London; *Pickwick Papers* is that of his passages as a political reporter through the counties of England. The latter relates a story of four highly unlikely travelers upon the highways. Oliver Twist, Nicholas Nickleby, Little Nell, and David Copperfield are a few of his characters who hit the road early; they not only are descendants of Dickens's favorite eighteenth-century novel characters but also reflect his personal passion for movement. Although most characters in the *Christmas Books* tend to be somewhat more stationary, *Bleak House, Little Dorrit, Great Expectations,* and *Our Mutual Friend* end with the characters still in transit or transition—each going, as Pip narrates it, "out of the ruined place." It is by means of this spatial image that Dickens could best represent human changes that are made in time but (as Carlyle said) not by time—changes that bespeak participation in being.

The physical movement of these characters symbolizes a fluidity of spirit—which is what Dickens prized most highly in the human personality. Notorious instances of his addiction to action, to movement, are: (1) his feats of hiking—even when his leg was going lame; (2) his nocturnal restlessness; (3) his need—almost to the point of craving—for the active streets of London; and (4) his return—against advice—to a demanding schedule of public readings. It is little wonder that his novels are instinct with the theme of fluidity—which implies social flexibility and psychological softening, changes of heart, self-revisions, and other forms of physical and spiritual transit. Granted, characters like Quilp and Carker, Steerforth and Headstone—and even the immature Martin Chuzzlewit and Pip—are seen in hectic movement; but they, like so many of the gentleman-villains, in their several ways want to fix things—to stop all movement. Quilp may seem a demon of abrupt action; yet in the end, he wants only to shut out the world by closing the gates of his waterfront place—"Strong and fast" (locs, 67). This final gesture epitomizes the effect of all of his actions—namely, to distance and alienate. Carker (DS)—at the moment that he believes that his despoiling of Dombey is successful—is thinking not of movement but of its cessation when he announces to Edith their destination: "Sicily shall be the place of our retreat. In the idlest and easiest part of the world, my soul, we'll both seek compensation for old slavery" (54). Carker and Quilp conceive it possible to end their commerce with the active world; and they find satisfaction in stasis—beyond the human pale. Dickens, perhaps making aesthetic virtue of his personal necessity, opposed to this false notion of satisfaction the values of fluidity in all its aspects. Fluidity—in the form of water and the moving train—provides a fitting end for those two mistaken characters Carker and Quilp.

The necessity of movement is prescribed by Goethe's "Lord" in the prologue to *Faust:* "Man finds relaxation too attractive / Too fond too soon of unconditional rest."[35] In Goethe's scheme of things, God's devil must be active—and must lure the human being on to increased activity. For only in action can the human being hope to make his reality a happy and secure one. Goethe depicted God as a vortex—the prime mover—and the world as an ever-changing phenomenon: "The changing Essence which ever works and lives, / Wall you around with love, serene, secure!"[36] Goethe's radical modification of the medieval legend consists in refusing to take Faust's psychological yearnings and wanderings as prima facie evidence of damnation. The Middle Ages are over. Faust's dissatisfactions and his motive for continuing activity have become problematic—if not meritorious—and seem in harmony with the nature of the universe as physics then described it. Indeed, Faust's flaw is simply his assumption that nothing he does scientifically or personally can permanently affect the material world—and that nothing in the world can permanently affect his spirit. Without a belief in the interaction of matter and spirit, Faust can never finally be walled "around with love, serene, secure." But Dickens's community would accomplish the thing— that is, make each person serene, secure.

Human society finds more than an analogue in the eternal universe of interconnected and interacting atoms that Babbage envisioned. Society participates in that universe. The links between existents buttress Dickens's theory of social connection. As I have tried to show, the notion of connection finds frequent reiteration in his work—for one is, willy-nilly, bound to the world. As he wrote to Collins, "Everything . . . shows beyond mistake that you can't shut out the world."[37] But not only the links of matter but the momentum of the whole is assumed. This line of thought helped Dickens to justify his own personal restlessness. He was in constant motion:

> I have always felt of myself that I must, please God, die in harness. . . . However strange it is to be never at rest, and never reached, and to be always laden with plot and plan and care and worry, how clear it is that it must be, and that one is driven by an irresistible might until the journey is worked out.[38]

But if this motion is universal, his image of a journey to be worked out implies an activity in harmony with the momentum of the universe.

Dickens's fascination with the past, the present, and the future is reflective of his general restlessness. As I have said elsewhere, his fiction consistently undermines a settling on the past and the future and the present per se. The contents of each dimension of time have their value largely as distractions—as ways of loosening one's concentration upon another dimension of time. Hence, what emerges from his fiction is an accentuation of the fluidity of being—a decentration in terms of both space and time. For temporal concentration—attending to only one dimension—is to lose everything of value, that is, the capacity to move and be moved.

In fact, the only thing that one can profitably draw from a particular dimension of time is precisely that which does not belong to it in isolation—namely, its effect on the other dimensions. To try to draw more than this from any time, to try to "have"— to use Gabriel Marcel's term—is to withdraw from "being." "Having" and "being" are not terms that Dickens himself used; nevertheless, he certainly would have understood Marcel's distinctions.[39] To describe what happens to the self that centers upon "having," Marcel uses such terms as *mortify* and *sclerosis*. To Dickens nothing was so likely to harden the self as a fixation upon one dimension of time. Life has the essential quality of momentum; and to call a halt in any human process is an act of bad faith—indeed, of satanic rebellion. Energy displays God's will. Dickens's characterizations bear this scheme out. Nevertheless, Dickens also sought for a serene eye in the storms of life—for security at the heart of the vortex. In his fiction, Dickens sought to anchor—in the eternal drift of things—to hearth and heart; but this was done, paradoxically, only to preclude the human being from becoming fixated upon movement itself. This is why Susan Horton's emphasis on the phatic function in *Dombey and Son* makes so much sense to me. The novel is, she has said, before all else, "intended as an apology (for no longer being the taleteller for his readers), [and] a celebration"[40] of the renewal of the community of communication. In the community of writer, novel, and reader, Dickens was establishing a model for life in the world. Reading is not a timeless circle but an act of perpetual motion— and, thus, an emblem of spiritual life.

His art is designed to relieve, to move, to soften the audience. In doing this, it disposes the audience to see the world as a site of harmony—and to see time as an assistant, not the master, of mankind. Time consumes men only when men become discrete, hardened, and unyielding atoms. But human beings who move and are moved, who find themselves in doing and not in having, who are links in the human chain and who thus become somebody to somebody, who find a companion in an other, and who draw value from all dimensions of time are rewarded with the active serenity that Goethe predicates.

Perhaps Dickens never personally achieved this serenity. Perhaps his own restless movement was spectral, self-haunting. As he wrote Collins,

> The domestic unhappiness remains so strong upon me that I can't write, and (waking) can't rest, one minute. I have never known a moment's peace or content, since the last night of The Frozen Deep. I suppose that there never was a man so seized and rended by one spirit. In this condition though nothing can alter or soften it, I have a turning notion that the mere physical effort and change of the Readings would be good, as another means of bearing it.[41]

Or, as he wrote Forster in October of 1857, "I am incapable of rest. Much better to die, doing."[42] But one may well question the legitimacy of attempting to evaluate his art by what little we know of his personal life and thoughts. One must remember that personal correspondence articulates only a limited zone of human experience, the limits of the zone changing with each age. But in any case, there can be little doubt that Dickens's personal restlessness invigorated his art—although his art cannot be reduced to it. For in writing as, perhaps, in the midst of a reading, Dickens seems to have found his serene sense of being—found his own emancipation from the kingdom of time—and seems to have truly reported to us his discovery of human potentialities, namely, the capacities to see, to feel, and to find new connections, new views, new selves, and new directions. I, for one, cannot doubt the sincerity with which Dickens directs us out of our dead conventions, temporal isolation, fixed selves, sepulchral society—out of that "ruined place" that all of us may know in our hearts.

Notes

Introduction

1. Mildred Newcomb, *The Imagined World of Charles Dickens* (Columbus: Ohio State University Press, 1989), 8.
2. Patrick C. Creevy, "In Time and Out: The Tempo of Life in *Bleak House*," *Dickens Studies Annual* 12 (1983): 63–80.
3. George Steiner, *After Babel* (New York: Oxford University Press, 1975), 132.
4. John Carey, *Here Comes Dickens: The Imagination of a Novelist* (New York: Schocken Books, 1974), 15.
5. Arnold Kettle, *An Introduction to the English Novel*, vol. 1 (London: Hutchinson, 1969), 24.
6. G. K. Chesterton, *Charles Dickens* (London, 1910), 80–81.
7. See Fred Kaplan, *Dickens: A Biography* (New York: William Morrow, 1988) and Peter Ackroyd, *Charles Dickens* (New York: Harper Collins, 1990).
8. Lawrence Frank, *Charles Dickens and the Romantic Self* (Lincoln: University of Nebraska Press, 1984), 93. Frank has also said that in *Edwin Drood* Dickens tried to "annul the romantic imperative to the unceasing creation of both history and the self" (237).
9. Ibid., 232.
10. Ibid., 222.
11. Ibid., 221.
12. Ibid., 250.
13. Badri Raina, *Dickens and the Dialectic of Growth* (Madison: University of Wisconsin Press, 1986), 10.
14. Ibid., 25.
15. Ibid., 27.
16. Ibid., 63.
17. Ibid., 96.
18. Ibid., 110.
19. Dirk den Hartog, *Dickens and Romantic Psychology: The Self in Time in Nineteenth-Century Literature* (New York: St. Martin's Press, 1987), 34.
20. Ibid., 41.
21. Ibid., 53.
22. Ibid., 82.
23. Ibid., 135.
24. Ibid., 155.
25. Carey, *Here Comes Dickens*, 7.
26. Ibid., 28.
27. Ibid., 71.
28. Ibid., 175.

29. Edwin Eigner, *The Dickens Pantomime* (Berkeley: University of California Press, 1989), 14.
30. Ibid., 45.
31. Susan Horton, *Interpreting Interpreting: Interpreting Dickens's Dombey and Son* (Baltimore: Johns Hopkins University Press, 1979).
32. S. J. Newman, *Dickens at Play* (New York: St. Martin's, 1981), 5.
33. Ibid., 58–59.
34. Ibid., 68.
35. Ibid., 86.
36. Ibid., 122.
37. Ibid.
38. M. M. Bakhtin and P. N. Medvedev, *The Formal Method in Literary Scholarship*, trans. Albert J. Wehrle (Baltimore: The John Hopkins University Press, 1978), 120.
39. Ibid., 121.
40. Horton, *Interpreting Interpreting*, 16.
41. Roy Harris, *The Language Myth* (New York: St. Martin's Press, 1981), 153.
42. Ackroyd, *Charles Dickens*, 81.
43. Jacques Derrida, *Of Grammatology*, trans. Gayatri Spivak (Baltimore: Johns Hopkins University Press, 1976), 19.
44. Horton, *Interpreting Interpreting*, 4.
45. Peter J. Rabinowitz, *Before Reading: Narrative Conventions and the Politics of Interpretation* (Ithaca: Cornell University Press, 1987), 43.
46. Ibid., 51.
47. John Forster, *The Life of Charles Dickens*, vol. 3 (London: Chapman and Hall, 1872), 235.
48. Roman Jakobson, "Linguistics and Poetics," in DeGeorge and DeGeorge, eds., *The Structuralists From Marx to Levi-Strauss* (Garden City, N.Y.: Doubleday-Anchor Books, 1972), 87.
49. Ibid., 89.
50. Ibid., 89.
51. Ibid.
52. Ibid., 93.
53. Barbara Herrnstein Smith, *On the Margins of Discourse* (Chicago: University of Chicago Press, 1978), 128.
54. Jakobson, "Linguistics and Poetics," 92.
55. Charles Dickens, in *Our Mutual Friend* (London: Oxford Illustrated Edition, 1967), 1. Hereafter, all references to Dickens's novels will be followed by chapter numbers in parentheses.
56. Ackroyd, *Charles Dickens*, 99.
57. Steiner, *After Babel*, 217–18.
58. John Searle, *Speech Acts: An Essay in the Philosophy of Language* (Cambridge: Cambridge University Press, 1969), 38.
59. Ibid., 47.
60. Ibid., 50.
61. Hans Robert Jauss, "Literary History as a Challenge to Literary Theory," *New Literary History* 2 (1970), 8.
62. Ackroyd, *Charles Dickens*, 35.
63. Ibid., 70.
64. Forster, *Life of Dickens*, 2:447.
65. Ibid., 3:349.

66. Newman, *Dickens at Play*, 22.
67. Robert Buchanan, "The Good Genie of Fiction: Thoughts While Reading Forster's Life of Charles Dickens," *St. Paul's Magazine* 10 (1872), 130.
68. Horton, *Interpreting Interpreting*, 16.
69. Steiner, *After Babel*, 18.
70. See especially Jacques Derrida, *Of Grammatology*.
71. Jean Paul Sartre, *Being and Nothingness*, trans. Hazel Barnes (New York: Philosophical Library, 1956), 263, 627, and *passim*.
72. Leszek Kolakowski, *Bergson* (Oxford: Oxford University Press, 1985), 21.
73. George Orwell, *Dickens, Dali and Others* (New York: Reynal and Hitchcock, 1946), 56.
74. Ibid., 22.
75. Ackroyd, *Charles Dickens*, 202.
76. Quoted by J. J. Gibson, "Events Are Perceivable But Time Is Not," in *The Study of Time*, ed. J. T. Fraser and N. Lawrence, vol. 2 (New York: Springer-Verlag, 1975), 300.

Chapter 1. The Dead Hand of the Past

1. John Ruskin in a letter to Charles Eliot Norton, 19 June 1870, quoted in *Charles Dickens*, ed. Stephen Wall (Harmondsworth, England: Penguin, 1970), 191. Hereafter this book will be referred to as "Wall."
2. Charles Dickens, "The Bemoaned Past," *All the Year Round* 7 (1862): 257. But see P. A. W. Collins, "Queen Mab's Chariot Among the Steam Engines: Dickens and Fancy," *English Studies* 42 (1961): 83. Collins has said of Dickens that "Ruskin was over-simple in describing him as a pure modernist."
3. Ibid., 261.
4. Peter Ackroyd, *Charles Dickens*, 416.
5. See Ian Watt, "Oral Dickens," *Dickens Studies Annual* 3 (1974), 165–81. Watt has suggested that the crucial biographical episode is more probably the five months or so at Warren's blacking warehouse. See also Edmund Wilson, "Dickens: The Two Scrooges," in *The Wound and the Bow* (New York: Oxford University Press, 1947). Wilson wrote that "these experiences produced in Charles Dickens a trauma from which he suffered all his life" (6).
6. Edgar Johnson, *Charles Dickens: His Tragedy and Triumph*, vol. 1 (New York: Simon & Schuster, 1952), 32.
7. Ibid., 44.
8. John Hollingshead, "Fetishes," *All the Year Round* 11 (1864): 571. As an editor, Dickens suggested, commissioned, and reworked many articles.
9. J. Hillis Miller, *Charles Dickens: The World of his Novels* (1958; reprint, Bloomington, Ind.: Midland, 1969), 295.
10. Friedrich Nietzsche, *The Will to Power* (New York: Vintage, 1968), 47.
11. Forster, *Life of Dickens*, 1:136.
12. See Fred Kaplan, *Dickens and Mesmerism* (Princeton: Princeton University Press, 1976).
13. See Raymond Chapman, *The Sense of the Past in Victorian Literature* (New York: St. Martin's, 1986), 148, where he has said that "*The Pickwick Papers* is imagined as set about 1827." *Oliver* was published a few years after the inception of the New Poor Law—which the book attacks; but the effect of that law in the narrative is in its practice—not in its history. There is no sense within the narra-

tive that it is a legacy. Oliver has a family, he later learns; but his antecedents are not an important part of his experience in the present time frame of the novel. What is important when one looks at the narratives is not so much the historical settings per se as the effect of prior circumstances on the action in the narrative.

14. Philip Rogers, "The Dynamics of Time in *The Old Curiosity Shop*," *Nineteenth Century Fiction* 28 (1973): 127–44. For an interpretation of time that is diametrically opposite to mine, cf. Stephan L. Franklin, "Dickens and Time: The Clock Without Hands," *Dickens Studies Annual* 4 (1975): 1–35. In this article, London represents the Victorian present, from which Nell and her grandfather flee. My problem with this reading is that the shop itself is repeatedly imaged as a representative of the past; the manufacturing midlands to which Nell and her grandfather flee can scarcely be seen as anything but the present; and as Nell wanders safely through it, London is not shown to be a threatening site of modernity. However, the major point, upon which he and I no doubt agree, is that the danger is fixation upon one dimension of time, with its consequence that the soul is petrified and alienated from itself and others. This distancing from present life would happen whether it was the past or the present from which they fled.

15. See Thomas Rice, "The Politics of *Barnaby Rudge*, in *The Changing World of Charles Dickens*, ed. Robert Giddings (London: Vision Press, 1983), 51–74. Rice has argued persuasively that "Dickens's writing of *Barnaby Rudge* was in part an atonement for the unexpected impact of *Oliver Twist*" (54).

16. Rosemarie Mundhenk, "*David Copperfield* and the Oppression of Remembrance," *Texas Studies in Language and Literature* 29 (1987): 324, has written that "most of Charles Dickens's novels are structured around an embedded return to the past in order to rediscover or clarify the meaning of the present."

17. Samuel Taylor Coleridge, "Frost at Midnight," in *The Norton Anthology of English Literature*, eds. M. H. Abrams et al., 5th edition, volume 2 (New York: W. W. Norton, 1985), 373. Hereafter this anthology is referred to as "*Norton*."

18. Chapman, *Sense of the Past*, 176.

19. K. J. Fielding, "Dickens and the Past: The Novelist of Memory," in *Experience in the Novel*, ed. R. H. Pearce (New York: Columbia University Press, 1968), 112.

20. Harold Bloom, "Introduction," *Charles Dickens* (New York: Chelsea, 1987), 6.

21. Fred Kaplan, *Dickens*, 217.

22. Percy Bysshe Shelley, "A Defense of Poetry," *Norton*, 785.

23. Charles Dickens, "Old Lamps for New," *Household Words* 1 (1850): 265–67.

24. Dickens's grandmother was the housekeeper for the Crewe family.

25. K. J. Fielding, "Dickens and the Past," 123.

26. Lionel Trilling, "Little Dorrit," in *Charles Dickens*, in Wall, 364.

27. K. J. Fielding, "Dickens and the Past," 129.

28. Albert Hutter, "The Novelist as Resurrectionist: Dickens and the Dilemma of Death," *Dickens Studies Annual* 12 (1983): 25.

29. Johnson, *Charles Dickens*, 2:980.

30. The immensity of the social force exercised by the imagination that has been trained by tales and dreams is shown by Dickens when he has Jenny Wren provide Wrayburn with the class-and-precedent destroying idea of marrying Lizzie—an idea born of the pure imagination and without concrete antecedent.

31. Frank, *Charles Dickens*, 23.

Chapter 2. The Presence of Hunger

1. For a detailed analysis of who looked in which direction, see Jerome Buckley, *The Triumph of Time* (Cambridge: Harvard University Press, 1966).
2. Douglas Jerrold, *The Chronicles of Clovernook* (London: Punch, 1847), 95.
3. Thomas Malthus, *An Essay on the Principle of Population* (New York: W. W. Norton, 1976). Cf. Wm. Prout, *Eighth Bridgewater Treatise*, 1835. He expatiates on the "system of universal voracity" (p. 472)
4. Thomas Carlyle, *The French Revolution* (New York: Modern Library, n.d.) and *Sartor Resartus* (New York: AMS Press, 1969).
5. Carlyle, "Chartism," in *Critical and Miscellaneous Essays*, vol. 4 (New York: AMS Press, 1969), 203.
6. Ibid., 128.
7. Ibid., 143.
8. Ibid.
9. Ibid., 203.
10. Richard D. Altick, *Victorian People and Ideas*, (New York: W. W. Norton, 1973), 1
11. Max Weber, *The Protestant Ethic and the Spirit of Capitalism*, trans. Talcott Parsons (1930; reprint, London: Allen & Unwin, 1962).
12. Charles Dickens, "Sunday Under Three Heads," in *The Uncommercial Traveller and Reprinted Pieces* (London: Oxford Illustrated Edition, 1964), 637.
13. Charles Dickens to John Forster, 27 April 1855, *The Letters of Charles Dickens*, ed. Walter Dexter, vol. 2 (London: Nonesuch, 1938), 6. Hereafter, these volumes will be cited as Letters (1938).
14. Barbara Hardy, *Charles Dickens*, in Wall, 478. See also Joyce S. Toomore's appreciative "Dining With Dickens," *Harvard Magazine* 82 (January-February 1979): 38–44. Less appreciative is John Carey, *Here Comes Dickens*, 25: "Food consumption, for instance, is an indispensable accompaniment of Dickensian bliss." Much the same charge can be made of Homer; and, unfortunately, in both Homer and Dickens, food is often consumed in situations anything but blissful—which is my point.
15. See W. F. Axton, "Dickens and Drink," paper read to the Dickens Section at the Modern Language Association Conference, New York, December 1979. Axton has said of *Pickwick Papers* that it contains "no fewer than 249 references to alcoholic beverages."
16. See my "Social Harmony and Dickens Revolutionary Cookery," *Dickens Studies Annual* 17 (1988): 145–78, for observations on articles on food and cookery in *Household Words* and *All the Year Round*. See also Chris R. Vanden Bossche's informative article, "Cookery, Not Rookery: Family and Class in *David Copperfield*," *Dickens Studies Annual* 15 (1986): 87–109. He has noted that Eliza Beeton's popular cookery book contained a recipe for "Ruth Pinch's Beef-Steak Pudding." Dickens would, no doubt, have agreed with Vander Bossche's point that "the division between the novelistic and the domestic is tenuous at best" (109, n.3).
17. If so, Pritchett's view that Dickens "pushed the note of jollity much too far"—by overemphasizing the pleasant meals only—is not tenable. See V. S. Pritchett, "The Comic World of Dickens," in *The Victorian Novel: Essays in Criticisim*, ed. Ian Watt (New York: Oxford University Press, 1971), 30.

18. The phrase "cup and lip" is one of those commonplaces that Dickens could not let stand but developed into a theme in one of his works—in this case, becoming the title of Book 1 of *Our Mutual Friend.*

19. Carlyle, *Sartor Resartus* (London: Chapman and Hall, 1896; reprint. New York, AMS Press, 1969), 94.

20. Garrett Stewart, *Charles Dickens and the Trials of the Imagination* (Cambridge: Harvard University Press, 1974).

21. The stove seems to be contrived to put an end to the fear of going hungry. Making the individual self-sufficient, it is, perhaps, a fantastical replacement for inadequate mothers. But it may well be an intuition of the coming technological rebuttals to Malthus's vision.

22. See my "English Cannibalism: Dickens After 1859," *Studies in English Literature* 23 (1983): 647–66.

23. Fyodor Dostoyevsky, *Notes from the Underground,* trans. Andrew MacAndrew (New York: Signet, 1961).

24. Carlyle, *Sartor Resartus,* 181.

25. Douglas Jerrold, *The Handbook of Swindling,* ed. Walter Jerrold (London: Scott, 1891), 27.

26. Jerrold, *Chronicles of Clovernook,* 42.

27. Pritchett, "Comic World of Dickens," 32.

28. Jerrold, *Chronicles of Clovernook,* 26.

29. Carlyle, *Sartor Resartus,* 146–47.

30. Carlyle, *The French Revolution,* 45.

Chapter 3. Great Expectations: Fixtures of the Future

1. Johnson, *Charles Dickens,* 2:922.

2. David Masson, *British Novelists and Their Styles* (Cambridge, 1859), quoted in *The Dickens Critics,* ed. George Ford and Lauriat Lane (Ithaca: Cornell Paperbacks, 1966), 37.

3. George Ford, "Dickens and the Voices of Time," *Nineteenth-Century Fiction* 24 (1970): 431.

4. Frank, *Romantic Self,* 98.

5. William Hazlitt, *An Essay on the Principle of Human Action* (1805; reprint Gainesville: University of Florida Press, 1969).

6. "Remonstrance with Dickens," *Blackwood's Magazine* 81 (April 1857): 497.

7. Northrop Frye, "Dickens and Humour," in *Experience in the Novel,* ed. R. H. Pearce (New York: Columbia University Press, 1968), 52.

8. See my "Pickwick's Writing," *English Literary History* 53 (1986): 939–63.

9. Raina, *Dialectic of Growth,* 70.

10. Claude Levi-Strauss, *The Savage Mind,* trans. George Weidenfeld and Nicolson Ltd. (Chicago: University of Chicago Press, 1966). See especially chapter eight, "Time Regained."

11. Thomas Carlyle, *Past and Present* (Boston: Houghton Mifflin, 1965), 112.

12. Orwell, *Dickens, Dali and Others,* 53.

13. Johnson, *Charles Dickens,* 2:1150.

14. Charles Dickens, "Preliminary Word," *Household Words* 1 (1850), 1.

15. "Article VI.—The Collected Works of Charles Dickens," *British Quarterly Review* 35 (1862): 155.

16. "I Have Done My Duty," *All the Your Round* 12 (1865): 543.

17. Carlyle, *Sartor Resartus*, 156.
18. Creevy, "In Time and Out," 78.
19. John Forster, *Life of Dickens*, 1:129.
20. Kolakowski, *Bergson*, 56.
21. Carlyle, "Characteristics," *Critical and Miscellaneous Essays*, vol. 3 (reprint. New York: AMS Press, 1969), 37.
22. Ibid.
23. Ibid., 39.
24. Henri Bergson, *Creative Evolution*, trans. Arthur Mitchell (New York: Modern Library, 1944), 53. Following quotations: 64; 43; 369.

Chapter 4. The Battle of Life

1. See den Hartog, *Dickens and Romantic Psychology*.
2. Cf. William Hazlitt, *An Essay on the Principles of Human Action*.
3. James Marlow, "Dickens's Romance: The Novel as Other," *Dickens Studies Annual* 5 (1976): 23–42.
4. Steven Marcus, *From Pickwick to Dombey* (London: Chatto & Windus, 1965), 107. In contrast to my reading, Marcus seems to have concluded that the lack of a "continuous imagination of a great world" is a failing of *Nicholas Nickleby* that "the plot, is inadequate" to redeem.
5. Cf. John Forster, *The Life*, 2:416, for a similar declaration by Dickens.
6. Charles Dickens to Wilkie Collins, 6 September 1858, *The Letters of Charles Dickens*, ed. Mamie Dickens and Georgina Hogarth, vol. 2 (New York: Scribners, 1879), 79–80.
7. I cannot agree with Steven Marcus at another point when, in his otherwise excellent analysis of *Nicholas Nickleby*, I read the following about Ralph: "But his suicide is not an act of despair, or hopelessness at being estranged from human society; it is an act of anger, of malice against it and against those impulses remaining in him which bind him to other men," (see Marcus, *From Pickwick to Dombey*, 111). I feel that the narrative's words, "let it go," clearly suggest despair and not the anger that Marcus has found. In the analysis of the novel I have been making, suicide is the final phase of Ralph's continuous abandonment of the world.
8. Jerrold, *Chronicles of Clovernook* 17.
9. Charlotte Bronte, *Villette* (1853; reprint. London: Everyman's Library, 1974), 28 and passim.
10. Forster, *Life of Dickens*, 2:460.
11. Ibid., 3:35.
12. Dickens to Mrs. Dickenson, 19 August 1860. *Letters of Dickens*, 3:172.
13. Samuel Smiles, *Self-Help* (New York: A. L. Burt, n.d.), 324.
14. The manuscript titled *Memoranda Book*, apparently written between 1855 and 1865, is now in the Berg Collection of the New York Public Library. The entry cited is assigned the date 1855 by Fred Kaplan in his edition. See *Charles Dickens Book of Memoranda*, ed. Fred Kaplan (New York: New York Public Library, 1981), 4.
15. Dickens quoted by Johnson, *Charles Dickens*, 2:1150.
16. *The Speeches of Charles Dickens*, ed. K. J. Fielding (Oxford: Oxford University Press, 1960), 409.
17. Samuel Beckett, *Proust* (New York: Grove Press, 1957), 8.

18. Arnold Kettle, "Our Mutual Friend," in *Dickens and the Twentieth Century*, ed. Gross and Pearson (London: Routledge, 1966), 216.
19. Charles Dickens, *Letters to Angela Burdett-Coutts*, ed. Edgar Johnson (Boston: Little Brown, 1952), 51–52.
20. Edgar Johnson, *Tragedy and Triumph*, 2:684. Originally published in the *Examiner* 22 April 1848.
21. *Speeches of Dickens*, 81–82. Given before the Mechanics Institution, Leeds, 1 December 1847.
22. Ibid., 82.
23. Charles Dickens, "The Late Mr. Justice Talfourd," *Household Words* 9 (1854): 117.
24. Charles Dickens, "Ignorance and Crime," *Examiner*, 22 April 1848, quoted by Alec W. C. Brice, "Ignorance and Its Victims: Another New Article by Dickens," *Dickensian* 63 (1966): 144.
25. *Letters to Angela*, 321.
26. Philip Collins, *Dickens and Education* (New York: Macmillan, 1964), 193, 198.
27. See Johnson, *Charles Dickens*, 2:1132.
28. G. H. Lewes, "Dickens in Relation to Criticism," *Fortnightly Review* 17 (February 1872): 151.
29. Dickens to Arthur Helps, 3 January 1854. *Letters* (1938), 2:531.
30. "Article 8: Modern Novelists," *Westminster Review* 82 (October 1864): 441.
31. Dickens to Wilkie Collins, 20 September 1862, *Letters* (1938), 3:304.
32. Collins, 160.
33. Horton, *Interpreting Interpreting*.
34. Ackroyd, *Charles Dickens*, 653.
35. Taylor Stoehr, *The Dreamer's Stance* (Ithaca: Cornell University Press, 1965), 240.
36. Henry James, *The Future of the Novel*, ed. Leon Edel (New York: Vintage, 1956), 79.
37. This is the standard idea of the Romantic heritage as it was modified in the Victorian Era. Jerrold expressed it nearly simultaneously: "How flat, monotonous may be the circumstances of daily existence, and yet how various the thoughts which spring from it." *The Chronicles of Clovernook*, 180.
38. Charles Dickens, "Preliminary Word," *Household Words* 1 (1850): 1. Cf. Robert Newsom, *Dickens on the Romantic Side of Familiar Things: "Bleak House" and the Novel Tradition* (New York: Columbia University Press, 1977). See especially p. 113 where Newsom notes that as "we view the Chancery, we can never be sure whether it is the familiar institution or the romantic symbolic conception of it that we are seeing—because it is always both together."
39. "Article 8: Modern Novelists," *Westminster Review*, 438–39.
40. *Speeches of Dickens*, 407. Given in Birmingham, 27 September 1869.
41. Dickens to W. H. Wills, *Letters* (1938) 2:420–21.
42. Robert Browning, "Fra Lippo Lippi" in *The Poetical Works* (London: Smith Elder, 1889), 4:216–17.
43. G. K. Chesterton, "A Defence of Defective Stories," in Dick Clark and David Chacko, eds., *Detective Fiction* (New York: Harcourt, Brace and Jovanovich, 1974), 384–85.
44. *The Letters of Charles Dickens to Wilkie Collins*, ed. Laurence Hutton (New York, Harper Bros., 1892), 41.
45. Dickens, *Memoranda Book*, 14.

46. John Ruskin, Essay 1 of "Fiction, Fair and Foul," in *The Genius of John Ruskin*, ed. John D. Rosenberg (Boston: Houghton Mifflin, 1963), 440.
47. See "The Poetry of Fact," *All the Year Round* 18 (1867): 277–79. In this article, the author, possibly Dickens, has cited Sir John Franklin as a figure "in the onward march of time" that would result in "proper sympathy between classes" (279). In this way, Dickens masterfully intertwined his primary themes.
48. "Small Beer Chronicles," *All the Year Round* 12 (1863): 513.
49. Gabriel Marcel, *Homo Viator* (New York: Harper Torchbooks, 1962), 36, 37.
50. Marcel, 40.
51. Marcel, 53.
52. Marcel, 53.
53. "Remonstrance with Dickens," *Blackwood's Magazine* 81 (April 1857): 502.
54. Earle Davis, *The Flint and the Flame* (Columbia: University of Missouri Press, 1963), 72.
55. *Letters* (1938), 2:194. To W. F. Cerjat, 29 December 1849.
56. Ibid., 3:717. To Georgina Hogarth, 4 April 1869.
57. Dorothy Van Ghent, "The Dickens World," in *The Dickens Critics*, ed. George Ford and Lauriat Lane (Ithaca: Cornell Paperbacks, 1966), 222–23.
58. Northrop Frye, "Dickens and Humour," 52.
59. Ira Progoff, *Jung, Synchronicity, and Human Destiny* (New York: Julian Press, 1973), 4.
60. *Letters to Wilkie Collins*, 95.
61. Henri Bergson, *Creative Evolution*, 106.
62. Ibid., 177.
63. Ibid., 200.
64. Ibid., 237.
65. Ibid., 271.
66. Forster, *The Life of Dickens*, 3:349.
67. About the social realities in *Oliver Twist*, Lord Melbourne said to Queen Victoria, "I don't *like* those things; I wish to avoid them; I don't like them in *reality*, and therefore I don't wish to see them presented" (see Collins, *Dickens and Education*, 112).

Chapter 5. Trust in the Present

1. Sigmund Freud, *The Problem of Anxiety* (New York: W. W. Norton, 1963), 34, has written that "the idea of being eaten by the father belongs to the primal stock of childhood ideas; analogies from mythology (Kronos) and from animal life are generally familiar."
2. Stewart, *Trials of the Imagination*, xvii.
3. Gwendolyn B. Needham, "The Undisciplined Heart of David Copperfield," *Nineteenth-Century Fiction* 9 (1954): 81–107.
4. See Newsom, *Romantic Side of Familiar Things*, chapter 1, for a study of the imagery of circles that is so prevalent in *Bleak House*.
5. Many twentieth-century readers derogate Dickens's choice of a circus to represent the spiritual antithesis of English cannibalism. Perhaps they would prefer Dickens to have used the Italian opera or the Bolshoi. But if low-brow shows can offer citizens a defense against the ideology of hunger, how much more could high-brow entertainment? After all, Dickens was interested in stimu-

lating the fancy in those who were suffering from deprivation (we must not fail to contextualize the element of the circus), not in evaluating means of aesthetic repletion. Condemning Dickens's use of a circus here, it seems to me, is like criticizing Hamlet for choosing an inferior drama for his "mouse-trap." Sleary's slurred speech suggests that Dickens did not mean him to be an ideal. Fowler—in his linguistic analysis of Sleary's idiolect, which is purposely "defamiliarizing"—has made the undeniable point that "at least Sleary is *meant* to be listened to," and, thus, "he serves as a significant voice against Gradgrind's in the polyphonic structure of the book" See Roger Fowler, "Polyphony and Problematic in *Hard Times*," in *The Changing World of Charles Dickens*, ed. Robert Giddings (London: Vision Press, 1983), 98–99.

6. In nineteenth-century England, cannibalism frequently cropped up in humor and in popular stories; but by and large, references to cannibalism in the serious periodicals were extremely rare, considering that England was a maritime nation. See my discussion of the public attitudes toward cannibalism in "The Fate of Franklin: Three Phases of Response in Victorian Periodicals," *Victorian Periodical Review* 25 (1982): 97–103.

7. *London Times* 23 October 1854, 7.

8. Charles Dickens, "The Lost Arctic Voyagers," *Household Words* 10 (1854): 361.

9. Charles Dickens, "The Lost Arctic Voyagers," 392.

10. "The Long Voyage," *The Uncommercial Traveler*, 369–78.

11. See Robert L. Brannan's excellent work in disclosing Dickens's part in the play in *"The Frozen Deep": Under the Management of Mr. Charles Dickens* (Ithaca: Cornell University Press, 1966).

12. See Watt, "Oral Dickens." Dickens's dislike of Mrs. Merdle likely stemmed not only from his own oral character—which, according to Watt, permitted "no threatening sibling rivals at the maternal board or bosom" (p. 176)—but also in Mrs. Merdle's case, from there being no satisfaction for anyone. Watt, allowing for the reductionism of all psychological studies, has also suggested that Dickens's plots attempt "to find magic providers for secret suckers" (p. 178). But as I tried to show, Dickens was more concerned with exposing and condemning the secret suckers, the solitary monsters, and the ideology of Hunger that seemed to justify them.

13. Ibid., 177.

14. St. Augustine, *Confessions*, trans. R. S. Pine-Coffin (Hammondsworth, England: Penguin, 1969), 339, (Book 13, ch. 26).

15. R. R. Roopernaraine, "Time and the Circle in *Little Dorrit*," *Dickens Studies Annual* 3 (1974): 75.

16. Iain Crawford, "Machinery in Motion: Time in *Little Dorrit*," *The Dickensian* 84 (1988): 39, has written that "if the narrative is thus securely dated in the 1820s . . . the actual feeling of the novel is very much that of the mid-50s."

17. J. M. Rignall, "Dickens and the Catastrophic Continuum of History in *A Tale of Two Cities*," *English Literary History* 51 (1984): 585. Elliot Gilbert, "To Awake from History: Carlyle, Thackeray, and *A Tale of Two Cities*," *Dickens Studies Annual* 12 (1983): 264, has offered a counterview: "Just to *imagine* a vital future, then (the novel suggests) is already a very practical way to have defeated the worst the past can do". To supplement this imagined future with a trust in the present is, as I have argued, the way to avoid what Gilbert called "the dead hand of history" (260).

18. W. H. Wills, "Good Plain Cooks," *Household Words* 1 (1850): 139–41.

19. See my article "Dickens's Revolutionary Cookery," 145–178, cited earlier (ch. 2, n. 9).

20. Because I have already discussed at length the topic of cannibalism in *Great Expectations* (see "English Cannibalism," 647–66, cited earlier [ch. 2, n.15]) I will not duplicate it here.

21. The so-called servant problem was a very common topic of conversation and journalism in the middle of the Victorian Era. Dickens's dialectical mind was at work here, suggesting that there was at least as much an employer problem.

22. Ian Watt, "Oral Dickens," 170.

23. Alfred Lord Tennyson, "In Memoriam, A. H. H," 108, in Abrams, et al., *Norton Anthology*, 2:1168.

24. Fellowship porters, we learn from "A Popular Delusion," *Household Words* 1 (1850): 217, were Billingsgate stevedores who, it was written, being "responsible individuals . . . prevent fraud."

25. Besides the nineteenth-century reviewer who wrote that Bella "becomes finally one of the weakest, a mere milk-and-water sort of girl, with more water than milk" (*Christian Spectator* 5 (5 December 1865): 727), such highly respected modern critics as Barbara Hardy, Grahame Smith, and Philip Collins have animadverted against the character of Bella. Some critics have also been troubled by the indefiniteness of John Rokesmith's employment during his first year of marriage to Bella. From the point of view of the hungry present, Rokesmith's occupation for that brief time is of mere incidental interest compared to the definiteness of his occupation before he returned to England. Finding himself among the Cape vineyards, he became a "small proprietor, farmer, grower." What occupation could be more fitting for a man who joins Bella in denying the principle that man must partake first?

26. It is on this point that my major disagreement occurs with Steven Franklin's excellent article (see Franklin, "Dickens and Time 1–35, cited earlier [ch. 1, n. 14]). Franklin is right, in my view, to emphasize the Bergsonian continuum—which is time; but he does not focus adequately on the dangerous possibility that the human spirit could be consumed by the present commercial age—although this danger is a hallmark of Romantic thought. When George Cruickshank altered fairy tales for the purpose of "propagating the doctrines of Total Abstinence . . . Free Trade, and Popular Education," Dickens remonstrated: "The world is too much with us, early and late. Leave this previous old escape from it, alone" ("Frauds on the Fairies," *Household Words* 8 (1853): 100). And if such beneficent aspects of "an utilitarian age" threatened to imprison the audience in the present, how much more did such an audience need complete relief from the voracious aspects of the age. By considering only time and not the world, Franklin has missed some of the dilemma in Dickens's thinking about time—for Franklin has not sympathized with the idea that the past and the future have their legitimate uses in preserving the individual's spirit from being consumed by the present. In other words, Franklin has considered only the nefarious mien of the past and future—and only the beneficent mien of the present.

27. Bergson, *Creative Evolution*, 219.

Chapter 6. Beyond Forgetting: The Uses of the Past

1. Ford, "Voices of Time," 437.
2. *Speeches of Dickens*, 403–4. Given in Birmingham, 27 September 1869.

3. Charles Dickens, "The Business of Pleasure," *All the Year Round* 10 (1863): 149–52.
4. *Letters to Angela,* 350.
5. Dickens to W. C. Macready, 4 October 1855, *Letters* (1938), 2:695.
6. Charles Dickens, "Gone Astray," *Household Words* 7 (1853): 556.
7. *Letters to Angela,* 133.
8. Ibid., 85.
9. Humphry House, *The Dickens World* (1941; reprint, London: Oxford Paperbacks, 1965), 220.
10. Forster, *Life of Dickens,* 1:50.
11. Charles Dickens, "A Nightly Scene in London," *Household Words* 13 (1856): 25.
12. Wilson, "The Two Scrooges," 47.
13. Freud commented on the phenomenon of resistance in many places. In his essay "On Psychotherapy," he wrote simply of "the *resistance* with which the patient clings to his disease and thus even fights against his own recovery" (Sigmund Freud, *The Complete Works,* trans. James Strachey and Anna Freud (London: Hogarth Press, 1968), 7:261). Laing has made it his primary task to examine—from the existential point of view—the benefits seemingly derived from schizophrenia and other diseases. See R. D. Laing, *Self and Others* (London: Penguin, 1971), 42, and *The Divided Self* (London: Penguin 1971), 45.
14. Sydney Smith, "Sketches of a Moral Philosophy," in *The Wit and Wisdom of the Reverend Sydney Smith,* ed. Evert Duykinck (New York: W. S. Widdleton, 1870), 248.
15. Dickens to Mrs. Richard Watson, 14 September 1860, *Letters* (1938), 3:178.
16. Gabriel Marcel, *Being and Having* (New York: Harper Torchbooks, 1965), 117.
17. Ernst Cassirer, *An Essay on Man* (New York: Doubleday Anchor, 1944), 72.
18. Michael Goldberg, *Dickens and Carlyle* (Athens: University of Georgia Press, 1972), 89.
19. See Jean Piaget, *The Child's Consciousness of Time* (1927; reprint, New York: Basic Books, 1969).
20. Paul Goodman, *The Structure of Literature* (1954; reprint, Chicago: University of Chicago Press, 1962. Goodman has written that "*reversal is the destruction of the apparent plot and the succession of the hidden plot*" (35).
21. William Hazlitt, "The Plain Speaker," in *The Complete Works of William Hazlitt,* ed. P. P. Howe (1930–34; reprint, New York, AMS Press, 1967), 12:194. Dickens's expression "subtle essences" (HT, 1, 15) echoes Hazlitt's "finer essence."
22. James E. Marlow, "Memory, Romance, and the Expressive Symbol in Dickens," *Nineteenth-Century Fiction* 30 (1975): 20–32.
23. Ackroyd, 1045. See my "Memory," 32.
24. Carlyle, *Sartor Resartus,* 31.
25. Murray Baumgarten, "Writing the Revoution," *Dickens Studies Annual* 19 (1983): 173.
26. *Letters,* 2:531. To Arthur Helps, 3 January 1854.
27. Forster, *Life of Dickens,* 2:37.

Chapter 7. Trancending Time: "Out of the Ruined Place"

1. Dickens to Forster, 14 July 1839, *The Letters of Charles Dickens* (Oxford: The Pilgrim Edition, 1965), 1:564.

2. Dickens to Charles Knight, *Letters* (1938), 2:334.
3. Quoted by Ford, "Voices of Time," 439.
4. Michael Goldberg (*Dickens and Carlyle,* 221) has written, "The whole sense Dickens projects of an inter-connected world, in which people and things act on one another, expresses itself also in the principle of coincidence. Coincidence usually involves the surprised discovery of connection in the unconnected. . . . Coincidence, like animism, is one of the laws by which the world of his novels is structured."
5. Charles Babbage, *The Ninth Bridgewater Treatise* (Philadelphia: Lea and Blanchard, 1841), 115.
6. *Speeches of Dickens,* 399. Given in Birmingham, 27 September 1869.
7. Babbage, *Ninth Bridgewater Treatise,* 113.
8. Percy Bysshe Shelley, "Adonais," 406–8, in *Norton,* 2:752.
9. John Camp, *Magic, Myth, and Medicine* (New York: Taplinger, 1974), 66.
10. Carlyle, "Characteristics," 38.
11. Babbage, 117.
12. Dickens to Lever, 21 February 1860, *Letters* (1938), 3:152.
13. William Hazlitt, "On Doctor Spurzheim's Theory," in *The Complete Works,* 12:137.
14. Babbage, 114.
15. Babbage, 37.
16. Babbage, 61.
17. See Carlyle, *Sartor Resartus:* "Deep has been, and is, the significance of miracles" (203).
18. Babbage, 95.
19. Thomas Carlyle, *Past and Present,* 290.
20. Carlyle, "Characteristics," 37.
21. Nicolas Berdyaev, Introduction to *Six Theosophic Points,* by Jacob Boehme (Ann Arbor, Mich.: Ann Arbor Paperbacks, 1958), xxvii.
22. Charles Dickens, "Nobody, Somebody, and Everybody," *Household Words* 14 (1856): 145–47.
23. Ibid., 146.
24. Ibid., 145.
25. Ibid., 146.
26. Carlyle, *Sartor Resartus,* 146.
27. *Defer* in the sense of Jacques Derrida's "differer"—that is, to put off or postpone in time. See Derrida, "Differance" in *Margins of Philosophy,* trans. Alan Bass (Chicago: University of Chicago, 1982), 1–27.
28. Carlyle, *Sartor Resartus,* 146.
29. Dickens to Emmely Gotschalk, 1 February 1850, *Letters* (1938), 2:203.
30. Babbage, *Ninth Bridgewater Treatise,* 87.
31. As if to tease his own style, Dickens presents some "angular" characters—like Betsey Trotwood in *David Copperfield* and Mr. Grewgious in *Edwin Drood*—who appear to be stiff and inflexible in physique and character; but, as their names so clearly indicate, they have anything but immovable hearts.
32. Charles Dickens, "The Late Mr. Justice Talfourd," *Household Words* 9 (1854): 117.
33. Charles Dickens, "Preliminary Word," *Household Words* 1 (1850): 1.
34. Ackroyd, *Charles Dickens,* 70.
35. Johann Wolfgang Goethe, *Faust,* trans. Louis MacNeice, in *The Norton Anthology of World Literature,* Maynard Mack et al., eds., 5th ed. (New York: W. W. Norton, 1985), 480.

36. Ibid.

37. Dickens to Collins, 6 September 1858. Quoted by Harry Stone, vol. 2, *Charles Dickens Uncollected Writings from Household Words* (Bloomington: Indiana University Press, 1968), 596. See *To Collins*, 86.

38. Dickens quoted by Johnson, *Charles Dickens* 2:860.

39. Marcel has written that "having as such seems to have a tendency to destroy and lose itself in the very thing it began by possessing, but which now absorbs the master who thought he controlled it" (see Marcel, *Being and Having*, 164). For Dickens, this is true a fortiori of the relationship between the individual and a single dimension of time.

40. Horton, 80. *Interpreting Interpreting*. Cf. Ackroyd, *Charles Dickens*, 495, for the acid remarks at the time in the *London Times* about Dickens's presuming on his past relationships with his readers.

41. Dickens to Collins, 25 March 1858, *Letters* (1938), 3:14.

42. Johnson, *Charles Dickens*, 2:904.

Bibliography

Altick, Richard D. *Victorian People and Ideas*. New York: W. W. Norton, 1973.

Ackroyd, Peter. *Charles Dickens*. New York: Harper Collins, 1990.

Babbage, Charles. *The Ninth Bridgewater Treatise*. Philadelphia: Lea and Blanchard, 1841.

Bakhtin, M. M. and P. N. Medvedev. *The Formal Method in Literary Scholarship*. Translated by Albert J. Wehrle. Baltimore: Johns Hopkins University Press, 1978.

Bakhtin, M. M. *Problems of Dostoevsky's Poetics*. Translated by R. W. Rotsel. Ann Arbor, Mich.: Ardis, 1973.

Barthes, Roland. *Image-Music-Text*. New York: Hill & Wang, 1977.

Baumgarten, Murray. "Writing the Revolution." *Dickens Studies Annual* 12 (1983): 161–76.

Berdyaev, Nicolas. "Introduction." In Jacob Boehme. *Six Theosophic Points*. Ann Arbor Paperbacks, 1958.

Bergson, Henri. *Creative Evolution*. New York: Modern Library, 1944.

——. *Matter and Memory*. Garden City, N.Y.: Doubleday, 1959.

Bloom, Harold. "Introduction" to *Charles Dickens*. New York: Chelsea, 1987.

——, ed. *Romanticism and Consciousness*. New York, 1970.

Booth, Wayne. *The Rhetoric of Fiction*. Chicago: University of Chicago Press, 1966.

Brannan, Robert L. *"The Frozen Deep": Under the Management of Mr. Charles Dickens*. Ithaca: Cornell University Press, 1966.

Brillat-Savarin, Jean. *Gastronomy as a Fine Art*. Translated by R. E. Anderson. London: Chatto & Windus, 1877.

Buber, Martin. *I And Thou*. New York: Scribner's, 1958.

Buchanan, Robert. "The Good Genie of Fiction: Thoughts While Reading Forster's *Life of Charles Dickens*." *St Paul's Magazine* 10 (1872): 130–47.

Buckley, J. H. *The Triumph of Time: A Study of the Victorian Concepts of Time, History, Progress, and Decadence*. New York: Oxford University Press, 1967.

Butt, John and Kathleen Tillotson. *Dickens at Work*. London: Metheun, 1957.

Cabanis, P. J. G. *An Essay on the Certainty of Medicine*. Translated by R. La Roche. Philadelphia, 1823.

Camp, John. *Magic, Myth, and Medicine*. New York: Taplinger, 1974.

Carey, John. *Here Comes Dickens: The Imagination of a Novelist*. New York: Schocken Books, 1974.

Carlyle, Thomas. *Critical and Miscellaneous Essays*. 5 volumes. New York: AMS Press, 1969.

——. *The French Revolution*. New York: Modern Library, n.d.

———. *Heroes and Hero-Worship.* Lincoln: University of Nebraska Press, 1966.

———. *Past and Present.* Boston: Houghton Mifflin, 1965.

———. *Sartor Resartus.* New York: AMS Press, 1969.

Carmichael, Virginia. "In Search of *Beein': Nom/Non Du Pere* in *David Copperfield.*" *English Literary History* 54 (1987): 653–67.

Cassirer, Ernst. *An Essay on Man.* Garden City, N.Y.: Doubleday & Co, 1955.

———. *The Philosophy of Symbolic Forms.* 3 volumes. New Haven: Yale University Press, 1966.

Chapman, Raymond. *The Sense of the Past in Victorian Literature.* New York: St. Martin's Press, 1986.

Chesterton, G. K. *Charles Dickens.* London, 1910.

Cockshut, A. O. J. *The Imagination of Charles Dickens.* London: Metheun, 1961.

Collins, P. A. W. *Dickens and Crime.* London: Macmillan, 1962.

———. *Dickens and Education.* New York: Macmillan, 1964.

———. "Keep Household Words Imaginative." *The Dickensian* 52 (1956): 78–90.

———. "Queen Mab's Chariot Among the Steam Engines: Dickens and Fancy." *English Studies* 42 (1961): 119–23.

Coombe, Andrew. *The Physiology of Digestion.* Edinburgh: Machlachlan & Stewart, 1836.

Crawford, Iain. "Machinery in Motion: Time in *Little Dorrit.*" *The Dickensian* 84 (1988): 30–41.

Creevy, Patrick J. "In Time and Out: The Tempo of Life in *Bleak House.*" *Dickens Studies Annual* 12 (1983): 63–80.

Davis, Earle. *The Flint and the Flame.* Columbia: University of Missouri Press, 1963.

Derrida, Jacques. *Of Grammatology.* Translated by Gayatri Spivak. Baltimore: Johns Hopkins University Press, 1976.

Dexter, Walter. *The Letters of Charles Dickens.* 3 volumes. London: Nonesuch, 1938.

Doran, Dr. *Table Traits. With Something on Them.* London: Richard Bentley, 1859.

Eagleton, Terry. *Literary Theory.* Minneapolis: University of Minnesota Press, 1983.

Eigner, Edwin. *The Dickens Pantomime.* Berkeley: University of California Press, 1989.

Engle, Monroe. *The Maturity of Dickens.* Cambridge: Harvard University Press, 1959.

Fielding, K. J. "Dickens and the Past: The Novelist of Memory." In *Experience in the Novel.* Edited by R. H. Pearce. New York: Columbia University Press, 1968.

———, ed. *The Speeches of Charles Dickens.* London: Oxford University Press, 1960.

Ford, George. *Dickens and His Readers.* Princeton: Princeton University Press, 1955.

———. "Dickens and the Voices of Time." *Nineteenth Century Fiction* 24 (1970): 428–48.

Forster, John. *The Life of Charles Dickens.* 3 Volumes. London: Chapman and Hall, 1872.

Foucault, Michel. *The Archaeology of Knowledge.* London: Tavistock, 1974.

———. *The Order of Things*. London: Tavistock, 1974.

Fowler, Roger. "Polyphony and Problematic in *Hard Times*." In *The Changing World of Charles Dickens*. Edited by Robert Giddings. London: Vision Press, 1983.

Frank, Lawrence. *Charles Dickens and the Romantic Self*. Lincoln: University of Nebraska Press, 1984.

Franklin, Stephen L. "Dickens and Time: The Clock Without Time." *Dickens Studies Annual* 4 (1975), 1–35.

Freud, Sigmund. *Jokes and their Relation to the Unconscious*. Translated by James Strachey. New York: Norton, 1963.

———. *The Interpretation of Dreams*. Translated by James Strachey. New York: Basic Books, 1959.

———. *The Problem of Anxiety*. New York: Norton, 1963.

Frye, Northrup. *The Anatomy of Criticism*. Princeton: University Press, 1957.

———. "Dickens and Humour." In *Experience in the Novel*. Edited by R. H. Pearce. New York: Columbia University Press, 1968.

Garis, Robert. *The Dickens Theatre*. London: Oxford University Press, 1965.

Gibson, J. J. "Events Are Perceivable But Time Is Not." In *The Study of Time*, II. Edited by J. T. Fraser and N. Lawrence. New York: Springer, 1975.

Gilbert, Elliot L. "To Awake From History: Carlyle, Thackeray, and *A Tale of Two Cities*." *Dickens Studies Annual* 12 (1983): 247–65.

Gissing, George. *Charles Dickens: A Critical Study*. New York: Dodd Mead & Co., 1904.

Goldberg, Michael. *Dickens and Carlyle*. Athens: University of Georgia Press, 1972.

Goodman, Paul. *The Structure of Literature*. Chicago: University of Chicago Phoenix Press, 1962.

Gottschalk, Paul. "Time in *Edwin Drood*." *Dickens Studies Annual* 1 (1970): 265–72.

Haley, Bruce. *The Healthy Body and Victorian Culture*. Cambridge: Harvard University Press, 1978.

Hardy, Barbara. "Food and Ceremony in *Great Expectations*." In *Charles Dickens*. Edited by Stephen Wall. London: Penguin, 1970.

Harris, Roy. *The Language Myth*. New York: St. Martin's, 1981.

Hartog, Dirk den. *Dickens and Romantic Psychology: The Self in Time in Nineteenth Century Literature*. New York: St. Martin's, 1987.

Hazlitt, William. *An Essay on the Principle of Human Action*. Gainesville: University of Florida Press, 1969.

———. "On Doctor Spurzheim's Theory." *In The Complete Works of William Hazlitt*. Edited by P. P. Howe. New York: AMS Press, 1967, vol. 12.

———. "The Plain Speaker," *In Complete Works*, vol. 12.

———. *The Round Table*. London: J. Templeman, 1841.

———. *The Spirit of the Age*. London: Scholar Press, 1971.

Himmelfarb, Gertrude. *Darwin and the Darwinian Revolution*. New York: W. W. Norton, 1968.

Holloway, John. "Dickens and the Symbol." In *Dickens 1970*. Edited by Michael Slater. New York: Stein & Day, 1970.

Horne, Lewis. "Hope and Memory in *Hard Times*" *The Dickensian* 75 (August 1979): 167–74.

Horton, Susan R. *Interpreting Interpreting: Interpreting Dickens's Dombey.* Baltimore: Johns Hopkins University Press, 1979.

House, Humphrey. *The Dickens World.* London: Oxford Paperback, 1965.

House, Madeline, Graham Storey, and Kathleen Tillotson, eds. *The Letters of Charles Dickens.* Volumes 1–6 (1820–1852). Oxford: Clarendon Press, 1965–1988.

Husserl, Edmund. *The Phenomenology of Internal Time-Consciousness.* Bloomington, Ind.: Midland, 1973.

Hutchins, Eleanor N. "Towards a Poetics of Fiction: The Novel as Chronomorph." *Novel* 5 (1972): 215–24.

Hutter, Albert. "Nation and Generation in *A Tale of Two Cities.*" *PMLA* 93 (1978): 448–62.

———. "The Novelist as Resurrectionist: Dickens and the Dilemma of Death." *Dickens Studies Annual* 12 (1983): 1–39.

Hutton, Laurence, ed. *The Letters of Charles Dickens to Wilkie Collins.* New York: 1892.

Iser, Wolfgang. *The Implied Reader.* Baltimore: Johns Hopkins University Press, 1974.

Jackson, T. A. *Charles Dickens: The Progress of a Radical.* 1937. Reprint. New York: Haskett House, 1971.

Jakobson, Roman. "Linguistics and Poetics." In *The Structuralists From Marx to Levi-Strauss.* Edited by Richard and Fernande DeGeorge. Garden City, N.Y.: Doubleday Anchor, 1972.

———. "Sign and System of Language: A Reassessment of Saussure's Doctrine." In *Roman Jakobson: Verbal Art, Verbal Sign, Verbal Time.* Edited by Krystyna Pomorska and Stephen Rudy. Minneapolis: University of Minnesota Press, 1985.

——— and Krystyna Pomorska. "Dialogue on Time in Language and Literature." In *Verbal Art, Verbal Sign, Verbal Time.*

——— and Morris Halle. *Fundamentals of Language.* The Hague: Mouton, 1971.

James, Henry. *The Future of the Novel.* Edited by Leon Edel. New York: Vintage, 1956.

Jauss, Hans Robert. *Toward An Aesthetic of Reception.* Minneapolis: University of Minnesota Press, 1982.

Johnson, Edgar. *Charles Dickens: His Tragedy and Triumph.* 2 Volumes. New York: Simon & Schuster, 1952.

———, ed. *The Letters of Charles Dickens to Angela Burdett-Coutts.* London: Jonathan Cape, 1953.

Jerrold, Douglas. *The Chronicles of Clovernook.* London: Punch, 1847.

———. *The Handbook of Swindling.* Edited by Walter Jerrold. London: Scott, 1891.

Kaplan, Fred, ed. *Charles Dickens Book of Memoranda.* New York: New York Public Library, 1981.

———. *Charles Dickens: A Biography.* New York: William Morrow, 1988.

———. *Dickens and Mesmerism.* Princeton: Princeton University Press, 1976.

Kermode, Frank. *The Sense of an Ending.* New York: Oxford University Press, 1967.
Kettle, Arnold. *An Introduction to the English Novel.* 2 vols. London: Hutchinson, 1969.
―――. *"Our Mutual Friend."* In *Dickens and the Twentieth Century.* Edited by Gross and Pearson. London: Routledge, 1966.
Kincaid, James R. "The Education of Mr. Pickwick." *Nineteenth Century Fiction* 24 (Sept, 1969): 127–41.
Kolakowski, Leszek. *Bergson.* London: Oxford University Press, 1985.
Laing, R. D. *The Divided Self.* Harmondsworth: Pelican, 1970.
―――. *Self and Others.* Harmondsworth: Pelican, 1971.
Lane, Margaret. "Dickens on the Hearth." *Dickens 1970.* Edited by Michael Slater. New York: Stein & Day, 1970.
Langer, Suzanne K. *Feeling and Form.* New York: Scriber's, 1953.
―――. *Philosophy in a New Key.* New York: NAL, n.d.
Levi-Strauss, Claude. *The Savage Mind.* Translated by George Weidenfeld and Nicolson Ltd. Chicago: University of Chicago Press, 1966.
Lewes, George H. "Dickens in Relation to Criticism." *Fortnightly* 17 (Feb 1872): 141–54.
Liebig, Julius von. *Familiar Letters on Chemistry.* London: Taylor Walton and Maberly, 1851.
Lohrli, Anne, ed. *Household Words.* Toronto: University of Toronto Press, 1973.
Marcel, Gabriel. *Homo Viator.* New York: Harper Torchbooks, 1962.
―――. *Being and Having.* New York: Harper Torchbooks, 1965.
Malthus, Thomas. *An Essay on the Principle of Population.* 1798. Reprint. New York: W. W. Norton, 1976.
Marcus, Steven. *From Pickwick to Dombey.* London: Chatto & Windus, 1965.
Marlow, James. "English Cannibalism: Dickens After 1859." *Studies in English Literature* 23 (1983): 647–66.
―――. "Social Harmony and Dickens Revolutionary Cookery." *Dickens Studies Annual* 17 (1988): 145–78.
Masson, David. *British Novelists and Their Styles.* Cambridge, England, 1859.
McMaster, Juliet. *Dickens the Designer.* Totowa, N.J.: Barnes and Noble, 1987.
Meckier, Jerome. "The Dickens Forum: How Modern the Victorians? A Plan to Have It Both Ways." *Dickens Studies Newsletter* 8 (Dec 1977): 109–18.
Mendilow, A. A. *Time and the Novel.* New York: Humanities Press, 1965.
Miller, J. Hillis. "Afterword." In *Our Mutual Friend.* New York: New American Library, 1964.
―――. *Charles Dickens: The World of His Novels.* Bloomington, Ind.: Midland, 1969.
Moynahan, Julian. "The Hero's Guilt" The Case of *Great Expectations.*" *Essays in Criticism* 10 (1960): 60–79.
Mundhenk, Rosemarie. "*David Copperfield* and the Oppression of Remembrance.'" *Texas Studies in Language and Literature* 27 (1987): 323–41.
Needham, Gwendolyn. "The Undisciplined Heart of David Copperfield." *Nineteenth Century Fiction* 9 (1954): 81–107.

Newcomb, Mildred. *The Imagined World of Charles Dickens.* Columbus: Ohio State University Press, 1989.

Newman, S. J. *Dickens At Play.* New York: St Martin's, 1981.

Newsom, Robert. *Dickens and the Romantic Side of Familiar Things: Bleak House and the Novel Tradition.* New York: Columbia University Press, 1977.

Nietzsche, Friedrich. *The Will to Power.* New York: Vintage, 1968.

Ortega y Gasset, José. *The Dehumanization of Art.* Translated by Willard Trask. Garden City, N.Y.: Anchor, 1956.

Orwell, George. *Dickens, Dali and Others.* New York: Reynal and Hitchcock, 1946.

Patten, Robert L. *Charles Dickens and His Publishers.* Oxford: Clarendon Press, 1978.

Piaget, Jean. *The Child's Consciousness of Time.* New York: Basic Books, 1969.

———. *The Moral Judgment of the Child.* New York: Free Press, 1965.

Poulet, Georges. *Studies in Human Time.* New York: Harper Torchbooks, 1956.

Pritchett, V. S. "The Comic World of Dickens." In *The Victorian Novel: Essays in Criticism.* Edited by Ian Watt. New York: Oxford University Press, 1971.

Progoff, Ira. *Jung, Synchronicity, and Human Destiny.* New York: Julian Press, 1973.

Prout, William. *Chemistry, Meteorology, and the Function of Digestion, Considered With Reference to Natural Theology.* Philadelphia: Carey, Lea and Blanchard, 1834. [8th Bridgewater Treatise]

Rabinowitz, Peter J. *Before Reading: Narrative Conventions and the Politics of Interpretation.* Ithaca: Cornell University Press, 1987.

Raina, Badri. *Dickens and the Dialectic of Growth.* Madison: University of Wisconsin Press, 1986.

Raleigh, John. "Dickens and the Sense of Time." *Nineteenth Century Fiction* 13 (1958): 127–37.

"Remonstrance With Dickens." *Blackwood's* 81 (Apr 1857): 490–503.

Rice, Thomas. "The Politics of *Barnaby Rudge.*" In *The Changing World of Charles Dickens.* Edited by Robert Giddings. London: Vision Press, 1983: 51–74.

Rignall, J. M. "Dickens and the Catastrophic Continuum of History in *A Tale of Two Cities.*" *English Literary History* 51 (1984): 575–87.

Rogers, Philip. "The Dynamics of Time in *The Old Curiosity Shop.*" *Nineteenth Century Fiction* 28 (1973): 127–44.

Roopernaraine, R. R. "Time and the Circle in *Little Dorrit.*" *Dickens Studies Annual* 3 (1974): 54–76.

Ruskin, John. "Essay I" from *Fiction, Fair and Foul.* In *The Genius of John Ruskin.* Edited by John D. Rosenberg. Boston: Houghton Mifflin, 1963.

Sartre, Jean-Paul. *Being and Nothingness.* Translated by Hazel Barnes. New York: Philosophical Library, 1965.

Saunders, A. L. *The Victorian Historical Novel 1840–1880.* London: Macmillan, 1978.

Schad, S. J. "The I and You of Time: Rhetoric and History in Dickens." *English Literary History* 56 (1989): 423–38.

Searle, John. *Speech Acts: An Essay in the Philosophy of Language.* Cambridge: Cambridge University Press, 1969.

Slater, Michael. "Carlyle and Jerrold in Dickens: A Study of *The Chimes.*" *Nineteenth Century Fiction* 24 (1970).

Smiles, Samuel. *Self-Help.* New York: A. L. Burt, n.d.
Smith, Barbara H. *On the Margins of Discourse.* Chicago: University of Chicago Press, 1978.
Smith, Sydney, Rev. *The Wit and Wisdom.* Edited by Evert A. Duyckinck. New York: W. J. Widdleton, 1870.
Soyer, Alexis. *The Modern Housewife, or Menagere.* London: Simpkin, Marshall, Co., 1851.
Stange, G. Robert. "Dickens and the Fiery Past: *A Tale of Two Cities* Reconsidered." *English Journal* 46 (1957): 381–96.
Sterrenburg, Lee. "Psychoanalysis and the Iconography of Revolution." *Victorian Studies* 19 (1975–76).
Steiner, George. *After Babel.* New York: Oxford University Press, 1975.
Stewart, Garrett. *Charles Dickens and the Trials of the Imagination.* Cambridge: Harvard University Press, 1974.
Stoehr, Taylor. *The Dreamer's Stance.* Ithaca: Cornell University Press, 1965.
Stone, Harry, ed. *Charles Dickens: The Uncollected Writings from Household Words 1850–1870.* 2 volumes. Bloomington: Indiana University Press, 1968
———, ed. *Dickens Working Notes for His Novels.* Chicago: University of Chicago Press, 1987.
Talon, Henri. "Space, Time, and Memory in *Great Expectations.*" *Dickens Studies Annual* 3 (1974): 122–33.
Trilling, Lionel. *"Little Dorrit."* In *Charles Dickens.* Edited by Stephen Wall. London: Penguin, 1970.
Vanden Bossche, Chris R. "Cookery, not Rookery: Family and Class in *David Copperfield.*" *Dickens Studies Annual* 15 (1986): 87–109.
Van Ghent, Dorothy. "The Dickens World." In *The Dickens Critics.* Edited by George Ford and Lauriat Lane. Ithaca: Cornell Paperbacks, 1966.
Walker, Thomas. *Aristology, or the Art of Dining.* London: Geo. Bell and Son, 1881.
Watt, Ian. "Oral Dickens." *Dickens Studies Annual* 3 (1974): 165–81.
Waugh, Linda R. "The Poetic Function and the Nature of Language." In *Roman Jakobson: Verbal Art, Verbal Sign, Verbal Time.* Minneapolis: University of Minnesota Press, 1985: 143–68.
Weber, Max. *The Protestant Ethic and the Spirit of Capitalism.* Translated by Talcott Parsons. London: Allen & Unwin, 1962.
Westburg, Barry. *The Confessional Fictions of Charles Dickens.* DeKalb: Northern Illinois University Press, 1977.
Wilson, Edmund. "Dickens: The Two Scrooges." In *The Wound and the Bow.* New York: Oxford University Press, 1947.
Yaker, Henri, ed. *The Future of Time.* Garden City, N.Y.: Anchor, 1972

Index

Ackroyd, Peter, 14, 16, 19, 24, 44, 143, 213
Augustine, Saint, 174, 175
Axton, W. F., 245 n.15

Babbage, Charles, 189, 225–30, 232, 233, 235, 236, 238
Bakhtin, M. M., 18, 19, 20
Baumgarten, Murray, 216
Beckett, Samuel, 137
Bentham, Jeremy, 72
Berdyaev, Nicholas, 123, 230–31
Bergson, Henri, 26, 120, 121–22, 152, 189
Bible, 51, 61, 72, 91, 111, 133, 136, 169, 231
Blackwood's, 103, 149
Blake, William, 40, 103
Boehme, Jakob, 230–31
Bradbury & Evans, publishers, 97
British Quarterly Review, 114
Brontë, Charlotte: *Villette*, 133
Browning, Robert, 146, 189, 223
Buchanan, Robert, 25, 147
Burdett-Coutts, Miss Angela, 138, 140, 197, 199

Carey, John, 13–14, 17–18, 19, 245 n.14
Carlyle, Thomas, 38, 69, 70–71, 73, 80, 91, 121, 133, 136, 152, 229, 230, 231, 235; "Characteristics," 120, 226; *Chartism*, 70, 71; *The French Revolution*, 70, 95; *Past and Present*, 230; *Sartor Resartus*, 70, 93–94, 95, 233, 234
Cassirer, Ernst, 7, 206
Chesterton, G. K., 14, 146, 225
Coincidence, 149–51
Coleridge, S. T., 40, 46
Collins, Philip, 141, 243 n.2
Collins, Wilkie, 132, 142, 143, 147–48, 151, 166, 238, 240; *The Frozen Deep*, 165–66, 234
Comedy and the comic in Dickens, 79, 81, 83, 88, 89, 104, 112, 118, 119, 128, 131, 156, 162, 171, 183, 187, 193, 206
Community, or "social harmony," 24–25, 27, 29, 41, 44, 51, 58, 80, 82, 85, 88, 89, 97, 109, 152, 164, 185–86, 231, 234, 235, 238, 239
Creevy, Patrick, 13, 120

Davis, Earle, 149
Derrida, Jacques, 19, 26
Diachronic criticism, 14–16
Diachrony, 104, 107–8
Dickens, Charles:
—*All the Year Round*, 38, 115, 141, 147, 177, 185
—*Barnaby Rudge*, 37, 38, 42–44, 54, 83–85
—*Battle of Life*, 45–47, 105, 133, 144
—*Bleak House*, 13, 37, 38, 40, 44, 52–56, 68, 94, 107, 110–11, 112, 117, 119–20, 135, 136–37, 146, 148, 155, 159–62, 195–96, 200, 206, 212–13, 225, 231, 233–34, 237
—*Child's History of England*, 36, 192–93
—*Chimes, The*, 45–46, 91, 92, 108, 197, 198, 202, 206
—*Christmas Carol*, 44–45, 91, 202
—*Cricket on the Hearth, The*, 91, 203
—*David Copperfield*, 15, 18, 37, 48, 49–52, 68, 98, 106, 107, 121, 134–35, 141, 149, 155–59, 204–5, 228
—*Dombey & Son*, 15, 37, 48–49, 92–93, 96, 106–7, 111–12, 114, 126, 235, 237

264 INDEX

—*Edwin Drood*, 15, 37, 68, 100, 106, 115–16, 138, 155, 189, 205, 227
—*Great Expectations*, 15, 16, 64–65, 96, 98–102, 114, 121, 177–78, 198–99, 202, 217, 228, 229, 237
—*Hard Times*, 38, 55–59, 68, 108–10, 162–64, 207–8, 210
—"Haunted House, The" (CS), 117
—*Haunted Man, The*, 47–48, 67, 91, 203–4
—*Household Words*, 113, 139, 141, 176–77, 185, 200, 224, 235–36
—*Little Dorrit*, 37, 38, 59–63, 100, 103, 106, 111, 113, 115, 118, 121, 167–76, 194, 196, 201, 205, 208–9, 210, 214, 218, 225, 233, 237
—"Long Voyage, The," (RP), 165–66
—*Martin Chuzzlewit*, 18, 44, 86–90, 193, 200, 226–27
—*Memoranda Book, The*, 135, 136
—"Mrs. Lirriper's Lodgings" (RP), 115, 214
—*Nicholas Nickleby*, 41, 68, 80–82, 126–33
—"Nobody's Story," 230–33
—*Old Curiosity Shop*, 18, 37, 41–42, 82–85, 105–6, 210, 237
—*Oliver Twist*, 15, 38, 39–40, 41, 68, 76–80, 92, 154, 198, 228
—*Our Mutual Friend*, 14, 23, 37, 65–67, 68, 72, 75, 87, 96, 100, 107, 114–15, 118–19, 121, 125, 135, 144, 149, 154, 155, 179–89, 190, 197, 206–7, 209, 210–11, 214–16, 217, 218–19, 237
—*Pickwick Papers*, 38, 41, 74–76, 103–5, 149, 154, 237
—*Pictures From Italy*, 56
—*Sketches by Boz*, 18, 73, 231, 234, 237
—*Sunday Under Three Heads*, 114
—*Tale of Two Cities, A*, 37, 44, 63–64, 74, 78, 176–77, 208, 216–17, 225, 228–29, 234
—"Tom Tiddler's Ground," 145
—*Uncommercial Traveller and Reprinted Pieces*, 114
—"Wreck of the Golden Mary, The," 166
Dickensian, The, 23
Domesticity, 143–46, 177, 185, 187

Dostoevsky, Fyodor, 92, 147
Duty, 110–16, 173–74

Education, 137–43
Eigner, Edwin, 17, 18
English cannibalism, 78, 89, 90, 91, 94–95, 155–61, 167–71, 183
Expressive symbols. *See* Stylistics

Fancy. *See* Imagination
Faust (Goethe), 13, 238
Field, James and Annie, 213
Fielding, K. J., 49, 59
Fluidity and flexibility in characters, 52, 67, 82, 102, 236–38, 239, 253n.31
Ford, George, 191
Forster, John, 20–21, 24–25, 39–40, 134, 200, 218, 240
Fowler, Roger, 250n.5
Frank, Lawrence, 15, 67, 99
Franklin, Sir John, 164–67, 173
Franklin, Stephan, 244n.14
Frye, Northrop, 103, 150

Gentleman, 51, 61, 65, 99–101, 168, 171, 231
Gilbert, Elliot, 250n.17
Goldberg, Michael, 207, 253n.4
Goodman, Paul, 210
Good old times, 42, 43, 46, 63, 69, 97, 192
Grinding, 109, 125, 133, 149, 151, 171

Harmony. *See* Community
Harris, Roy, 19
Hartog, Dirk den, 16, 125
Hazlitt, William, 101, 126, 211, 228
Hirsch, E. D., 20
Hogarth, Georgina, 173
Horton, Susan, 18, 19, 20, 24, 25–26, 143, 239
House, Humphrey, 199–200

Imagination, 97, 101, 109, 113, 116, 125–26, 147, 148, 161, 212–13, 219

Jakobson, Roman, 21–23
James, Henry, 22, 144

James, William, 29
Jauss, Hans R., 24
Jerrold, Douglas, 69, 133, 147, 184; *The Chronicle of Clovernook*, 94, 248n.7; *The Handbook of Swindling*, 94
Jung, Carl, 151

Kaplan, Fred, 14, 25, 40, 50
Kettle, Arnold, 14, 138

LaMettrie, J. O. de: *Man the Machine*, 206
Lemon, Mark (editor of *Punch*), 97
Levi-Strauss, Claude, 107
Lewes, G. H., 141

Malthus, J. T., 28, 70, 71, 72, 73, 74, 78, 80, 84, 88, 90, 91, 92, 93, 94, 134, 154, 159, 162, 167, 195
Marcel, Gabriel, 148, 149, 152, 158, 206, 239, 254n.39
Marcus, Steven, 126, 247nn. 4 and 7
Masson, David, 97
Melbourne, William, Lord, 153
Melodrama, 24, 169
Mesmer, Anton, 213; mesmerism, 40, 212
Mill, John Stuart, 39
Miller, J. Hillis, 38–39
Milton, John, 112, 132, 210
Mortmain (dead hand), 38

Names, 53, 55, 82, 85, 93, 109, 141, 157, 162, 164, 171, 173, 174, 175, 181, 184, 185, 186, 216, 224, 232, 236, 253n.31
Needham, Gwendolyn, 156
Newcomb, Mildred, 13, 17
Newman, S. J., 17, 18, 19, 25
Nietzsche, Friedrich, 39

Odyssey (Homer), 85
Orwell, George, 27, 113

Paul Clifford (Bulwer-Lytton), 80
Philosophical Radicals. *See* Utilitarians
Phrenology, 101, 228
Physiognomy, 227–28
Poe, Edgar Allen, 199

Poetic justice, 180, 205, 209–10, 234
Poor Law of 1834, 80
Pritchett, V. S., 94
Puysegur, Marquis de, 213

Rabinowitz, Peter, 20. *See also* Rules of notice
Raina, Badri, 15, 106
Respectability, 54–55, 63, 66, 67, 85, 88, 92, 96, 111, 112, 160, 168, 171, 180, 181
Revenge, 47, 60, 61, 64, 65, 66, 81, 98–99, 100, 102, 169, 171, 205, 229
Rignall, J. M., 176
Rogers, Philip, 41
Romantic side of familiar things, 25, 144, 146–47, 149
Roopernaraine, R. R., 175
Rules of notice, 20, 21, 182, 187, 208
Ruskin, John, 25, 35, 147

Sabbatarians, 73
Sartre, Jean-Paul, 26, 61
Searle, John, 24
Shakespeare, William, 147
Shaw, George Bernard, 167
Shelley, Percy Bysshe, 52
Shuttleworth, Mr. Kay, 139
Smiles, Samuel, 134
Smith, Barbara, 23
Smith, Rev. Sydney, 154, 202
Solitary monster, the, 166–67, 178
Sow/reap imagery, 22, 27, 44, 45, 112, 135, 136, 163–64, 204, 210
Steiner, George, 15, 24, 26
Stewart, Garret, 155–56
Stoehr, Taylor, 143–44
Stylistics, 23–25, 27, 66, 67, 75, 77, 82, 99, 100, 113, 146, 192, 214; expressive symbol, 211–14; plot construction, 149–51, 156, 160, 172, 207, 209
Synchronic criticism, 17–19
Synchrony, 108, 112; synchronicity, 161

Tennyson, Alfred, Lord, 183
Thackeray, William, 97
Trilling, Lionel, 59

Utilitarianism, 44–45, 55–56, 73, 79, 93, 94, 108, 110, 162, 173

Vander Bossche, Chris, 245 n.16
Van Ghent, Dorothy, 150

Watt, Ian, 171, 183, 243 n.5
Weber, Max, 72

Westminster Review, 142, 145
Wills, William H. (sub-editor of HW), 146
Wilson, Edmund, 201
Wollstonecraft, Mary, 202
Wordsworth, William, 16, 28, 52, 101, 133, 195, 211, 212, 215
Work, 136–38